The perspective of ethnomethodology

THE PERSPECTIVE
OF ETHNOMETHODOLOGY

Douglas Benson
and
John A. Hughes

LONGMAN
London and New York

LONGMAN GROUP LIMITED
Longman House, Burnt Mill, Harlow
Essex CM20 2JE, England
Associated companies throughout the world

*Published in the United States of America
by Longman Inc., New York*

First published 1983

BRITISH LIBRARY CATALOGUING IN PUBLICATION DATA

Benson, Douglas
 The perspective of ethnomethodology.
 1. Ethnomethodology
 I. Title   II. Hughes, John A.
 301   HM24
 ISBN 0–582–29584–X

LIBRARY OF CONGRESS CATALOGING IN PUBLICATION DATA

Benson, Douglas.
 The perspective of ethnomethodology.

 Includes index.
 1. Ethnomethodology. I. Hughes, John A.,
1941–.   II. Title.
HM24.B3867   1983   306'.01'8   82–10113
 ISBN 0–582–29584–X (pbk.)

Set in 10/11pt Linotron 202 Plantin Roman

Printed in Hong Kong by
Astros Printing Ltd

 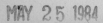

CONTENTS

PREFACE

What we have tried to do in this volume is present an account of ethnomethodology for those who have little or no knowledge of its antecedents, and what, as a sociological discipline, it aims to achieve. Even though its birth as an identifiable discipline is only recent, we have by no means covered all the aspects of the enterprise, or been as comprehensive in our coverage as the considerable amount of ethnomethodological work allows. Instead, our aims have been more modest, and restricted to giving, as faithfully as possible, a taste of what is involved in ethnomethodology in as comprehensible a way as possible. Accordingly we have restricted ourselves to only a relatively small segment of the work available, hoping that the reader will be encouraged to follow up the further readings.

As far as the organization of the book is concerned, we have assumed that most readers will have some acquaintance with what we call, not pejoratively, 'conventional' sociology. Accordingly, we have taken a great deal of space contrasting ethnomethodology with many of the theories and methods which will be more familiar. The reasons for this are mainly heuristic not polemical. So, Chapters 1, 2 and 3 constitute a section in which we are concerned to show the differences between 'conventional' sociology and ethnomethodology from a number of different directions. Chapter 1 is suggestive of ideas and concepts used in ethnomethodology. Chapter 2 deals more formally with the 'submerged tradition' which has informed ethnomethodology, and Chapter 3, from another direction, reinforces many ideas already mentioned and prepares the ground more directly for a discussion of the central ideas and some of the work done in ethnomethodology. Chapter 4 is organized around the basic ideas and concepts of ethnomethodology, while Chapter 5 deals, in the main, with some of Harvey Sacks' work. In this chapter we try to give an idea of the breadth of style of ethnomethodological work as displayed by one of its most important figures, and his investigations of 'practical reasoning'. Chapter 6 deals with the more prolific of investigative areas in ethnomethodology, namely, conversation analysis. It is perhaps time for someone to write a text solely devoted to this work, especially since it is so very technical. What we have done is to wander, we hope informatively, through some of the more interesting topics in this field, and, by doing so, to have illustrated its relevance for the ethnomethodological enterprise. The final chapter tries to indicate some other areas which have not been fully dealt with in the earlier parts of the book and which might be of some interest to the reader.

Although the situation has changed, much of the early ethnomethodological work was only available in mimeo form and, therefore, not widely or easily accessible. To date the most serious gap is the lectures which Harvey Sacks gave through the 1960s until his tragic death in 1975. We have, accordingly, minimized the number of references we give to these even though some of the ideas found there do appear in the book. Here we can only record a general debt to his influence and hope that the lectures soon appear in published form.

One other presentational point. Much of the data ethnomethodologists present, especially that from conversations, is heavily annotated with transcription symbols. Where we felt it appropriate, we have simplified these.

There are, as always, many people we need to thank for their contributions, both direct and indirect, to this book. We would specifically like to mention two members of the Manchester Boddington's Appreciation Society and Boozing Team, Wes Sharrock and Bob Anderson, both of whom appear throughout in various guises, some grotesque, some plagiarized, some acknowledged. John Lee, who has the best wine cellar east of Runcorn, Paul Drew, Nina, Nicole Marie-Claude, Graham Button, Ruth, Sue, Terry, Bill Roper and members of Ronnies, all of whom in various and kindly ways make their unknowing contributions. Maeve, Wendy and Heather at Lancaster, Jane, Susanne and Kay at Plymouth, all bore the heavy responsibility for typing. Special thanks, too, to Jacky, who had the unenviable task of looking after the only two and a half year-old to have a trial for Wakefield Trinity during the final stages. For all these we wish the book could have been better.

D. B., J. A. H.

DB – my parents
JAH – Jacky

to whom we are more than reflexively tied.

Chapter one
AN INVITATION TO ETHNOMETHODOLOGY

In recent years the sociological community, especially in this country, has witnessed a debate about the merits and demerits of an approach to sociology known as ethnomethodology. For many, its appearance on the sociological scene caused no little concern since, on the face of it at least, ethnomethodology seemed to deny the hard-won scientific status of sociology and challenged many of its cherished principles: a challenge met with some vigour and anxiety.[1] For others, the appearance of ethnomethodology was largely greeted with indifference, its problems and concerns seemingly too remote from the central issues of the discipline. More recently, however, the debate has cooled somewhat and ethnomethodology has been embraced, if reluctantly, by the sociology community as another way of engaging in sociology. Like most reasonably successful radical movements, with acceptance its critical force appears spent and its practitioners tolerated as slightly wayward, if not eccentric, members of the sociological profession. Yet ethnomethodology seems as little understood today as it was when Garfinkel first produced his *Studies in Ethnomethodology* in 1967.[2] Now much of the turmoil has subsided it is perhaps a more opportune moment to try to present some systematic account of what ethnomethodology is and what its practitioners do.

In order to begin such an account, in this chapter we intend to illustrate the approach of ethnomethodology by contrasting it with the approaches taken by 'conventional' sociology to some traditional sociological issues. The first of these is that of crime, the second that of sexual identity, while the third concerns 'story telling'. We are not claiming that these are in any sense 'typical' sociological problems, whatever this might mean, merely that they provide us with an opportunity to highlight some of the differences between ethnomethodology and what we are calling for the sake of convenience, 'conventional' sociology.[3] Our concern at the moment is to note and discuss some of the observations ethnomethodology is likely to make about the 'conventional' sociological treatment of such topics, leaving fuller development of these for subsequent chapters. We have avoided offering a sentence-length definition of ethnomethodology mainly for the reason that such definitions are rarely helpful to the reader until he has some insight to give the definition life. This is the purpose of what follows.

CRIME

For sociologists, and social scientists generally, crime constitutes a problem to be explained. While the nature of the explanation may and indeed does vary, the questions asked about crime tend to be of the following order: "What are the causes of crime?'; 'How much crime is there?'; 'How is it distributed amongst the population?'; 'Is the volume of crime increasing or decreasing?'; 'How can crime be prevented?' and so on. The first thing to notice about these questions (and this is a point which will be developed later in the discussion) is that they are the kind of questions and concerns that an ordinary member of society might ask. Despite this similarity of concern, it is claimed that the sociologist, as a social scientist, has access to methods which enable these questions to be answered precisely, systematically and theoretically: in short, scientifically. In other words, involved here is a distinction between the kind of knowledge of the social order produced by the sociologist as social scientist and the common-sense knowledge produced or acquired by the ordinary member of society. One of the ways in which this distinction is made and warranted is in terms of the data the sociologist brings to bear on the questions asked compared with that used by the ordinary member who, it is argued, makes judgements on the basis of inadequate empirical materials. The ordinary person is often subjective in his selection and treatment of those materials, not to say prejudiced, is unlikely to have a perspicuous view of the social order and its workings, and, finally, is generally atheoretical: in short, is unscientific in approach.

How then does the sociologist go about answering the questions just posed? An important, indeed an essential requirement of any sociological answer to the questions is an adequate empirical data base. Clearly, what this data base will consist of, its content if you like, will depend upon the particular question asked. If the question concerns the social and geographical distribution of crime within a society then, obviously, the data base will need to consist of crime statistics which show the relative rates of criminal activities within specified regions or social groups. If, on the other hand, one is interested in the attitudinal dispositions of known offenders compared with non-criminals, then an adequate data base might consist of attitude scales, personality inventories, and the like, filled in by the members of relevant groups, such as prisoners and college students. In other words, the obvious point to make is that the data base must be germane to the research question being posed. From a scientific point of view, there are other requirements essential to an adequate data base, including statistical adequacy, representativeness, random selection, and so on, again depending on the nature of the question asked. Thus, it is claimed that an adequate data base constituted according to the kind of requirements just mentioned will go some way to avoid problems noted in connection with the ordinary member's everyday view of crime such as its subjectivity, partiality, bias, and so on.

Of course, an adequate data base while necessary is not, by itself, sufficient for a 'conventional' sociological analysis of crime which aims at scientific respectability. Of equal importance is a theory which explains the patterns found within the data. It is this theoretical knowledge of crime, that is, knowledge derived from the systematic application of a warrantably scientific method upon the phenomena of the world, which distinguishes the social scientist's account from that of the ordinary member of society.[4]

An example of work in the style we are discussing here is Morris' study, *The Criminal Area*.[5] In the course of this work he examines the social class distribution of probation and approved school cases. The data base consisted of the official figures produced by the probation and approved school services along with the social class distribution, the latter given in terms of the Registrar General's definition of social class.[6] Morris notes that not one child in the listings came from Classes I or II, while for the other three classes the relative rates were as follows: Class III, 1 case per 3,003; Class IV, 1 case per 380; and Class V, 1 case per 187. He concludes:

The assumption that there is a valid class differential suggests that delinquency may be studied within a class frame of reference. This is not saying that morality varies inversely with social status, but merely that *legally defined* deliquency is a social characteristic of the working classes in general and the family of the unskilled worker in particular. The behaviour of individuals in other social classes is so organised that departure from established norms is far less likely to bring the non-conformist into collision with the criminal law.[7]

Using this data base, then, Morris has been able to find a characteristic of persons on probation and in approved schools, namely, that such persons tend to cluster toward the lower end of the social scale. This is a 'finding' derived from the data and the next step is to account for it. To accomplish this a theoretical framework is called into play based upon notions of family type and the kind of socialization that occurs in each. Briefly, Morris holds that there is a marked difference between the patterns of behaviour and conduct in middle-class as opposed to working-class families; in the former the child is brought up in an 'atmosphere of controlled care', while in the latter child-rearing takes place 'in an atmosphere in which restraint is often conspicuous by its absence'.[8] In this way the data base and the theoretical frame are brought together such that the social class distribution of probation and approved school offenders is explained in terms of differential family types and related socialization patterns.

The model of sociological explanation we have just outlined is, we would contend, a familiar one in 'conventional' sociology, extending beyond the province of criminology. Accordingly, in what follows we are not criticizing Morris in particular but, as we said at the outset, using his work as a means of pointing to features which can be found in sociological work generally. We will begin by considering how Morris defines the parameters of his data base and, hence, his phenomenon of interest.

Morris claims that he is merely considering the social class distribution of *legally defined* delinquency. This could be taken as meaning that there are other instances of delinquency, presumably undetected, which might not be distributed in the same way. Indeed, one way in which some sociologists attempt to subvert studies similar to Morris' is to claim that there are numerous instances of undetected crimes and delinquencies which could or do show a different social class distribution of criminality.[9] These accounts, by pointing to such things as the variable rates of detection, the occupational specificity of some types of crime, police and judicial discretion, poor statistics, and so on, argue that detected crimes and delinquencies constitute merely a sample, and a biased one at that, of the total level of delinquency within a society at any point in time. But, regardless of whether one wishes merely to describe official delinquents and their social class distribution, or whether

one wishes to fill out this picture by including undetected delinquents one is, nevertheless, trading on the common-sense notion
familiar to ordinary members of society that there is such a 'thing'
as a delinquent that is detectable and countable.[10] This is only to be
expected since from the earliest days the whole aim of sociology,
even as traditionally conceived, has been to address the everyday
world in which we all live. This being the case, sociology must,
perforce, use the concepts of that social world. This is not yet a
criticism merely an observation upon the traditional aims of the
discipline.

Of course, 'conventional' sociology does not take the everyday
vocabulary of the ordinary member of society unchanged. As we
have already indicated, everyday language is transformed in order
to achieve greater theoretical and empirical rigour. In this respect,
the attitude of 'conventional' sociology to everyday language was
established early on with Durkheim's pronouncements on the
vagaries of the language used by the layman.

... the words of everyday language, like the concepts they express, are
always susceptible of more than one meaning, and the scholar employing
them in their accepted use without further definition would risk serious
misunderstanding. Not only is their meaning so indefinite as to vary, from
case to case, with the needs of argument, but, as the clarification from
which they derive is not analytic, but merely translates the confused impressions of the crowd, categories of very different sorts of fact are indis-
tinctly combined under the same heading, or similar realities are differently
named.[11]

and, even more passionately,

The sociologist... must emancipate himself from the fallacious ideas
that dominate the mind of the layman; he must throw off, once and for all,
the yoke of those empirical categories, which from long continued habit
have become tyrannical. At the very least, if at times he is obliged to resort
to them, he ought to do so fully conscious of their trifling value, so that he
will not assign to them a role out of proportion to their real importance.[12]

Accordingly, although the language of the everday may form the
starting point of social scientific investigation, in itself it cannot
constitute the language of scientific inquiry; at least not without
major modifications to make it more precise, more rigorous, more
analytically usable.

However, it is our claim, which we will substantiate in more detail later, that the *sense* of concepts so transformed still largely depends on their everyday usage. Understanding Morris' explanation,

for example and, by implication, other 'conventional' sociological accounts, depends upon our understanding of what 'an atmosphere of controlled care' may look like, what bedtime as an 'institutional ritual' is, what 'working-class' and 'middle-class' family life is like, and so on: all essential to the analysis but rarely adumbrated in any detail and then only discursively. The reasonableness of the explanation that differential socialization patterns produce variations in delinquency, depends heavily upon the reader using the social knowledge acquired in his or her everyday world to 'fill in' the sociological account of family life which Morris provides. It is this very social knowledge which members must use and bring to bear on sociological accounts to render them reasonable and plausible. It is this otherwise unanalysed and undescribed social knowledge which ethnomethodology seeks to examine. Let us look at this in a little more detail.

It is a commonplace to observe that in the course of their daily lives the ordinary members of society regularly make use of categories in order to describe the world around them, including other members of society. This is so pervasive a practice that it hardly needs illustration. Similarly, sociologists make use of categories in order to map out their phenomena of interest. In Morris' case these categories include 'delinquents', 'criminals', 'working-class', 'middle class', 'members of families', and more, all of them referring to types of social actors, institutions, or activities. We have also made the point that the *sense* of many of these sociological categories depends heavily upon the kind of common-sense knowledge used by the ordinary members of society. For both the sociologist and the lay person, it is presumed that these categories are 'seeable', describable and detectable. Indeed, criminals of various kinds and their activities are to be found in records, they are reported in the press, talked about and even appear on television. It is their seeability, their describability, their detectability which is of interest to ethnomethodology. How do 'crimes' and 'criminals' come to be seen and described? And, more generally, how are identifications and categorizations done and how do they contribute to the construction of the social order?

These questions pose a number of problems for the practices of 'conventional' sociology. One of them concerns the relationship between the sociologist's account of the social order and those offered by the members of society. In work of the kind illustrated by Morris' research on the relationship between social class and delinquency, this issue emerges out of the very data base he has used to investigate the relationship; the official records produced by the probation and approved school services. These records are the product of a long and complex social process of categorization done by those responsible for 'dealing with' crime and delinquency, including members of the police, legal officials, social workers, and more. In other words, the data is the outcome of many anonymous individuals' own procedures for accounting for the social order in the course of doing their respective jobs. But, none of this categorization work is dealt with by Morris or, by implication, the others who adopt this style of sociological research.[13] How the social actors involved make sense of their environment and construct courses of action over time on a moment-to-moment basis is not a fundamental issue, despite the fact that part of the sense made of their environment and the lines of action constructed by those who 'deal with crime' include the very records used by Morris and other researchers in their tabular presentations and analyses.

In order to see where this point might lead us, let us look briefly at the kind of categorization and descriptive work involved in what we have summarily referred to as 'dealing with crime'. The long journey of an act and its perpetrator to its final enshrinement as a 'crime' in official records begins with the point at which it is brought to the notice of the police. This can happen in any number of ways including reports by private citizens as well as detection by the police themselves. In any event, neither of these processes is to be understood as automatic; that is, 'crimes' and 'criminal acts' do not come to the police neatly packaged and appropriately labelled, but have to be assembled out of all the particularities that constitute a report, an event, or a person. Is this report of a stolen car an instance of a criminal act or a case of an owner forgetting where he parked his vehicle? Is that young long-haired man dressed in denims and driving a new car a likely car thief or a University lecturer on his way home? Is this smashed shop window an act of vandalism, an accident, or the result of a successful rugby team's high spirits? The point is that the police do not, can not, encounter everyday scenes as clear, unambiguous displays of some legal code. The police, like all members of society, engage with the world through an assemblage of background expectancies and norms; what Cicourel calls, 'a sense of social structure'.[14] It is this which enables them to 'read' the social environment as recognizable displays of the everyday world. It enables them to distinguish between the 'normal' and 'abnormal' features of the environments they police. It enables them to describe an area in terms of the likely types of offences and offenders to be found there, to know what 'trouble' to expect, to decide whether or not something 'strange', 'routine', 'harmless', 'wrong' is happening, and so on.[15] In other words, the police, in the course of doing their job, faced with the day-to-day scenes they encounter are able, as occasions arise, to determine, or at least suspect, that something is happening with which they have to deal. Much of this background knowledge is tacitly held rather than explicitly listed as a set of descriptions or rules in advance of an occasion when they may be used. A traffic policeman may not be able in advance to say why he stopped the bedenimed young man in the new car beyond a vague statement of a feeling that it 'looked suspicious' or 'not quite right', or why he suspected the car reported as stolen had, in fact, only been mislaid. Nonetheless, the policeman can sense when things stand out from the texture of the routine, can detect anomalies, by using his background knowledge of the world which is his responsibility to police.

Of course, 'hunches' or 'suspicions' are not enough. In each and every case, the matters with which the policeman deals have to be assembled into one or more of the categories deemed relevant by the legal code: a process that involves transforming all the particularities of the actual scene encountered with instances of socially and legally relevant categories which can serve as the basis of inference and action by himself and by others. The initial 'hunch' based on the incongruity of the driver's denim clothes and relatively new family car, might become more firmly based if, for example, the driver cannot produce his driver's licence or other documents certifying ownership of the vehicle. In this event, the policeman has legal grounds for proceeding further in whatever ways he may think appropriate. But, as with any event, other features of the scene may be used to assemble and warrant another description of 'what is going on'. If the driver's voice, demeanour, comportment, and speech style along with the books strewn on the back seat, do not quite fit the standard image of a 'joy rider' or 'car thief', the policeman may well decide to proceed no further. The point is that the policeman engages in a massive amount of interpretative work deciding and assembling an account of 'what is happening'. Some of this process of practical reasoning makes use of the policeman's stock of knowledge about the social types likely to be encountered in the district, some of the customs and lore of policing, some of the conceptions of the 'normal' and the 'abnormal', some of the law itself: all, however, as a swarm of particulars as revealed and displayed in each concrete case.[16]

Of course, this kind of street contact of police with crime is not the end of the story. The final product, the successful determination and categorization of a criminal act and its perpetrator, is the outcome of a long and bureaucratically shaped process in which other officials are also engaged. And, just as the legal rules are insufficient for, understanding how the policeman on the beat goes about his job, so they are also poor guides for understanding how cases are recorded, how evidence is assembled, how courts decide matters, and more. As Cicourel's study shows, police and probation officers developed and used perspectives that closely paralleled typifications held by members of the community. For example, they knew the city in which they worked as consisting of areas where police could routinely expect difficulty, areas where little trouble was to be expected, and areas where care should be taken in dealing with the populace because of political, economic and ethnic influences. Such typifications enabled them in the course of their routine day-to-day work, to make quick inferences about 'what is going on' in some setting despite the lack of information which must, sooner or later, be used in oral or written form.[17] At the beginning of each encounter the officials concerned often attributed typical circumstances, social causes, and careers to juveniles. Their encounters with delinquents, assessment of situations and ways of thinking, had an unfolding situated character as well as a more formal status as exemplified in the written reports.

From the point of view of official statistics, the interest lies in the written reports which culminate in the official record itself. Like most bureaucratic officials, the police and probation officers investigated by Cicourel are faced with the problem of transforming their conversations with putative law-breakers into oral and written reports that represent not only decisions taken with respect to each case but also serve to justify that decision as right and proper and prepare the subject for further classification and treatment. These accounts standardize the business at hand so that activities falling under the official's practical domain of interest are made meaningful for themselves and others who were not witnesses to the actual events recorded. So, there is always a discrepancy between the unfolding dialogue among the persons involved, say, an offender and interviewing officials, and how the exchange is written up as a report of 'what happened'. As Cicourel demonstrates, the exchange between an officer and a juvenile is an occasion for 'lecturing', 'fact-finding', character assessment, threats of dire consequences to come, and more, carried out using a variety of interrogation techni-

ques ranging from 'buddy-buddy' to 'threatening'.[18] The policeman's conception of 'typical' juveniles, 'punks', 'good kids', his
recognition of typical ecological arrangements, family organization
and background, personality, basic attitude, and so on, are all integral to understanding how behaviour comes to be labelled as 'delinquent' or 'criminal' and how some general rule or policy can be
invoked to deal with the case at hand. Little of any of this process
of practical reasoning and the contingent consideration which
prompted a particular decision in a particular case, appear in the
written record. Yet, it is the written record which invariably forms
the basis for further action with regard to the offender. Other officials, such as probation officers, who have to use the written record can, as 'insiders', interpret the record using their own background knowledge alluded to earlier, to determine 'what happened'
even though, from some points of view, the record is an 'incomplete' and certainly a 'glossed' version of all that transpired between
a delinquent and a policeman. The written record, in other words,
is inextricably part of and produced by a pattern of social organization from which it takes its sense.

The sociologically problematic character of the 'facts' and
'assessments' contained in the written records can be illustrated
from one of Cicourel's own cases, that of 'Robert'.[19] His family was
described as a 'middle income' home; his mother had remarried
though Robert's natural father lived nearby. The probation officer
was aware of a number of incidents at school in which Robert was
considered to be 'incorrigible'. The probation file contained mention of 15 incidents at school prior to his court appearance, ranging
from 'smoking' to 'continued defiance'. The probation officer's
assessment and recommendations for Robert contained a fairly detailed citation of a number of factors explaining Robert's 'complete
lack of responsibility toward society' with the recommendation that
he be placed in a school or state hospital. Among the factors mentioned were the mother's 'severe depression', divorced parents, un-
stable marriage, and his inability to comprehend his environment:
the kind of factors, we should note, assembled in conventional
sociological reasoning explaining the causes of delinquency. The
family, however, retained a lawyer for the hearing on Robert's case,
a step regarded by the probation officer with some amusement since
the case seemed so 'clear'. During the hearings the lawyer reviewed
each of the allegations and incidents said to comprise a picture of
Robert's 'complete incorrigibility' and suggested that the court was
imputing motivational connections between each difficulty and

argued instead that each could be seen as independent events arbitrarily connected by the officials of the court. The lawyer also pointed out that there were no explicit references in the reports to when Robert was 'doing well'. Eventually it was agreed that the boy should change schools and the entire family participate in a therapy programme so overturning the tacit decisions of the officials, adopting as they did a criminal view of the case, that Robert should be 'sent away' for 'his own good'. Two months later Robert was arrested for taking a car without its owner's consent. This time a psychiatrist came to his defence arguing that although the violation of probation was a serious matter, any disruption of his therapy programme might 'precipitate a regression'. The police and probation officials viewed subsequent offences such as this as yet further evidence of the delinquent's criminality, while from the clinical perspective of the psychiatrist they were not 'obviously' so, but rather a 'regression' from otherwise 'good progress'.

This and the other cases discussed by Cicourel show how 'delinquents get that way' as a process managed and negotiated through the socially organized activities that constitute 'dealing with crime'. The case of Robert illustrates how the object or act can be transformed by invoking a different frame of reference, or ideology, to reread the 'facts', character structure, family structure, mental stability, and the like.[20]

In addition, other materials examined in some detail by Cicourel reveal the contingencies associated with day-to-day police, probation, and court activities. What turns out to be crucial is how the differences in the official's relationship to the juvenile influence the individual's immediate disposition and his long-range career consequences. Even within the same community, differences in law enforcement personnels' perspectives on juveniles who are in 'defiance of authority' or possess a 'bad attitude' can have different consequences for the juvenile. Middle-income families, largely because of their wish to avoid the stigma of incarceration, mobilize resources to avoid this through legal and other efforts to change probation or court recommendations.[21]

There are a number of implications of Cicourel's work for the kind of research illustrated by Morris which are worth mentioning. First, the official records as a data base do not 'stand for ' or 'indicate' the amount and type of criminality in the way conventionally taken: that is, as indices of some Durkheimian 'social fact'.[22] Although conventional sociologists have long complained about 'bad' statistics, poor record keeping, and other 'biases' imported to official statistics by such things as changes in policy, fashion, or whatever, few have examined the procedures which produce these 'bad' materials. In the main, these have been viewed as irritating obstacles to understanding the 'real' distribution and nature of crime, or whatever phenomenon the official statistics record, however imperfectly. Yet, as Cicourel's work shows, understanding how official statistics are assembled illustrates how, in the case of crime, 'delinquents' are produced by the 'socially organized and socially sanctioned activities of members of the community and representatives of law-enforcement agencies'.[23] From this perspective, the meaning of official statistics has to do with the transformation of vague and disconnected everyday events into an ordered 'happening': a process which requires us to examine how deviations from the law, as imputed and described by members of the community or law-enforcement officials, come to be recognized, acted upon, in a legal way. The oral and written reports that are one of the outcomes of this process continually simplify, abstract, interpret and reinterpret the original event or action so that it is seen to 'fit' the logic of the law which is more accustomed to dealing with standardized recipes for explaining the relationship between legal rules and behaviour.[24] Legal thinking and its view of social reality removes the contingent and particular features of everyday life in the course of successive transformations from the original event to its legal adjudication. The net result, and one taken for granted by most conventional sociologists, is an 'obvious', a 'clear' picture of causality and 'what happened'. As Cicourel states it, 'Legal reasoning formalizes the premises of commonsense thinking about the world as taken for granted and known in common by 'everyone' and understood by 'any man', and 'closes' ambiguities in the language . . . as a means of making decisions and arguing the validity of concrete events in terms of taken-for-granted assumptions about everyday life.'[25] One consequence of all this for sociologists using official statistics to study delinquency and crime is that there is a premature specification of 'explanatory factors' in terms of the ready-made categories provided by the official organizations which have no 'obvious' correspondence with the daily events and the practical reasoning that led to the official statistics. In other words, according to Cicourel, using the official records as data we have no warrant for 'reading into' them the meaning of the events at the time for the personnel who recorded them. We do not know, nor can we infer, what precisely went on, what kind of contingencies were deemed relevant at the time, what kind of particulars and principles were brought to bear, and so on, when the events and the individuals recorded in the official statistics were dealt with. What Cicourel proposes instead is that the meaning of official statistics must be sought in the processes through which men, resources, policies, strategies, cover a given community, interpret incoming calls, assign men, screen complaints routinize reports, and so on.

A second point, which arises out of the preceding discussion, is that Cicourel's study challenges the conventional view found in lay and professional sociological reasoning that 'delinquents' are social types distributed in some systematic fashion produced by the social structure and its processes. It is this view which Morris seems to exploit by trying to trace the causes of the pattern of delinquency in variations in socialization practices between the social classes. The official statistics and other records stand as evidence for the existence of delinquents, despite problems of bias, error, and the like. In other words and as we pointed out at the beginning of this section of the conventional sociological investigation of crime, both lay and professional sociology assumes the existence of 'criminality' as something that is detectable and countable: an assumption which is, of course, supported by the official statistics themselves since they do count and record crime. The members of society 'know' this commonsensically in the way that they 'know' what 'defiance of authority' is; what to expect from people who live in Toxteth; what a 'good home background' is; what 'lurking on street corners' implies; and more. They have a 'sense of social structure' which enables them to 'know' what the social world with which they have to deal looks like, how it works, and so on. So, the official figures, for the members of society at least, have much of the circular quality of a self-fulfilling prophecy: crime and criminality exist and can be recorded as is evidenced by the records themselves. But the commonsense knowledge which actors use in the course of 'dealing with' crime, of which the official records are a part, is not examined by conventional researchers, although it is taken for granted in the analyses produced and in the understanding of them. Morris' conclusion about the differential class distribution of probationary and approved school cases and his explanation in terms of variations in family background, have all the flavour of explanations or accounts that might be offered by police, probation officers, and so on. Indeed, one might hazard the suggestion that if the official statistics index anything it is the theories officials use in 'dealing with' crime, and to this extent, represent another feature of a self-fulfilling prophecy. So far as Morris' own explanation is concerned, as reported earlier Cicourel's detailed investigation of how particular cases were dealt with, shows that middle-class families are often more prepared to mobilize legal resources on behalf of their delinquent members and are able to do so successfully because it is 'known', by relevant officials and others, that middle-class families are less likely to produce delinquents.

None of this is to deny that certain members of society do criminal things; that is, acts which the members of society could describe as 'criminal'. But the issue of how 'something' can be so objectified and communicated to others as part of their practical circumstances is seldom, if ever, addressed in conventional research. Abstract, statistically correlated information on age, sex, ethnicity, number of offences, social class, age at first offence, and so on, do not provide the researcher with the material for understanding how delinquency is produced. Such data provides only truncated indices or versions of 'what happened' in the day-to-day occurrences of actual school, police, probation and court practices. The negotiated character of phenomena labelled by community and law enforcement members as delinquent cannot be shown from the statistical data.

By way of summarizing the discussion so far, let us point to an important contrast between the kind of sociological work illustrated by Morris and that exemplified by ethnomethodology. Morris begins with the category of delinquent persons found in the official records and then selects a further set of categories by which those persons might also be described, namely, by 'social class'. The criminal population is then found to cluster in terms of the social class categories: more 'working class' being found among the delinquent category than other classes.[26] This 'interesting' distribution is accounted for in terms of a theory of the socialization practices and family structures found within the various social classes. By contrast, the concerns which might exercise the interests of the ethnomethodologist could include the following. Rather than the official records, police station log books, and other organizational artifacts being used as a source of information to be extracted as data in terms of age, sex, social class, etc., of offenders (which are then taken as indexing some further underlying social structure), these records are seen as embedded in an organization and used as a resource for organizational action by the members concerned. As Beatrice and Sydney Webb noted many years ago in regard to an organization's documents: 'They are not written with any view to inform historians or sociologists, or other persons unconcerned with the activities in question. They are, in fact, secreted exclusively for the purposes of action. They are, in a sense facts themselves, not merely representations of facts.'[27] Ethnomethodological interest in records might then centre on how records are used in the course of other activities. These 'other activities' might include such matters as arguing with a colleague as to whether certain information had been collected, as a source for determining whether one had remembered a case correctly, or for comparing one case with another. And, of course, using records in arguing, as a check on one's memory, and the like, are not activities restricted to police records. They are activities which go beyond the bounds of criminal records and crime as matters of concern. In this way, we can see that ethnomethodological concerns might begin to dissolve the common-sense notion of crime as a topic of enquiry and focus instead upon general procedures whereby members construct and make sense of the world in which they live. It is also worth noting here that while members themselves divide the social world into such categories as crime, industry, the family, education, politics, and so on, this does not necessarily mean that the analyst *qua* analyst must also organize his description of social organizations at this level. Since members themselves use such categories, how they use them becomes a topic of enquiry and not merely an unexplicated resource in analysis and description. We can see this, too, in the way in which Morris, along with other sociologists, make use of identifications which are also used by the members of society, such as 'working class', 'middle class', 'black' or 'white', 'male', 'female', 'friends', and so on. For social actors, the interactional significance and relevance of such categories of identification is a situated matter decided upon each and every occasion by the parties concerned. The fact that there is some sense in which one could 'correctly' identify a person as 'black' as 'working class', as 'female', says little about the relevance of such categories and their instant-by-instant interactional use and significance. For while it may be the case that any particular person could be identified as 'working class', or whatever, there is an indefinite list of other identifications, which could be used, such as 'son', 'father', 'mechanic', 'boozer', 'captain of the darts team', etc. While all may be 'correct' not all, depending on the occasion, would be 'right' or 'fitting' for the purposes at hand. What makes them 'right' or 'fitting' is a routine matter for the members of society and their 'sense of social structure'. To the extent that sociologists use them for analytic purposes, no matter how precisely defined, illustrates once again the way in which they 'trade on' actors' own common-sense knowledge as a resource. This is a point to which we shall return.

A further interest ethnomethodologists might have in records, official statistics, newspaper cuttings, documents, or whatever, would be concerned not so much with the content of those documents, records, etc., but rather with how such documents come to be understood. So, what might be of interest in a report of criminal offence is not *that* it is a report of a criminal offence but *how* we came to read it that way. In other words, the aim would be to obtain a description of the cultural knowledge and procedures of understanding required to read the report *that* way. Again it is to be expected that the description of such structures of cultural knowledge and interpretative procedures would not be restricted to a domain constrained by a notion of 'crime'. Such procedures would obtain for a wider level of analytic generality.[28]

Clearly more could be said about the ethnomethodological approaches to what is conventionally referred to as crime, as indeed more could be said on behalf of the traditional sociological approaches to this topic. However, let us now move on to a rather different matter to illustrate, once again, what might be seen as some features of ethnomethodological interest, in this case arising from the topic of transsexuality.

TRANSSEXUALITY

Although this topic might seem exotic, the issue of gender identity is of massive importance within all cultures. Even within relatively undifferentiated societies, gender, along with age, tends to form one of the major axes around which the division of labour is organized. Women tend, on the whole, to be drawn into what could broadly be termed domestic roles, while men become warriors, hunters and, often later in their lives, important political figures. Even as societies become more differentiated, gender still constitutes one of the major criteria of role allocation and attainment. Explanations of why gender status tends to be all pervasive in its social consequences vary between disciplines. On the whole biologists favour explanations which stress innate genetic differences between the sexes, while sociologists identify, instead, such factors as socialization and cultural patterns as responsible for producing the variations just noted. But, in either case, the picture becomes more complex when one has to take into account those cases, albeit rarities, where some kind of transfer is effected between the categories 'male' and 'female'. Accordingly, both the biologist and the sociologist might arguably have an interest in studying these 'deviant cases' since they could conceivably throw some light on what gender consists in, either biologically or sociologically. Our major concern here is with sociological conceptions of gender identity.

As Garfinkel points out, every society exerts strict controls over the transfer of sexual status.[29] When such events occur these are normally only permitted on ceremonial occasions and regarded as 'temporary' and 'playful' variations on what the person truly is. Certainly, from the point of view of the member of society the 'natural' gender composition of the environment consists of two categories, 'male' and 'female'. Except for a legal alteration of the birth certificate, there is no legitimate path between what Garfinkel calls the 'moral entities' of male and female, and even the change just referred to is ambiguously regarded by societal members. The overwhelming commonsense conception of gender identity consists in the dichotomy in which persons are 'naturally', 'originally', 'in the first place', 'in the beginning', 'all along' and 'forever', one or the other.[30] Given that this is the standpoint taken in our society, then those persons who elect for a transformation of sexual status from one category to another became a topic of some interest. A typical sociological approach to these persons would be to examine the possible personal, family and general social conditions which create such gender ambiguity. Leaving on one side, then, the possible hereditary genetic and hormonal influences, the sociologist would be concerned with such matters as, say, the child's relationship with his/her parents. Was the child subject to ambivalent and ambiguous role-models? Was there an absent parent of the same sex as the child thus subjecting it to overstrong cross-gender influence? These and many more would be the kinds of question that the social scientist could pose, the basic concern being with how and why intersexed persons came to be as they are. By contrast the problem that exercised Garfinkel's interest in his study of the intersexed person, Agnes, was how Agnes 'passed' as a normal natural female despite the fact that she ran the constant risk of exposure. Agnes, at the time of the study, was a 19 year-old girl who had been raised as a boy and whilst having female measurements of 38–25–38, these co-existed with a fully developed penis and scrotum. In other words. Agnes continually had to achieve her claimed rights to female status while possessing bodily features which were manifestly male. For Garfinkel, Agnes was a practical methodologist. Because of her position she had to be extremely sensitive to the background and largely tacit features of interaction which 'normals' might see but not notice.

There are many fascinating features of Garfinkel's account we could discuss. However, those on which we wish to concentrate are, first of all, Garfinkel's discussion of Agnes's discovery and creation of the social order from within and, secondly, how accounts of social phenomena are tied to and are part of the scene, or social setting, in which those accounts are provided.

Common sociological conceptions of the manner in which the routine and organized features of social settings are produced tend to rely upon some neo-Durkheimian notion of rules which organize, 'externally' as it were, the behaviour which takes place within the social setting. That is, the rules which specify appropriate behaviour in particular settings, be they situated at work, at home, at play, on the road, in the cinema, at a party, or whatever, are regarded as external to the settings, at least in the sense that their existence is independent of, and extends beyond, the *particular* setting and its participants. The rules, or norms, are used by participants, in the relevant situations, to guide their behaviour and others in the roles in which they find themselves. In this way, patterns of interaction are made generally stable and, hence, predictable, and since many norms are learned early in life, the roles and behaviour they generate often have an automatic and unreflective quality to them. Thus, the conceptions of 'normal' sexuality, for example, could be theorized in terms of the stable patterns of behaviour induced from early childhood socialization. The case of Agnes, however, illustrates the ethnomethodological view that the stable, rational, intelligible, reasonable, understandable, justifiable, etc., features of a situation are a practical and continuous accomplishment of members throughout the course of their daily lives. One of the examples Garfinkel cites on this point is bound up with the description of Agnes as a 'secret apprentice'. Agnes had occasion to be in the home of Bill, her boyfriend, and was learning from Bill's mother how to cook Dutch food. But not only was Agnes learning how to cook Dutch food she was also learning to cook: in other words, acquiring a 'normal' female accomplishment or skill rather than adding to it by learning a specialized facet or development of the skill. Thus, under the guise of the overt goal, held mutually by Agnes and Bill's mother of learning to cook Dutch food, Agnes was, for herself, learning other components of what it is to be female. A further example of this 'secret apprenticeship' occurred when Agnes was with her girlfriends. On many of these occasions when the girls would be discussing their boyfriends, other girls, various events that had occurred, and so on, Agnes took a largely passive and acquiescent part. Again, not only did Agnes find out from the girls how women talked about such issues but, in addition, she learned from the girls that her passivity and acquiescence was itself a desirable female trait. The point here is not so much that Agnes learned one thing in the course of doing another, which she did, but, rather, in attending to the features of the setting in which she was involved, and by manipulating the relevant textures of that situation, she was at one and the same time 'producing' herself as a 'normal natural' female, and, in so doing, contributing to the development of the interaction.

All of this was a continuing practical accomplishment by Agnes, and a general feature we want to note here, of which the study of Agnes is a particularly perspicuous example, is that ethnomethodology views *all* social settings as produced in this manner. The *sense* of social order, the *sense* of social structure, the *sense* of the stable features of personality, sexuality, social settings, etc., is a continuous production by members. The case of Agnes illustrates that for 'normals', too, their situated displays of sexuality are also practical accomplishments in that they must perforce take cognizance of the particular setting, the particular partner they are with, the particular topic at hand, and manipulate these in such a way as to produce themselves as 'normally sexed' persons. As Garfinkel puts it:

Agnes' methodological practices are our sources of authority for the finding ... that normally sexed persons are cultural events in societies whose character as visible orders of practical activities consist of members' recognition and production practices. We learned from Agnes, who treated sexed persons as cultural events that members make happen, that members' practices alone produce the observable-tellable normal sexuality of persons, and do so only, entirely, exclusively in actual, singular, particular occasions through actual witnessed displays of common talk and conduct.[31]

Thus, we can say that one of ethnomethodology's abiding interests is the explication of the ways in which members, through their practices, produce the social structure of everyday activities, the aim being to describe those practices and show how they work.

One of the most pervasive features of social settings is the talk that goes on within them. In a fundamental sense we can say that talk is constitutive of the settings in which it takes place. Indeed, this was one of the interesting features which emerged from Garfinkel's study of Agnes. Here we are not simply pointing to the fact that Garfinkel was interviewing Agnes and tape-recording 35 hours of conversation in which she reported on her past experiences, much as a travelogue reports on the scenes projected on the screen. Rather, the point is that Agnes' talk, like all talk, took place within a setting, was consequential for further action within that setting, and in this sense was constitutive of the setting and the relationship of the parties to it. Some of the import of this conception can be gleaned from another feature arising from Agnes' 'secret apprenticeship'. Agnes herself had remarked on a problem she encountered whenever the issue of her childhood or early days came up as a topic with her friends. Agnes had been raised until the age of 17 as a boy and, accordingly, one of the problems she faced was not only to display herself as currently a female, but also as one who had a biography as a female. The strategy Agnes adopted was to talk about herself in terms of vague generalities, a side feature of this being that her friends saw this as a sign of 'natural female modesty'. While it might seem from this that Agnes was telling her biography for manipulative and Machiavellian purposes, (and Garfinkel himself notes he experienced this feeling when he interviewed Agnes), the point we wish to stress here is that there is no such thing as a biography for all purposes. The 'stories' one tells about one's past life will vary according to whether they are for a curriculum vitae for a university teaching post, or whether they are for the amusement of friends, talking to a member of the appropriate sex to awaken their interest in you, eliciting sympathy in a court of law, attempting to justify a less than sober life style, and so on. Also the significance, humour, relevance, effectiveness, etc., of events in one's past life will themselves vary with time. The 'wasted' years spent as an apprentice motor mechanic prior to gaining a university degree and becoming a teacher might look rather different in a period of educational recession.[32]

But not only were Agnes' observations about presenting her biography relevant to the problem of presenting herself as a woman with a seamless biography of being a woman, they were also pertinent to the interviews she had with Garfinkel and the other researchers. Agnes had portrayed herself as someone who had always been a girl and her possession of male genitalia some ghastly accident of nature. However, it turned out that she had been taking oestrogens since the age of 12. Prior to this disclosure Agnes had said that from an early age she had always expected to grow into a woman's body and that, in puberty, this had spontaneously, gradually but unwaveringly, happened. It now appeared that the dosages of oestrogen, which by chance she had started to take about the right time, prevented the development of all secondary sex characteristics that would have been produced by the male hormone, androgen. Nonetheless, her body continued to produce the androgens with the result that she became a 'lovely looking young "woman", though with a normal-sized penis'.[33]

The point to be drawn from this is not that Agnes had 'lied', nor that Garfinkel had been misled, or whatever, but that it reveals Garfinkel's article to be a feature of the very circumstances it reported, that is, it was a 'situated report'. In other words, Agnes' disclosure displayed the fact that the events which occurred and were reported in the interviews and which Garfinkel then assembled into articles, were themselves the product of the practical work Garfinkel and Agnes had engaged in to produce and maintain the setting as an interview. That is, the plausibility, reasonableness, warrantableness, groundedness or rational character of the talk, actions, stories, behavioural displays, etc., that took place between Garfinkel and Agnes were themselves 'worked up' as a practical accomplishment; *that* and *how* they were 'worked up' was masked from the participants. It was Agnes' disclosure that revealed, yet again, this fact as a feature of how the social order is produced by and displayed by and to members.[34]

Once again, we can see that when ethnomethodology begins to address common-sense topics, in this case 'transsexually', the focus begins to shift as issues of rather more general import emerge. In the case of Agnes, Garfinkel's investigations begin to address not transexuality as commonsensically conceived but the 'passing' practices that Agnes, because of her ambivalent gender identity, had to learn as a 'secret apprentice': practices which, in the normal course of events are viewed by 'normals' as routine, unquestioned methods of producing and sustaining the social order. The interest, then, is not so much in Agnes as a deviant, as a sexual oddity, a victim of sexual politics, or some pitiable unfortunate, but in focusing on the ways in which identities, any identities, are displayed and on the methods used to display them. The use of 'passing' techniques, of course, are not exclusive to transsexuals. Garfinkel himself notes that he had many occasions upon which he was endeavouring to 'pass' with Agnes as someone with adequate medical knowledge. Roy Turner has noted that one of the practical day-to-day problems faced by ex-mental patients is to 'pass' as normal, sane persons who have never been other than normal or sane.[35] Turner, in discussing the problems encountered by mental patients, suggests the generic usefulness of the notion of 'disclosure norms' concerning who gets told what and when. Ex-mental patients, for example, justified the non-disclosure of their mental illness to employers by using an analogy from physical illness; after all, that one had a broken leg when a teenager is arguably an irrelevant disclosure when applying for a clerical post. Sacks notes that there seems to be an ordering of persons to whom 'troubles' can be disclosed, it not being the case that one tells these 'willy-nilly', 'to all and sundry' with impunity. An illustration of this would be the 'typical trouble' occurring between spouses if the husband, or the wife, tells someone else of his, or her, promotion before the spouse.[36]

Passing techniques are not confined to 'deviants' but are something in which we are all engaged, be it as students, teachers, shopkeepers, customers, poets or peasants. There are occasions when we are all involved in something similar to Goffman's 'management of identity'.[37] In Goffman's analysis people are seen as strategically employed in episodic encounters, manipulating appearances in some Machiavellian manner. Against this, however, Garfinkel indicates that occasions of interaction are not typically 'seeable' as episodic, nor are they set up with some predetermined goal in view. Thus, not only are people unable to 'leave the field of play' at will, but the 'game' itself, to put it this way, is situated within the stream and flow of living. In other words, encounters, interactions, and so on, are not games or episodes detached from the social world, but are part of the unfolding process in which sense and understanding are mutually established. Importantly the bedrock upon which this comprehension is established is that of 'trust' and tacit acceptance of background appearances and expectancies.[38] Even Agnes, 'aware' to a degree that most of us never attain for any sustained period of time, depended upon 'trust' and the requirement of treating words and appearances at face value, thus belying the Machiavellian approach to much of her behaviour. Further to this, most encounters do not have any set goal which provides 'sense' to the developing interaction. Rather people find out where they have been and where they are *in the course of the interaction*. The sense or meaning of words and actions are revealed and can change across the course of social time. In this way we are all 'secret apprentices' to the settings and encounters in which we are engaged. We are continually discovering the social world anew *from within*, and one of ethnomethodology's abiding interests is to elucidate how this process of discovering the social order from within the culture, the setting, and the society is achieved by members.[39]

Another point of some methodological as well as theoretical importance, and a contrast with what is a prevailing practice in 'conventional' sociology, is that Garfinkel's study was based on a sample of one case. Yet, much of what we would want to characterize as of a general nature emerges from this close and detailed study of Agnes. Not only about transsexuality but also about particular aspects of social interaction, such as passing practices, the achievements and disclosure of identities, the importance of 'trust', and so forth. We are not claiming that large samples of transsexuals are useless for sociological investigation, merely pointing out that much can be achieved by a close and detailed attention to a case which, from a 'conventional' sociological view, might seen untypical if not unique.[40] This feature of ethnomethodological work will appear again.

Finally, as the 'disclosure' by Agnes of her early pill-taking activities revealed, accounts, including Garfinkel's own account, are irretrievably tied to settings as part-and-parcel of those settings. This would also, by implication, be true of sociological accounts of social settings.

Now we turn to a phenomenon, one already mentioned, namely talk, which though hardly of central importance to 'conventional' sociology as a phenomenon of itself is, nonetheless, a vital and essential resource for engaging in sociology.

TALK

It is a commonplace to remark that talk is a pervasive feature of social life in that much of social interaction is carried on by means of talk between participants to social scenes or settings. One could hardly imagine families, industrial organizations, schools, political systems, even revolutions, being carried on without talk. Yet, rarely has 'conventional' sociology addressed the topic of talk in its own terms. However, possible exceptions to this general lack of interest in talk might include the work of such people as Bales, Bernstein and the general area of socio-linguistics.

By and large these scholars have treated talk not as a phenomenon in its own right but as an index of some other matters in which they are interested. For example, Bernstein explores the effects of differential access to aspects of the language on the ability to conceptualize and perform other intellectual tasks, and hence, derive benefit from educational provisions.[41] His central argument, much simplified, is that the working class, unlike the middle class, can only use a 'restricted' subset of the language which, in turn, explains their relative lack of success in the educational system compared with their middle-class counterparts. Although the data upon which Bernstein bases his case is somewhat sparse, relying in the main upon fairly commonly held cultural conceptions of the differences in speech styles between the English middle and working class, the main point we want to make here is that his work is not directed to the operation of talk in itself.[42] The 'restricted code', supposedly typical of working-class speech, is described as consisting of short, ungrammatical sentences, poor syntax, and an over-reliance upon proverbs and proverbial expressions, and the like. Nowhere is the structure of talk itself described, which is perhaps not surprising since this was not Bernstein's concern. For him, what was of major concern was the way in which the talk, as characterized by the speech styles detected, indexed conceptual abilities.

A similar use of talk can be seen in Bales' technique for measuring small group structures and dynamics, which consists of 12 categories derived from Parson's action schema.[43] Each of the categories is based on a conception of the kind of talk which can transpire in group interaction. For example, members of a group can 'aim for an orientation', can 'show approval', 'give support' to others, and so on. Thus, the talk that actually occurs within an observed group is mapped onto the 12 categories such that frequencies of types of talk can be used to describe the structure and dynamics of the group. A consequence of this procedure is that the actual talk and the context in which it occurs is lost through the process of codifying and abstracting into the categories. Once again, as we saw with Bernstein, the talk itself serves as an index of, in this case, group processes and group structures. The talk, in effect, is detached from the setting in which it occurs, with some perverse consequences. For example, only an interactional dullard would see the question, 'Are you doing anything this evening?', as merely and always, a 'request for information', ignoring, in other words, the massive and varied amount of interactional work that talk can do extending far beyond the categories used by Bales. While Bales, in a fashion, sees that talk can be illocutionary in that it performs actions, his categories are far too gross to capture the often delicate and often indefinite activities that can be and are done through talk.[44]

In both these examples, the talk that 'emerges' from interaction is used as an index for social processes other than the talk itself. The talk, to put it this way, is a resource rather than a topic of inquiry in its own right. One can also see this in the research technology currently used by much of 'conventional' sociology, such as questionnaires, attitude scales, interviews, participant observation, and so on: all of which essentially rely upon eliciting talk in some form or another from subjects or respondents. In the light of this it is perhaps surprising, given the emphasis 'conventional' sociology places upon enhancing the precision, accuracy and validity of its research instruments, that little attention has been given to the phenomenon of talk itself.

Particularly revealing in this connection is Cicourel's study of the interviewing process in a study of fertility conducted in Buenos Aires.[45] The study aimed at investigating the social factors affecting fertility among a sample of families selected from Buenos Aires. The main research instrument was an interview schedule consisting of many open-ended items in which interviewers could explore the ramifications of particular responses. One theme concerned the notion of ideal family size. The responses to the various items concerned to assess what the respondent felt about this varied, often within the same interview. By the normal rules of questionnaire and interview evaluation this variation would be taken as indicative of 'inconsistency' on the part of the respondent; a sign of confusion, a poor questionnaire, an inadequate interviewer, or lack of attention and interest by the respondent. In any event, a mark of poor or deficient data. However, when examining the transcripts Cicourel made of the actual interviews, it became clear that the responses to the questions on ideal family size were closely tied to the particular topic that was currently being discussed. In one case, for example, when the question of ideal size was embedded in the topic of the expense of bringing up families, the respondent indicated a low figure for ideal family size, whereas, when the talk was about the pleasures of family meals, then the figure mentioned was higher.

This and other points of a similar kind made by Cicourel should alert us not only to the fact that talk about a topic is tied to an environment which includes the talk itself, what has been talked about, by whom, what was said, and so on, but also that current sociological conceptions of the stability of attitudes, personality and beliefs, might need re-examination.[46] That is, 'inconsistent' responses might not only be indications of the fact that respondents are 'lying', 'failing to come clean', 'trying to conceal their true feelings', etc., but might also be indicative of the ways in which such things as attitudes, beliefs and personality, are expressed in the course of talk-as-interaction. Through talk people do things such as complaining about their husbands, praising their children, making jokes, giving ironic descriptions of family life, change topics, interrupt, deliver news, etc., and it is from these, by various processes of abstraction, that personality, attitudes and beliefs are inferred by *both* sociologists and other members of society. We will discuss in later chapters some points arising from these remarks. Of more immediate concern is the ethnomethodological approach to talk.

The examination of talk has for some time been a central ethnomethodological concern and the study of ordinary, naturally occurring, everyday talk has come to be widely known as conversation analysis. This area of study was developed by the late Harvey Sacks who had studied at the University of California Los Angeles with Harold Garfinkel. Whilst no adequate summary of the nature of this work can be given here (see Chapter 6), an example of Sacks' work will be presented for flavour. It is well to point out, however, that conversation analysis is not an enterprise designed to repair some perceived deficiency in 'conventional' sociology: a position it shares with ethnomethodology itself. Rather, it is geared to the description of the highly organized structure that talk, particularly as conversation, takes in all its extremely fine detail. As such, it could be claimed that conversation analysis represents a discipline in its own right, with its own internal interests, concerns and methods of study. To borrow a phrase from Althusserian Marxism, conversation analysis has its own 'problematic', even though its origins lie in not unfamiliar sociological terrain.

The topic we have chosen to illustrate the approach of conversation analysis concerns some aspects of story telling in conversation.[47] An initial feature we can note about the way in which stories get to be told in conversation is that they take more than one utterance to deliver. That is, if A is telling B a story the way in which the story is told is typically formatted as follows:

A: Something terrible has just happened.

B: What's that?

A: (STORY)

B: Oh that was awful.

We can call A's first utterance, following Sacks, a 'story preface' and suggest that it has at least three interactional jobs to perform. First, the utterance operates to get A conversational space in which to build a possible multi-sentence length utterance, that is, a story. Second, it gives B some information as to what the end of the story will be: the end is to be located by listening until something describable as 'terrible' has been told. Third, it provides B with some material with which to give an appropriate response to A, namely, something like 'Oh that is terrible/awful/wonderful.' The significance of the first point is that ordinarily a listener has potential rights and sometimes obligations to start speaking at 'speaker transition' points which, for current purposes, can be glossed as occurring at the potential end of sentences.

The fact that story prefaces can provide a listener with a proto term with which to respond to the story in terms of both its completion and appropriate manner of response, means that when B utters, 'Oh that was awful' it could be said that he was displaying understanding of the story that had just been told. It is however a particularly weak way of indicating to another person that one has 'understood' what was being talked about. This being the case, it raises the question as to whether there is any strong way in which people can demonstrate to each other that a story has been heard and understood? One possible way in which a stronger demonstration can be made is through the production of a second story. That is, one gross observation that can be made about story telling in conversation is that one can get a return story from the recipient of the first, where, significantly, the second story is produced and organized as a *second* to the first story. It is not simply the case that one gets a story told, and then another is told by the listener to the first, and that 'firstness' and 'secondness' is a matter of mere happenstance. Rather, what Sacks argues is that the second story is constructed and delivered as a second to a first. Such an organization of story telling can be noted in the similarities that often obtain between the two stories such that if the first story is about an automobile accident, then the second story is also about an automobile accident. Similarly, the two stories are often told with the respective tellers occupying the same 'position' in each story. That is, if the first story is about an automobile accident which the teller had witnessed, then the second story will tend also be from the point of view of a witness. If this is not the case then it is possible that different interactional work is being performed. Instead of demonstrating understanding – 'I know exactly what you mean, hear my similar story' – a second story concerning an automobile accident in which the teller was a victim might operate, say, as a put-down to the first story in that it might get mentioned that the ambulance had a hard time getting to the victim because of the gawping onlookers!

Second stories, then, delivered at the completion of a first story, and produced and told to display similarities to the first, are thus a strong way in which persons can demonstrate that they have understood somebody's first story. Such second stories show that the hearer had listened closely to the story and that, out of all the many things that had happended to them, they were able to select one event and describe it in such a way as to produce detailed similarities.

Having described the operation of second stories, Sacks goes on to suggest some further interesting points. One has to do with how memory might possibly be organized. A common and prevailing view sees it in terms of an analogy with computer storage systems in which events get remembered in terms of their programmed importance. While this may hold for some items, for others it does not seem to fit in with the way in which memory gets to be displayed through talk. A common example here would be the way in which people remember the death of John Kennedy and will remember that of John Lennon. Typically, this event is recalled in terms of what one was doing at the time one was first told of the shooting. Although the incident itself had wide, indeed global, significance, it is remembered, typically, in egocentric terms – where 'I' was in the scheme of things. At first glance this might seem a perverse way in which to build a common culture. How on earth can people get to understand one another when events in the world are remembered from a totally unique individual position? One answer, Sacks suggests, is provided in the very operation of second stories. The availability of the skill to produce stories which 'match' other people's stories is one of the ways in which people can come to see that they inhabit a common culture and common social world. Sacks further suggests that second stories also enable people to become aware that they are *not* 'unique' or 'alone' in the world in regard to any particular problems they might have, but that others have had similar experiences, witnessed similar tragedies, enjoyed similar pleasures, been exposed to life's little heartbreaks that nearly kill you, and so on. A person with a newly discovered heart disease can locate others who have similar problems merely by telling a story relating to the illness. In this way we can become aware that others are in the same boat; this being one way in which the 'trouble' can be handled.

Many more things could be said about stories, as Sacks does. Also conversation analysis is concerned with more than story-telling. It includes, for example, close order sequencing, that is, ways in which a current utterance is tied to a preceding one; the opening and closing of conversations; topical change and continuity; the way in which news is delivered and received; and generally the whole range of procedures persons use in interacting with one another. Although second stories are only a small part of the interest of conversation analysts they do illustrate, nonetheless, some of the general points about talk which we can summarize as follows.

First, the very notion of *second* stories involves the important idea of sequencing. That is, it is not simply the case that the second story occurs after the first one, but that it is *produced* as a second to a first in a similar way that a second 'hello' of a greeting is produced as a response to a first 'hello'. Sequencing points to the fact that interaction, not just conversation, proceeds in a step-wise fashion. The sense of an utterance or action is dependent on its position within a sequence of other utterances or actions. This demonstrates a general ethnomethodological observation that the sense and rationality of events is closely bound up with their temporal ordering. Conversation analysis has shown that this operates in fine detail including such an apparently trivial and inconsequential phenomenon as laughter. People can engage in competitive laughter, for example, through the highly organized placement of 'laugh-units'.[48]

Second, the data used for conversation analysis consists of tape and video recordings, and the transcripts thereof, of naturally occurring talk.[49] This facilitates the continuous review of the data so that any detail which escapes first notice can be retrieved on second, third, fourth or however many analyses. The raw data is not abstracted into categories such as Bales might devise prior to its analysis, or laundered and cleansed of the natural pauses, hitches, 'um's' and 'er's', etc., which, while irrelevant for the linguistic analysis of sentences *per se*, turn out to have significant interactional consequences.

Third, the fact that the raw data is 'bottled' in transcript form means that others can propose alternative analyses on the same set of data: a condition rare in 'conventional' sociology not to say social science in general. One could argue that 'bottled' data in this form makes possible a more extensive cumulative knowledge about conversational interaction than is perhaps possible with other areas of sociology.

Fourth, and finally, although conversation analysis would seem on the face of it to be addressing issues remote from those which concern 'conventional' sociology, Sacks' remarks on memory suggest this is far from the case. In so far as 'conventional' sociology is interested in, for example, mind, personality and social structures as the product of interaction, talk is one place where these are located and revealed. Seen in this way conversation analysis is very much a sociology of everyday life.

CONCLUSION

Through these three examples we hope to have given the reader some idea of the different ways in which what we have termed conventional sociology and ethnomethodology approach the social world, and given hints on how this world is respectively conceptualized and investigated. A point that perhaps needs to be stressed here is that although we started with three topics of conventional sociological interest, crime, transsexuality, talk, these served as the catalysts for bringing out some features of ethnomethodology's approach to the study of social interaction. They were, to put it another way, occasions or tags on which to hang illustrations of the kind of observations ethnomethodology makes about aspects of the social world. What we are not saying is that 'conventional' sociology and ethnomethodology are in competition with each other; that, for example, the ethnomethodologist's approach to the study of crime is a better alternative to those exemplified in criminology or sociology. As we saw in this example, under ethnomethodological treatment the topic as conceived by 'conventional' sociology tends to dissolve or disappear, suggesting, to put it no stronger than this, that ethnomethodology's interest lies in a different direction pointing to different phenomena. Clearly, more could be said on this matter but we have, hopefully, come closer to a characterization of what ethnomethodology is about. It aims to examine the ordinary, common-sense, mundane world in which members live and do so in a way that remains faithful to the methods, procedures, practices, etc., that members themselves use in constructing and making sense of this social world.[50]

NOTES AND REFERENCES

1. Indeed, one might speculate that the personal direction many of those attacks took suggests that all was not well with sociology and that ethnomethodological critiques had found one or two tender spots. Garfinkel, for example, had difficulty renewing his membership of the American Sociological Association on the grounds that he was not doing sociology. Only after the intervention of Parsons was he reinstated. Some of the flavour of the disputes can be gleaned from R. J. Hill and K. S. Crittenden (eds), *Proceedings of the Purdue Symposium on Ethnomethodology*, Institute for the Study of Social Change: Purdue, 1968.

2. H. Garfinkel, *Studies in Ethnomethodology*, Prentice Hall: Englewood Cliffs, 1967. See also review symposium in *American Sociological Review*, **33**, 1968.

3. 'Conventional' sociology we merely intend as a shorthand expression for sociological practices other than ethnomethodology. No pejorative tone is implied. Further ramifications of this characterization will, of course, be explained in later chapters.

4. We are aware that even within conventional social science there is dispute over the precise value of theory and its relation to empirical data. These issues, by and large, are not germane to the case we are making here.

5. T. Morris, *The Criminal Area*, Routledge & Kegan Paul: London, 1957.

6. The rationale of the Registrar General's classification of occupational groupings is that 'each category is homogeneous in relation to the basic criterion of the general standing within the community of the occupations concerned', and includes educational and economic factors. Until 1971, the social classes were titled as follows: I Professional, etc. occupations, II Intermediate occupations; III Skilled occupations; IV Partly skilled occupations; V Unskilled occupations. See *Classification of Occupations*, HMSO: London, 1960. The classification is periodically updated. For a discussion of recent changes see I. Reid, *Social Class Differences in Britain*, Open Books: London, 1977, pp. 34–42.

7. *op. cit.*, p. 10.

8. *ibid.*

9. See, for example, E. H. Sutherland, *White Collar Crime*, Holt,

Rinehart and Winston: New York, 1949; S. Box, *Deviance, Reality and Society*, Holt, Rinehart and Winston: New York, 1971; H. Becker, *Outsiders*, The Free Press: New York, 1963, among many others.

10. This is true even of those sociologists who have attempted to 'relativize' the notion of deviance by using some variant of the idea that deviant behaviour is so defined by relevant audiences. See M. Pollner, 'Sociological and Common-sense Models of the Labelling Process', in R. Turner (ed.), *Ethnomethodology*, Penguin: Harmondsworth, 1974, pp. 27–40; P. McHugh, 'A Commonsense Perception of Deviance', in J. D. Douglas (ed.), *Deviance and Respectability*, Basic Books: New York, 1970.

11. E. Durkheim, *Suicide* (trans. J. A. Spaulding and G. Simpson), Routledge & Kegan Paul: London, 1952, p. 41.

12. E. Durkheim, *The Rules of Sociological Method* (trans. G. E. C. Catlin) The Free Press: New York, 1966, p. 32.

13. When it is dealt with it is often conceived as a source of 'error' or 'bias' in the official figures and, hence, a process that interferes with accurate recording. See our earlier remarks on the deficiencies of official crime rates.

14. A. V. Cicourel, *The Social Organisation of Juvenile Justice*, Heinemann: London, 1976, p. 328.

15. See, for example, E. Bittner, 'The police on skid row', *American Sociological Review*, **32**, 1967, pp. 699–715; Cicourel, *op. cit.*; H. Sacks, 'Notes on the Police Assessment of Moral Character', in D. Sudnow (ed.) *Studies in Social Interaction*, The Free Press: New York, 1972, pp. 280–93; Ch. 4 of this volume.

16. See, for example, D. Sudnow, 'Normal crimes: sociological features of the penal code in a public defender's office', *Social Problems*, **12**, 1965, pp. 255–76.

17. A. V. Cicourel, *op. cit.*, p. xiv.

18. *ibid.*, pp. 166–7.

19. *ibid.*, pp. 319–27.

20. *ibid.*, p. 327.

21. *ibid.*, p. 331.

22. E. Durkheim, *The Rules of Sociological Method, op. cit.*, and his *Suicide, op. cit.* Similar points we are making with respect to criminality have been made in connection with Durkheim's study of suicide based as it is on official statistical records. See, for example, J. M. Atkinson, *Discovering Suicide*, Macmillan: London, 1978.

23. *op. cit.*, p. 27.

24. *ibid.*, pp. 27–8.
25. *ibid.*, p. 28.
26. Note that, in principle, other categories could have been selected to describe the criminal population: gender, hair or eye colour, height, weight, ethnicity, shoe-size, marital status, leisure pursuits, body odour and so on, not all of which, of course, would produce 'interesting' distributions. This illustrates, once again, how social scientists routinely use their prior cultural knowledge in order to investigate the social world and, in advance, 'construct the reasonableness' of their findings. Who would imagine that body odour or shoe-size had anything to do with criminality? And, then again, who would not?
27. B. and S. Webb, *Methods of Social Study*, Longman: London, 1932, p. 10, and H. Garfinkel, *op. cit.* Chapter 6, and E. Bittner, 'The Concept of Organization', in R. Turner (ed.), *op. cit.*, pp. 69–81.
28. As an example of work in such a vein see H. Sacks, 'On the Analyzability of Stories by Children', *op. cit.* It is also discussed in Ch. 6 of this volume.
29. H. Garfinkel, 'Passing and the Managed Achievement of Sex Status in an Intersexed Person', in Garfinkel, *op. cit.*, pp. 116–85
30. *ibid.*, p. 116.
31. *ibid.*, p. 181. In talking about the sense of social order, etc., as a practical ongoing accomplishment by members we are not saying that they are conscious of the practices in which they are engaged. For them it is a matter of knowing 'how' rather than knowing 'that'.
32. We are, of course, talking here about the 'retrospective interpretation of events' There is also a 'prospective interpretation of events' where the view taken of future events is heavily dependent on current happenings. See also Ch. 3. of this volume.
33. This later disclosure is recounted in the Appendix to Garfinkel, *op. cit.*, pp. 185–228. The quotation is from R. T Stoller, Garfinkel's collaborator. The disclosure was not made known to Garfinkel until sometime after the study was in press.
34. Garfinkel, *ibid.*, p. 288.
35. R. Turner in seminar given at Plymouth Polytechnic, 1975.
36. Sudnow notes the same phenomenon in informing family members and friends of a death. See his *Passing On*, Prentice Hall: Englewood Cliffs, 1967. and Sacks' remarks in Hill and Crittenden (eds), *op. cit.*, and Ch. 5 of this volume.

37. E. Goffman, *The Presentation of Self in Everyday Life*, Penguin: Harmondsworth, 1959.
38. H. Garfinkel, 'A Conception of, and Experiments with, "Trust" as a condition of stable concerted actions', in O. J. Harney (ed.), *Motivation and Social Interaction*, Ronald Penn: New York, 1963.
39. One little discussed but intriguing implication of this observation is how children learn language and, of course, acquire the culture. Children are, if you like, the 'secret apprentices' *par excellence*. Moreover, although all adults began as members of this 'closed order of children' it is difficult, if not impossible, to retrieve what the pre-linguistic world of the child is/was like except through adult conceptions.
40. The usual position adopted is that since there is a sense in which all individual cases are unique then any 'general' sociological description must be based upon a significant number of such cases giving an averaged description. Since, however, this still retains the initial problems of how to articulate any given individual case in terms of this averaged description then it is difficult to see what gains are made over describing the structure of any given individual datum. H. Sacks, 'Sociological descriptions', *Berkeley Journal of Sociology*, 8, 1963, pp. 1–19.
41. B. Bernstein, *Class, Codes and Control*, vol. 1., Routledge & Kegan Paul: London 1971.
42. Bernstein's argument was avidly adopted in America where, not having the typical English concern with matters relating to social class, it was used to account for the lack of success of blacks in the American School system. The notion developed that blacks suffered from 'linguistic deprivation'. The major critic of this position is W. Labov. See his 'The Logic of Non-Standard English' in P. Giglioli (ed.) *Language and Social Context*, Penguin: Harmondsworth, 1972, pp. 179–218.
43. The choice of 12 categories is extremely fortuitous since there are 12 vertical positions on an IBM computer card! We merely note this fact. See for an account of the techniques R. F. Bales, *Interaction Process Analysis*, Addison-Wesley: New York 1950.
44. This has been forcefully expressed by such philosophers as L. Wittgenstein, *Philosophical Investigations*, Blackwell: Oxford, 1958 and J. L. Austin, *How To Do Things with Words*, Oxford University Press: Oxford 1965.
45. A. V. Cicourel, *Theory and Method in a Study of Argentine Fertility*, Wiley: New York, 1973.

46. See for example, J. Heritage, 'Assessing People' in N. Armistead (ed.), *Reconstructing Social Psychology*, Penguin; Harmondsworth, 1974, pp. 260–81.
47. Sacks' Lectures, 1970.
48. G. Jefferson's transcription procedures highlight, among others, this phenomenon. See also, G. Jefferson, et al., 'Preliminary notes on the segmental organisation of laughter' Unpublished draft.
49. It will be obvious to those with any familiarity with the relevant literature that much of the data consists of telephone calls. The reason for this is to obviate arguments about non-verbal communications in the early stage of analysis.
50. 'Methods', 'procedures' and 'practices' as a list is intended to convey the fact that there is a whole host of variety of ways in which people assemble the social world. The list contains some aspects of those ways.

Chapter two

ETHNOMETHODOLOGY AND THE SUBMERGED TRADITION: A BIOGRAPHICAL VERSION

Tracing the origins of any body of thought is a hazardous enterprise at best but in this case made worse by the fact that most of ethnomethodology's pioneers, with the tragic exception of Harvey Sacks, are very much alive and kicking, and more than capable of contributing their own 'insider's' versions. Few, however, seem keen on so doing. Unlike many of their colleagues in conventional sociology, ethnomethodologists seem less inclined to establish much of an intellectual geneology for their work. Apart from references to the works of the putative founder, Harold Garfinkel, and to Sacks, they rarely indulge in the sport of footnoting the works of major, or even minor, forebears. Nevertheless, if only for didactic purposes some discussion of the traditions to which ethnomethodology is connected can be valuable. Accordingly in what follows we merely offer an outline of some of the main ideas that have, arguably, influenced the character of ethnomethodology in an effort to place it within a wider intellectual context. We are not so much concerned to establish a pedigree for ethnomethodology; its validity is its own affair and not a matter of having the right ancestors. As with all accounts, pedigrees and biographies are constructed for particular purposes and this one is no exception. The parts of the story we have selected identify, or so we hope, the sociological questions and issues to which ethnomethodology offers answers, and in this way are intended to illustrate its profoundly sociological inspiration. Biographies have another feature worth mentioning: they are constructed with hindsight and it is easy to give the impression that ethnomethodology, or any other approach for that matter, is a direct logical descendant of identified antecedents. For some purposes this may be a valuable insight, but here our aims are more limited. To establish a case of direct lineal descent we would need to know a great deal more than we do about the personal history of the participants, their teachers, their intellectual biographies, and other details. Failing this all we can offer is a discussion of the wider traditions which could have played their part. It is a little like a traveller who, on reaching a destination, buys a map to see through where he may have travelled.

THE SUBMERGED TRADITION

Ethnomethodology is normally lumped together with other so-called 'humanistic' sociologies, or what Morris calls, 'creative sociologies': a heading which includes phenomenological sociology, Weberian sociology, existential sociology, symbolic interactionism, interpretative sociologies, sociology of the absurd, and more.[1] Though often very different in both the theories they espouse and the methods they recommend, each of these approaches to the study of social life, according to Morris, share two key assumptions. The first is that 'human beings are not merely acted upon by social facts or social forces' but 'are constantly shaping and "creating" their own social worlds in interaction with others'. Second, that 'special methods are required for the study and understanding of these uniquely human processes'.[2] These approaches belong, in other words, to what has been referred to as the 'subjectivist' tradition of social inquiry in contrast to the 'objectivist' or 'positivist' tradition.[3]

The intellectual origins of both these traditions go back at least to the philosophical debates of the seventeenth century concerning the nature of human knowledge and its relationship to the world. The view which eventually predominated, and from which the 'objectivist' or 'positivist' tradition derives, was that reality consisted of what was available to the senses, and that all knowledge, properly so-called, had to have its basis in sensory experience. This empiricist theory of knowledge posited the independent existence of an external world which was made known to us by its action upon our senses. The knower contributed very little to the organization of this experience and the knowledge it provided of the external world. There was no knowledge independent of experience which was at the same time informative about the world.[4]

As far as the social sciences are concerned, this epistemology is generally associated with the claim that there are logical and methodological affinities between the natural and the social sciences. Not that they share precisely the same techniques or methods since, pragmatically, their respective subject-matters require different methods of study, but that they share the same logic of enquiry, the same scientific method. Ontologically, this claim was predicated on the argument that, essentially, there was little difference between the natural and the social worlds. Both constituted a world external to and independent of human subjectivity, a world subject to impersonal laws which could be revealed by the application of the scientific method. As a subject of enquiry, then, human beings and their products were logically identical to the inanimate objects of nature. Man was not only *in* the world but also he was *of* the world. It was not denied, of course, that human beings had qualities not possessed by rocks, chemical compounds, atoms, etc., such as beliefs, language, attitudes, values, and so forth. What *was* denied was that these facts has any consequential epistemological implications for the nature of social scientific inquiry. Values, beliefs, and so on, could be studied in much the same way as inanimate nature; indeed, the very success of the social sciences as interpreted positivistically depended on this very possibility.

By the conclusion of the Second World War, the tradition just discussed had become the orthodoxy of professional social science. Not unconnected with this state of affairs was the tremendous growth in the number of social scientists practising not only in universities and other centres of learning, but also in government agencies of various kinds advising on policy, researching into social problems, gathering statistics, and so on. No longer was social science the activity of a few eccentric intellectuals ensconced in cold, damp attic rooms, suffering from carbuncles and cadging money off their richer and more fortunate friends. Social science became a large industry, if that is not too inappropriate a word, committed to a particular conception of society and to a method of study. Although each social science formulated theories specific to its own subject-matter and drew upon different traditions, they did share a conception of society, and of social actors, which made them amenable to scientific study in the sense discussed earlier. Society, organizations, groups, institutions, and such like, had a structure and dynamics explicable in terms of causal principles or laws appropriate to their status as phenomena independent, as it were, of the individual persons who could be said to compose them. For example, one particularly important sociological theory of the mid-1950s, structural functionalism, adapted an older analogy comparing society with an organism. While trying hard to avoid many of the crasser implications of this by now ancient analogy, functionalism modelled society, and any group for that matter, as an open, changing system which operated according to principles and constraints which characterized all systems.[5] Although this is not the place to go into the details of this particular theory, the important point to note about it is that the social actor plays only a minor and dependent role. In Morris' terms, the social actor is acted upon by the systemic forces rather than being the shaper or creator of the social world.

The positivist tradition encouraged the development of an empirical research technology designed to emulate the impressive achievements of the natural sciences. The aim was to produce knowledge of society which was precise, objective, predictive and, ultimately, formulable as causal laws. Research methodology became more systematic, influenced by the logic of experimental designs derived largely from biological science. The survey and the questionnaire were brought to the foreground of empirical research and used to investigate a wide range of topics. Measurement models were developed and the use of statistical measures of association became endemic. Knowledge of social life had to satisfy the requirements of scientific knowledge in the sense that it was objectively produced; the product, in other words, of scientifically accredited methods correctly applied to the investigation of social phenomena. Methods which, among other things, annihilated the individual scientist's standpoint and, as rules of procedure, made agreement on specific versions of the world possible. The language of social research became the language of variables: a way of talking about social phenomena in terms of their attributes and properties, and how they varied among and between one another.[6] The social actor became a bundle of discrete and measurable properties described as chunks of data ready and waiting for processing. Society became a system of vectors and forces.

Of course, the authority of orthodox social science did not go unchallenged, and the challengers had a tradition to draw upon equally as venerable as the positivist. The 'humanistic' tradition drew a firm distinction between natural and human phenomena and, further, claimed that each realm required different methods of study.[7] Though variously argued and conceived, this distinction depended on the claim that human society and its history could only be understood in terms of meaning and not in the causal categories of natural science. Nature and culture were inherently different. Society and history, as the products of human consciousness, were subjective, emotive as well as cognitive phenomena, and the causal, mechanistic and measurement oriented models of explanation, typical of the positivist approach, inappropriate to their understanding. Knowledge of society and its culture could be gained only by isolating the common ideas, the feelings, the goals of the people living in a particular, historically specified, society. It was these cultural themes that made each social act subjectively meaningful for those living in the society. Social science should concern itself with understanding these meanings and the ways in which the members of society shape and create their social roles through them.

One issue arising from this debate and which beset in different ways both the 'positivistic' and 'humanistic' traditions was how the 'inner' or 'subjective' dimension should be treated. Although what we are calling the 'humanistic' tradition made meaning central to its programme the 'positivistic' approach, as we have suggested, did not ignore the subjective dimension. The notions of culture, beliefs, ideologies, values, and more are all concepts which attest to the fact that social actors live a rich and highly varied mental life. The problem was how to deal with it. For both traditions, the issue boiled down to one of accessibility. Almost be definition, certainly by conceptualization, the 'inner life' was private, beyond public access except through indirect, often ingenious devices. For 'positivistic' social science, the solution lay in treating such things as values, beliefs, and so forth, as phenomena which shared, in all important respects, the properties of natural phenomena, in that they were part of a causal pattern, varied systematically with other 'objective' phenomena, and hence measurable, if only indirectly. Once the problem of accessibility was solved through the design of appropriate measuring instruments, such as questionnaires, depth-interviews, attitude scales, personality inventories, and the like, to disclose their latent structure, 'subjective' phenomena could be correlated with 'objective' structural variables, such as age, class, education, and more, to build up a more complete picture of the workings of the social order.

The 'humanistic' tradition, on the other hand, because of its very presuppositions could not take this route quite so confidently. For one thing, intellectual constructs including sociology itself were simply one way of interpreting the world and, as such, influenced by all the historical and social factors which shaped the ways in which human beings made sense of their lives and environments. The 'interpretative method' seemed irretrievably locked in an infinite regress, there being no way to escape the social conditioning of interpretations to reach the kind of transcendental ways of knowing which positivism claimed for itself. Yet, for much of its history, the humanistic tradition remained locked within the idea that the 'subjective' elements of human life were fundamentally inaccessible. Its own solutions to the problems this posed for sociological knowledge focused largely on finding a method which did not depend upon positivistic precepts but which, instead, made the 'interpretative method' respectable.

MAX WEBER AND THE INTERPRETATIVE METHOD

A key figure in the humanistic tradition is Max Weber who belongs to that vein of German social thought which first seriously tried to face the theoretical and methodological consequences of the distinction between nature and society.[8] One of the major difficulties which beset this conception of social and historical inquiry was the matter of the criteria by which the results of enquiry could be judged. Unlike the positivist conception that the truth of a scientific statement lies in its correspondence, however indirectly, with facts derived from sensory experience, the fruits of interpretative understanding seemed intangible, too open to the personal inclinations of the scholar, and, above all, open to the charge that, as a form of knowledge, it is socially determined and, hence, merely relative. It was the search for a resolution to this particular problem which consumed much of the energy of Weber's predecessors, such as Dilthey and Rikert. By and large, these efforts concerned themselves with finding a philosophical basis for conceptions of knowledge which did not rely so exclusively, as did positivism, on sensory experience.[9] From a sociological point of view, however, Weber is important because he did not see causal explanation and interpretation as separate and autonomous modes of social scientific explanation. On the contrary, each was necessary to the other in order to produce a social science that was both scientific and faithful to the nature of its subject matter.

Weber argued, in brief, that since the causal relationships among the elements studied by natural science are devoid of meaning for the elements concerned, the methodology of natural science cannot be transferred, *in toto*, to the study of social life where meaning does play not only a critical but an essential role. For Weber, social action occurs when a social actor assigns a meaning to his or her conduct and/or environment and, through this meaning, relates it to the actions of others. Actions, then, are reciprocally oriented to each other not in any mechanistic fashion of stimulus and response but through an interpretative process. Accordingly, to grasp the meaning and significance of social phenomena it is necessary to understand this interpretative process and discover the motives, the reasons, and the goals which lead people to act in the ways they do. Before we can ask questions calling for causal explanation we must know and understand what it is we wish to ask such questions about. Thus, for Weber, at least as interpreted by most social scientists, understanding and interpretation logically precedes causal explanation.[10] Interpretation in this view is not an end in itself. While a necessary process for social science, it is never sufficient. Nor was it a simple matter of spontaneous insight or intuition, of fancifully imagining oneself in the position, say, of a Trobriand Islander, a Protestant manufacturer, a drug addict, or Attila the Hun. The process of *verstehen*, or understanding, is a matter of hard work and reflection and, above all, like any method, subject to the authority of logic and the criteria of science.[11] Accordingly, the products of understanding and interpretation had to be checked and endorsed by the appropriate methods of science. Sociological knowledge in Weber's terms, was a combination of the interpretation of meaning coupled with rigorous scientific procedures.

However important Weber might have been in Germany at the beginning of this century, his ideas were to become widely available in the English-speaking world only after the publication of Parsons' *The Structure of Social Action* in 1937.[12] For our purposes two features of Weber's work are worth noting. The first, and one which in the hands of Schutz was to prove consequential for ethnomethodology, was the emphasis Weber placed on individual social action. Although the vast bulk of his work embraces the massive sweep of comparative history, Weber's fundamental concept of social action and other concepts associated with it, are defined in individualistic terms; that is, social action is the result of an individual actor attributing meaning to some object, event, or person taking the orientation of other actors into account. Weber's core conceptual unit, then, is the individual in meaningful interaction with other individuals. Collective categories such as status groups, classes, religious sects, organizations, and so on, while often indispensible for intelligibility, are to be understood as shorthand expressions referring to 'actual or possible courses of actions of individual persons'.[13] Such collective phenomena have no ontological status apart from this. Concepts referring to collectivities have, of course, a meaning in the minds of individuals but have no other concreteness. Although, as we have suggested, Weber's preference in his empirical work was for the analysis of civilizations rather than the minutae of the individual's day-to-day interactions, his theoretical emphasis on the individual's subjective orientation was to provide an opportunity for Alfred Schutz to complement Weber's work by providing a fuller analysis of what he was to refer to as the 'life-world'.

The second feature of Weber's work we wish to point to concerns the reception of his writings when they became more accessible to English-speaking scholars. As far as sociology was concerned, Weber seemed to offer a solution to the problem of dealing with particular human qualities, such as beliefs, motives, reasons, etc., in a rigorously scientific manner. Unintentionally, then, he served to legitimate not only sociological styles which did not wish to go too far along the positivistic road, as well as providing some authoritative gloss for those who, while endeavouring to make social science scientific in the positivistic sense, wanted to escape some of its worst excesses. The interpretative method became respectable, while Weber's notion of the 'ideal type' was interpreted as a methodological device by which social scientists could approximate the generalized descriptions of the natural sciences. The net effect of this incorporation of Weber into orthodox professional sociology, for which Parsons must bear some credit and responsibility, was that it brought into the mainstream an alternative social and philosophical tradition with issues and problems that, sooner or later, would have to be confronted.

SYMBOLIC INTERACTIONISM

However, before discussing the consequences of Weber's thought, we first need to look at a particularly American tradition of 'humanistic' sociological practice which, we would argue, prepared much of the ground for the reception of ethnomethodology. In the 1920s and 1930s, Robert Park, Ernest Burgess, W. I. Thomas and others at the University of Chicago, pioneered participant observation as a method for studying social life, in particular the rapidly changing social milieux of the city of Chicago itself. An ex-journalist, Park's 'muckraking' style epitomized the spirit of many of the early studies. For the Chicago school of sociologists the little communities springing up throughout the city, the result of wave after wave of immigration, were 'natural' communities; social entities that were essentially self-regulating symbolic worlds perpetuating a distinctive moral and social organization. The aim was to interpret and analyse these communities in order to identify the processes through which their organization was created and sustained. We must also add to this conception a traditional American concern with the small community, and the disdain American pragmatic social philosophy had for highly rationalistic and formalized theories as reflected in its preference for first-hand practical knowledge. Both of these themes, as elements in the intellectual context of the early participant observation studies, served to shape and mould their distinctive style.[14] The earliest, Anderson's study of the hobo was published in 1923, to be followed by Thrasher's study of gangs and Cressey's of taxi dance halls.[15] During the 1920s and onwards, the theoretical framework underlying this method of research was refined and became widely known as symbolic interactionism, owing much to the work of the philosopher, G. H. Mead.[16]

As a theory of social action, symbolic interactionism stressed, as its name suggests, the symbolic nature of human social life. For symbolic interactionists, meanings are 'social products formed through activities of people interacting'.[17] Earlier, Mead had united a conception of the individual with that of society and culture through a notion of 'the self' which was seen as the internalization of the social processes by which groups of people interact with each other. Social action takes others into account through 'the self' which is able to take an imaginative view of their interests, possible reactions and circumstances into account. An actor learns to construct his or her own 'self' and those of 'others' through interactions with those 'others'.[18] In this way, individual action cannot be mechanical but must be seen as the mutual creation of interacting 'selves'. It was this insight which, in one form or another, provided the basis for the symbolic interactionist enterprise. 'Selves' and meaning become pre-eminently social, and hence sociological phenomena, and constitute the 'worlds' in which individuals spend their lives. Social life, then, is very much a creation of individuals interacting with each other and the study of this life must, of necessity, concern itself with exploring the processes by and through which social actors mutually adjust lines of action on the basis of their interpretations of the world in which they live.

Symbolic interactionism, then, gives pride of theoretical place to the interpreting social actor and, thus, commits itself to a method of enquiry which emphasizes the actor's point of view and which concerns itself with elucidating the meanings and understandings actors themselves use to construct their social world. By and large, symbolic interactionists rejected efforts to make a science of social life through adherence to formally rigorous, deductive, causal and quantitative models of enquiry. Sociological knowledge could not be gained through methodological formulae but must needs be gathered through living in the world; the result, in other words, of praxis. Efforts to reduce social research to routine and rule according to the accepted canons of scientific method distort the social world in elemental ways and merely 'gloss over the character of the real operating factors in group life, and the real interaction and relations between such factors'.[19] Instead hypotheses should develop out of engagement with the social life under investigation and sociological knowledge be an emergent consequence of enquiry rather than predetermined by abstracted intellectualizing. Symbolic interactionists, in other words, deny that adequate sociological knowledge can be gained by the rule-like application of methodological principles aimed at providing objective, detached, and rigorously formulated data. Questionnaires, interviews, scaling methods, research assistants, data processing procedures, statistical tables, and so on, all serve to distance the researcher from the real social world, albeit in the name of objectivity. The result is a 'scientized' conception of social actors as human beings having little or no relationship to the naturally occurring social world inhabited by men and women of flesh and blood. For the symbolic interactionist, authentic knowledge of social life is furnished by immediate experience which explains, to a large degree, the intimate association of symbolic interactionism with the method of participant observation: in fact, in this case theory and method become virtually inseparable and not some more or less casual association.

This commitment of symbolic interactionism to the study of everyday interaction entails taking very seriously the viewpoint of the actors concerned. Whether a researcher is studying a military unit, a religious sect, a hospital, drug users, professional footballers, or whatever, he must begin with the social world as constructed by the actors concerned, since it is through the meanings they impart to the objects and people around them and the symbols they use, that their social world is formed in the first place. This, to repeat, is one reason why much of symbolic interactionism emphasizes participant observation not only as a preferred method but the only proper way of doing social research. In this way, it is argued, the integrity of the social world being investigated is preserved undistorted by concepts, categories, methods, and such like, brought in from outside as alienating and 'dehumanizing' frameworks: as one commentator pithily expresses it, 'research is not . . . a disembodied agent of pure logic, but a social encounter'.[20] Accordingly, the social reality of symbolic interactionism is very much the reality of immediate experience. Unlike orthodox social theories, including Marxism, structural–functionalism, conflict theory and more, which presuppose deeper social processes at work beneath the phenomenal world of appearances that must be uncovered through rigorous theoretical and methodological work, interactionism attends to the visible social world, the world as understood and seen as such by the social actors concerned. To quote Rock again: 'interaction is defined as an order which is *sui generis*, not simply as the vehicle for the manifestation by the sovereign and deep structures of society'.[21] Social phenomena are to be studied on their own grounds and revealed in their own terms.

As far as the professional sociological world was concerned, symbolic interactionism remained, after a brief but colourful flowering in the 1930s and 1940s, a submerged edentulous tradition that just about held its own against the theoretical and methodological orthodoxy we spoke of earlier. For most professional sociologists it represented an unscientific brand of social investigation, little better than journalism though, perhaps, of some small use as a tool of preliminary investigation. Pride of place, however, was taken by the social survey and the questionnaire on the methodological front, and by variants of structural-functionalism on the theoretical. Symbolic interactionism did not disappear but carried on its research tradition in the United States, especially in the field of deviance.

For us, the importance of symbolic interactionism is that it did maintain a posture in professional sociology which emphasized the meaningful nature of social life and the creative role played by social actors in constructing and sustaining that life. It is also important in the stress it placed on the detailed, *in situ*, investigation of the processes by which individuals construct their everyday social worlds. An investigation which, moreover, must be entered into with the minimum of preconceptions derived from abstracted theorizing of a 'scientific' nature. But theoretical preconceptions it did have and despite its seeming eagerness to assert the contrary when giving advice on empirical research, symbolic interactionism did have a lively theoretical tradition. Its basic stance toward the social world, as we have said, emphasized the creative role of the social actor. In interaction, persons routinely use symbols, especially those embedded in language, and orient their actions toward others. While much social interaction of this kind is habitual, persons can and do self-consciously construct new lines of action. Social objects are constructs not 'self-existing entities with intrinsic natures'.[22] An object possesses social meaning because of the meanings brought to it by persons in the interaction process. Some meanings may remain stable over time, but frequently they must be worked out and negotiated at the time for organized joint action. Interaction, and the social patterning that results, is seen as a negotiated order, a temporary, often fragile thing created by meaning attributing, interpreting beings, interacting through time. Actors construct their actions together rather than merely acting in common, and concepts referring to macro or collective phenomena, such as culture, institution, group, even society, are to be regarded, *pace* Weber, as merely convenient expressions decomposable, without residue, into their fundamental interpersonal units.

Within this framework, however, symbolic interactionism embraces a number of varieties, some leaning more toward the aims and aspirations of orthodox social science, others maintaining the subjective interpretative critique of positivism. Becker, for example, certainly in his earlier investigations, argued that symbolic interactionism and its participant method were better suited to meeting the aims of a sociological science than the conventional positivist methods.[23] Similarly, the self and role theory branches tend to adopt a style of research and theorizing more in tune with those of orthodox social science.[24] To this extent, some versions of interactionism have been incorporated into mainstream sociology as the micro companion to the predominantly macro emphasis. Douglas refers to the distinction between these strains of interactionist thought as a conflict between 'behavioural interactionism' and 'phenomenological interactionism'.[25] Both take seriously the view that the fundamental social reality consists in the meaningful everyday interactions in which actors engage, but then lead off in rather different directions: a crossroads formed by their respective attitudes toward the role of the actor's point of view in sociological enquiry. 'Behavioural interactionism', broadly speaking, places more emphasis on the construction of a proper scientific vocabulary of ordering concepts held together by abstracted theory than do the 'phenomenological' brands of interactionism. These latter seek to conduct sociological enquiry through the description and analysis of the concepts and form of reasoning used by actors themselves.

This commitment to preserving the integrity of the phenomena under investigation by refusing to import presuppositions from 'outside', as it were, a commitment held extremely strongly in some interactionist quarters, can lead to what Matza calls, 'sociological naturalism' whose 'loyalty is to the world with whatever measure of variety or universality happens to inhere in it'.[26] From this stance the aim seems to be to reproduce as faithfully as possible the world of the actors as understood and as perceived by them with a minimum of interpretation on the part of the investigator. This aim, even as a minimal requirement of social research, influences and shapes the style of much interactionist writing: long quotations from the people being studied, often retaining the argot and slang typical of the group, the celebration of the details, often intimate, of people's lives, the sense of an almost indecent peek into a private world, the lack of abstract theory and quantification, and so on. It is for many, merely sophisticated, in-depth journalism, often exciting, provoking, giving insight, but representing no real or systematic attempt to address the important theoretical questions of the discipline. But, of course, the dilemma is clear: to do more than this is to run the risk of flirting with orthodox 'scientific' sociology. In any event, the idea of a researcher entering a scene or social setting without any ideas or preconceptions whatsoever is an absurdity. As a number of accounts show, participant observation as a method of direct engagement with the social world is by no means straight forward. The necessity of retaining some objectivity in presenting an analysis to the professional collegiate compounds an already ambiguous stance toward sociological research.[27] Indeed, on some renderings of symbolic interactionism the criterion of a successfully completed research project is when the investigator 'goes native' and is fully socialized into the group he is investigating. This, at least, is some evidence that the researcher has grasped and understood the life he was studying.

The difficulties we have noted with respect to symbolic interactionism arise mainly out of the injunction that social phenomena must be interpreted rather than analysed by means of causal, mechanistic models. Interpretation as a process seems altogether too dependent on individual whimsy or imagination ever to contribute to a consensus about the results of its investigations. Could two researchers using the theory and the method of symbolic interactionism ever reproduce similar findings with respect to the same phenomenon? Faced with the necessity of choosing between contrary findings, the practitioners of interpretative methods could hardly refer to 'impersonal rules which could govern so thoroughly a personal act as sympathetic insight and self-identification'.[28] Moreover, the validation of interpretations of meaning appears somewhat questionable since there are no 'external' criteria by which this may be done, given their approach. As we saw earlier with Weber, these particular problems are by no means new and constitute one of the predominant problems addressed by German social thought throughout the nineteenth and early twentieth centuries. One attempt to solve them, however, is important with respect to the intellectual background of ethnomethodology, namely, phenomenology, especially in the variant propounded by Alfred Schutz.

SCHUTZ AND PHENOMENOLOGY

In the span of this volume it is impossible to present more than a brief account of phenomenology and its relationship to sociology.[29] As developed by Husserl the aim of phenomenology is to describe the constitution of experience uncontaminated by scientific theory and other preconceptions. As Luckman puts it: 'The goal of phenomenology is to *describe* the *universal* structures of *subjective* orientation in the world, not to explain the *general* features of the *objective* world.'[30] In this way Husserl hoped to overcome the problem of the historical and cultural relativity of our knowledge of the world.

The means Husserl devised to overcome this relativity is the method of phenomenological reduction, or epoché, by which consciousness, the fundamental and undeniable existent, cleanses itself of all its social and historical baggage and constitutes itself as an absolute. Husserl held that whatever is genuinely true must be so universally and eternally. Yet, the attainment of this truth is inhibited by the fact that human experience is spatially and temporally bounded, a product of history, culture and society, and, hence, subject to the various distortions of prejudice, interest, incompleteness, cognitive preselection, and more. To reach the untarnished truth one must suspend or 'bracket' what Husserl called 'the natural attitude': that is, the ordinary cognitive posture we adopt toward the world in which we are naively immersed. For us this everyday world is taken for granted. We do not question its reality. We refrain from doubt, accepting it as it presents itself to us. Normal doubts and illusions leave intact the belief that *the* world, as a fact-world, is always there, self-evidently being. Even the unusual appears within an horizon of the taken-for-granted ordinariness typical of the 'natural attitude'. We are not motivated to question the meaningful structures of this 'life-world' in general and our interest in it is the practical one of living rather than studying it. It is a world of everyday experiences unquestionably accepted as they present themselves to us. This is the natural stance.

The 'life-world', for Husserl, is prescientific in that it exists prior to the growth of the modern sciences and is, furthermore, presupposed in all scientific endeavour. In the West, as early as Galileo, what took place was 'the surreptitious substitution of the mathematically substructured world of idealities for the only real world, the one that is actually given through our perception, that is experienced and experienceable – our everyday life world'.[31] In other words, science imposed an image of mathematical, objectified nature which became the measure of all that is genuinely real, and neglected to study reality as it is primordially given in experience. The phenomenologist must refuse to accept the validity of any conceptual scheme, rationalistic or otherwise, must doubt even the findings of science, adopting instead a philosophical stance which suspends judgement on all socially accepted knowledge until absolutely confirmed by 'transcendental consciousness'. Husserl's aim was nothing less than the gigantic enterprise of tracing back the essential meanings at the core of all disciplines to their source in this 'transcendental consciousness'.[32] The reconstruction, or recovery, of the life world was only a step along the way to reaching the destination of 'pure consciousness'. The life world, too, must be rendered 'strange' and its mundanity made the subject of a radical epoché, suspending the natural attitude and exposing its presuppositions. Perhaps not surprisingly Husserl failed to complete this project before his death. In any event the sociological relevance of his phenomenology owes much of the transformation wrought by one of his not uncritical followers, Alfred Schutz.

It is important to point out that though Schutz was heavily influenced by Husserl the point of departure for his own work was Weber's ideas on the philosophy of science. Schutz was convinced that 'while Max Weber's problematic has definitively fixed the starting point of every genuine philosophy of the social sciences, his analyses were not conducted down into that depth layer from which alone many important tasks that grow out of the procedure of the human studies itself can be accomplished'.[33] Among the problems that Weber had left buried included the central concept of subjective meaning which included a host of other issues that Weber failed to deal with in any detail. Like Husserl, Schutz argued that to achieve true understanding reason must penetrate to that level where 'the work of universal subjectivity is given in its pure form, unpolluted by contingent and particularistic admixtures'.[34] Such understanding would need to be based on an examination of the invariant and essential structures of the mind. So, like Husserl,

Schutz sought to establish an 'objective' study of 'subjective' meanings; that is, to discover the essential knowledge of human reality uncontaminated by the particularistic, the unique and the contingent. But there the correspondence ends. Far from wanting to bracket away the life world, as Husserl wished to do, Schutz regards this as the natural locus of understanding. Instead of, as in Husserl, a station on the way to the rarified realms of the transcendental ego where universally valid knowledge roams, the life world is, for Schutz, the primary focus of attention. In this respect Schutz saw himself as extending Weber's theory of social action by providing a conception of meaning as an intersubjective phenomenon.

Schutz's social world is that of everyday life as lived by common-sense actors carrying on the cognitive and emotive traffic of daily existence. As common-sense beings, we all of us act and live in this world taking no theoretical interest in its constitution while in the natural attitude. In the stance of the natural attitude, one's being in the world is taken for granted as objective and pregiven, as is the existence of others like oneself. The social world is an intersubjective one: a notion that Weber's theory of action took for granted and failed to analyse. It is also a world of routine in which the tasks of everyday life are accomplished largely unconsciously: it is not a world of *reflective* interpretation. It has the accent of a reality which seems both natural and unproblematic.[35] In Schutz's own words, 'social reality' is:

... the sum total of objects and occurrences within the social cultural world as experienced by the commonsense thinking of men living their daily lives among their fellow men, connected with them in manifold relations of interaction. It is the world of cultural objects and social institutions into which we are all born, within which we have to find our bearings, and with which we have to come to terms. From the outset, we, the actors on the social scene, experience the world we live in as a world both of nature and of culture, not as a private but as an intersubjective one, that is, as a world common to all of us, either actually given or potentially accessible to everyone; and this involves intercommunication and language.[36]

This reality is constituted as the object, the phenomenon, of social science by the social scientist deciding 'no longer to place himself and his own condition of interest as the centre of this world'.[37] By a process of epoché the mundane world, a world, by the way, taken for granted by all the orthodox forms of social science, is revealed and made available for a disinterested analysis. Intersubjectivity, interaction, communication, language, indeed, the very possibility of the social world, all presupposed as the unclarified foundations of orthodox social science, become the proper objects of phenomenological social science.

For Schutz, what we have called positivistic or orthodox social science, which he refers to as 'naturalism', fails to account for the way in which social reality is constituted and maintained as a subjective phenomenon, in what ways it is intersubjective, or how actors in their common-sense thinking interpret their own and others' actions. A more adequate foundation for the social sciences requires the elucidation of the basic structures of the life world. Weber was right to stress the importance of *verstehen* and the subjective point of view of the social actor, but failed to clarify whether this referred to the common-sense knowledge of human affairs, or to an epistemological problem, or to a method peculiar to the social sciences.[38] In Schutz's conception, *verstehen* refers mainly to the process by which we all, in our everyday life, interpret the meaning of our own actions and those with whom we interact. The epistemological problem arises when we ask how it is that common-sense understanding is possible. Schutz saw this as the 'scandal of philosophy' until Husserl furnished the tools to understand what is presupposed in our common-sense interpretations.[39] To obtain knowledge of the constitution of the familiar we must transform it into an enigma by the employment of epoché. For Schutz, meaning has to be constructed; it is a property of interpretative procedures and is not an immanent feature of social objects themselves. Accordingly, Schutz's critique of conventional sociological reasoning involves investigating the *a priori* possibility of meanings; in other words, elaborating the conditions of the meaningful world as we know it. These conditions are to be found in the analysis of the intersubjective world of daily life.

Every individual approaches his world with a 'stock of knowledge at hand', which includes such things as beliefs, expectations, rules and norms, etc., by which we interpret the world. Without this action would be inconceivable. The stock of knowledge is formed by our experiences and by the socially preformed knowledge we inherit, and is constantly being tested, refined, modified, and altered in the course of our lives. Much of this knowledge is tacitly held only to be called into operation when relevant. However, although this knowledge is under continual change, overall it is structured through common-sense constructs with which the individual approaches the world moment by moment. These 'typifications' organize our impressions, at the start, into objects, events, and categories and so structure our experience. As mentioned earlier, many of these 'typifications' are tacitly held in the sense that, in the 'natural attitude', we lack the explicit awareness of what they consist in, how they become relevant, how they connect with others, and so on. They serve, to put it another way, as the unquestioned starting points for action and, as such, are self-evident, apodictic, incontrovertible facts of life.

Another key element in the stock of knowledge is the information that others like ourselves exist and that their actions have the same qualities as our own. This makes them partners to communication in a reciprocal and perpetual process of interpretation. The ordinary individual is continually clarifying, ordering, interpreting his on-going experiences according to various schemes. These schemes are essentially social and intersubjective. We are continuously endowing our experiences with meaning through these schemes which are, cannot be anything else but, social and held in common.

If the goal of the social sciences is the understanding of social reality as experienced by social actors in their everyday lives, and if that life is characterized by the intersubjective context in which common-sense interpretation takes place, then a scientific understanding of the life world requires categories and constructs adequate to explaining these structures. Here Schutz offers his postulate of subjective interpretation which requires that the constructs of social science, constructs of the second level, include a first level reference to the meanings used by social actors.[40] These second level constructs are closely akin to Weber's 'ideal types'; artificial devices or models, 'puppets' or 'homunculi' Schutz calls them, which bring the intersubjective world into view. These models of the life world are not peopled by human beings in their full rounded humanity, but with 'puppets' constructed as though they could perform working actions and reactions. Since they do not originate in a living consciousness these actions and reactions are fictitious. But, if they are constructed in an appropriate way they will remain consistent with the 'pre-experiences of the world of daily life which the observer acquired within the natural attitude before he leaped into the theoretical province.'[41] In this way Schutz connects with some of Weber's key methodological concepts. *Verstehen* becomes a first order process by which we all interpret the world and also a second order one by which social scientists interpret and understand the first order process. The 'ideal types' of the second level become ways of characterizing the typifications used at the first level in making everyday interpretations.

Obviously, the position of the social scientist becomes an incredibly difficult one. While Schutz recognizes that social scientists are also human beings and, as such, participants in the life world, he also requires them, *qua* scientists, to pursue an objective study of this life world. That is, though as a participant in the life world he engages in its interpretation like any other actor, as a social scientist he must present an objective representation and explanation of the structure and dynamics of the everyday world. How is this possible? Part of Schutz's answer we have already mentioned in connection with *verstehen* and the construction of second order concepts. In addition, the social scientist must adopt a theoretic posture to the everyday world; that is, assume an attitude of disinterest and aloofness. Scientific theorizing does not serve any practical purpose; on the contrary, the theorist 'is interested in problems and solutions valid in their own right for anyone, at any place, and at any time . . . The "leap" into the province of theoretical thought involves the resolution of the individual to suspend his subjective point of view.'[42] The pragmatic, private concerns of everyday life must be bracketed away.

There is little doubt that Schutz's contribution to ethnomethodology is immense, and we will point to some of these connections in a moment when we discuss some of the ideas of Harold Garfinkel. Schutz also forms a link, albeit a sympathetic rather than a logical one, between the German debates on the foundation of the social sciences and the American interactionist tradition. Soon after arriving in the United States, Schutz discovered in the works of James, Mead and Dewey, American philosophers who had a considerable influence on the formation of symbolic interactionism, ideas that seemed to complement and support the insights of phenomenology. One of Schutz's first papers published in English was an exploration of phenomenological themes in the philosophy of William James.[43] He also exerted a profound influence on students and colleagues including Natanson, Berger and Luckmann, and both Garfinkel and Cicourel record their indebtedness to Schutz's work. More directly, Schutz is responsible for much of the basic posture of ethnomethodology, especially the recognition that the social sciences have their foundations in the everyday social world. As Schutz pointed out and, as we shall see, Garfinkel and other ethnomethodologists have elaborated, orthodox social science uses the 'attitude of everyday life' as a resource for doing social scientific work, but have rarely treated it as a topic. As Zimmerman and Pollner argue:

The formal properties of the social world encountered under the attitude of everyday life are the formal properties that Durkheim attributed to the social structures that were to be sociology's topic. For both lay and professional investigation, the social world presents itself as an exterior field of events amenable to lawful investigation. For both lay and professional investigation, however, the fundamental 'facticity' of those structures . . . is an unexplicated and invisible premise, condition, and resource of these investigations.[44]

It is in this sense that social science retains the presuppositions of the phenomenon it seeks to describe as presuppositions of *its* own investigations. The problem is, as Schutz pointed out, to make available the work, methods, processes through which this mundane world is produced. In other words, to make the life world visible as a topic of enquiry and not merely a resource of enquiry. Although the micro sociology of symbolic interactionism had, to put it this way, made the everyday world part of its special interest, it had failed to go far enough. While much symbolic interactionism for example, had developed a lapidary style of investigation into the everyday world of drug users, pool room hustlers, teenage fellators and others, it still placed complete reliance on the very taken-for-granted features of common sense which members themselves used to construct their social interactions. The everyday world did not become a phenomenon in the sense required by Schutz and later by ethnomethodology. The 'insiders' view, while substantively appealing and impressive in its sensitivity, lacks any explicit treatment of how both actor and observer went about constructing and negotiating the scenes they created. As Cicourel says, its 'descriptive statements are prematurely coded, that is, interpreted by the observer, infused with substance that must be taken for granted, and subsumed under abstract categories without telling the reader how all of this was recognised and accomplished'.[45]

At this point we now turn to the ideas of Harold Garfinkel in an effort to see how he develops Schutz's ideas into a sociological programme.

HAROLD GARFINKEL AND ETHNOMETHODOLOGY[46]

For the record, it was Garfinkel who coined the term, 'ethnomethodology' in an effort to characterize some phenomena he had disco-vered in the course of an investigation, during 1954, into the ways in which jury members went about their deliberations.[47] The jury room had been 'bugged' and Garfinkel's job, after listening to the tapes, was to interview the jurors. At first he and a colleague tried to use Bales' technique to analyse the recorded conversations as instances of small group interactions. Working through the material the following year, Garfinkel noticed that the jurors dur-ing their deliberations were interested in such things as the adequa-cy of accounts, descriptions, evidence, and so on. In short, to get the work of deliberation done they had to be concerned with no-tions of evidence, truth, falsity, relevance, justice, fact, proof, and a host of other methodic issues. To Garfinkel, the jurors were con-cerned every bit as much with methodological matters as they were with the guilt or otherwise of the accused parties. Later, while us-ing the Yale cross-cultural area file, he came across the headings 'ethnobotany', 'ethnophysiology', 'ethnophysics', etc. The 'ethno' prefix, for Garfinkel, seemed to refer to the ordinary member of society's knowledge of biological, botanical, physical, or whatever, phenomena. However, the phenomenon Garfinkel wished to point to was not the folk knowledge ordinary social actors had of botanic-al things or biological things, etc., but to the 'adequate grounds of inference and action' held in common by the members of so-ciety concerned with any matter whatsoever; as, if you like, folk methodologists.[48] Thus, in the context of jury deliberations, 'ethnomethodology' pointed to those ways in which members came to see and report on those features or arrangements of their setting as the practical matter of 'doing deliberations'. Widening the refer-ence of the term, ethnomethodology becomes the study of 'how persons, as parties to ordinary arrangements, use the features of the arrangement to make for members the visibly organised characteris-tics happen'.[49] Or, somewhat less elliptically, it is concerned with the procedures members use to do 'going about knowing the world'.

However, in order to elaborate on this characterization and to see the very strong not to say intimate connections Garfinkel has with Schutz's work, in this section we want to undertake the task of dealing with what we might call, not too happily, Garfinkel's 'meta-theoretical' position. Garfinkel himself has not devoted much of his energies to promulgating any sociological doctrine or theoretical approach in the traditional sense.[50] His main concern has not been to reorder, justify, or philosophize about his sociological position, but to get on with the task of investigating what difference his ideas, including those derived from Schutz, make to the practice of sociology. The impulse of Garfinkel's work has always been methodological if only in the sense of asking what difference an idea or proposition might make to the practices of sociology. His overriding concern has been to pursue the consequences of Schutz's social philosophy and in this respect he has been pragmatic and instrumental in seeing what phenomena it identifies as worthy of sociological interest. As Anderson puts it, Garfinkel's work is 'a demonstration of the methodological implications of adopting the social philosophy of Schutz as a set of theoretical elections'.[51] He is asking, in other words, what problems and puzzles are made available for study if we take Schutz's philosophy seriously.

Garfinkel subscribes to the phenomenological distinction, and one firmly entrenched in Schutz's work as we have seen, between the natural and other attitudes on daily life. One of these 'other' attitudes or stances is that of science. Under the scientific attitude no proposition is taken as indubitable-in-principle. On the contrary, compared with the activities of daily life, 'the activities of scientific theorising are governed by the strange ideal of doubt that is in principle unlimited and that specifically does not recognize the normative social structures as constraining conditions'.[52] That is, the scientific attitude provides for interpretation while holding to a posture of 'official neutrality' toward the belief that the world is as it appears to be. Although the practical theorist holding to the attitude of everyday life may also doubt that objects are as they appear, this doubt is limited by 'practical considerations' and a respect for the valued and more or less routine features of the social order as 'seen from within' which are not called into question, as they are in the scientific attitude. By contrast, scientific theories constitute the world under varying conditions and choices: the world, in other words, is given within the theory itself.[53] That is, in common with fellow phenomenologists, Schutz rejects the 'correspondence theory' of scientific truth which sees the purpose of scientific activity as finding a correspondence between theoretical objects and the referents of those objects in the world 'as it really is': a view we have already met in our discussion of positivism. It is a view predicated upon a distinction between the *perceived* object in the 'world out there' and the object itself; a distinction, to put it in a slightly different way, between the appearance of an object and the object in the real world. The concreteness or the reality of the object in the real world is seen as a property of the object and quite independent of the various ways in which it might appear to an observer or an experiencer. Thus, for positivistic philosophy of science, one of the major issues which arises at an early stage is the question of how objective knowledge of the object, whatever it might be, can be obtained despite its appearance and despite differences in observers. In short, a question about the criteria needed to assess the fit between the theory and the world.

The answer provided in the correspondence theory is through an appeal to invariant and universal categories of understanding and knowledge by which we can be sure that the logic of the theory matches the logic of the world. These categories are seen as incorporated in logico-empirical procedures or, for short, the scientific method, which serve as rules by which any observer can obtain a more or less accurate view of real objects independent of his or her particular circumstances.

By contrast, the Schutzian 'congruence view of reality', as Garfinkel calls it, holds that the terms 'perceived object' and 'concrete object' or, alternatively, 'object' and 'appearance', are synonymous and interchangeable; that is, the perceived object of the 'world out there', whether it be sensorily or ideally founded, *is* the concrete object. Its concreteness, its fullness, its invariance, its stability, or otherwise, is to be found in its constitution through a unity of meanings and only in that. Indeed, an object, whether it be a table, a motive, a society, a conversation, a noise, a reasonable decision, a scientific finding, or whatever, can never appear except through a constituting schema of meaning and interpretation. Thus, whereas in the correspondence theory the function of a theory or conceptual schema is to provide an approximation to what is 'really out there', the congruence theory holds that however the experiencer experiences something 'out there', is 'out there' in the way he or she experiences it. For example, the doubt someone might experience as to whether they had or had not heard a noise is specifiable as a 'doubted noise': the thing, the object, stands along with its doubted character. Furthermore in the congruence theory one is concerned with the varieties of objective worlds and varieties of objective knowledge; in short, with multiple realities, all of which are objective in their own way. The alternative to an objective world is, on this view, a world without sense, a meaningless world which an experiencer has failed to actualize. The 'subjective' becomes not a perception influenced by personal and other idiosyncrasies of circumstance, but a failure to intend a meaning.

One major consequence of the Schutzian view is that both actor and observer, as experiencing beings, are in much the same situation as organizers of their experiences and, through this process, actualizers of their worlds, their realities. While on the correspondence view a theory's correctness is established through some process of 'fitting' or 'matching' its propositions to the actual world 'out there', as far as Schutzian phenomenology is concerned this 'fitting' process is seen as a constitutive operation in which the objective character of the relevant objects and events is given to an observer through the operations of the theory itself. Hence, and for example, determinism is not an ontological characteristic of a set of natural events but is a property of the theory that relates the events to each other. An empirical law is not a reflection of the uniformities found in nature but of the observer's experiences. Thus, a theory serves the function of organizing the possibilities of experience to present the theorist, *whether lay or professional*, with one of many objective worlds. Phenomenologically speaking, there is no disjuncture between experience and reality and, accordingly, little point in seeking a correspondence between them. Nothing more lies behind our experiences and has a greater reality than they do. So, for Schutz, the problem in the correspondence theory of finding transcendent and universal criteria for evaluating the correspondence between a theory and reality does not arise. Instead, the task of theorizing is to reflect upon our experiences of the world reducing our conceptualizations to the essence of reality as we experience it by the use of the phenomenological epoché.

One major consequence of this philosophical stance is to make understanding, both lay and scientific, a deeply problematic activity. For Schutz, the social world is continually constituted in experience as an endless series of activities which are *accounted* for as rational, just, factual, logical, or whatever attributes may be accorded them. The phenomenon for investigation, then, becomes the methods by which experience is *found* to be rational, just, factual, logical, or whatever. Thus, one cannot resort, as Parsons and many others do, to the notion of a widespread cultural integration of values and normative orientations as a solution to the problem of social order. Such a notion becomes an unreflected upon presupposition which can be suspended to reveal a totally new set of phenomena for investigation. Parsons' picture of social life sees it as a system of action operating via the contingencies of rewards and sanctions. Such a model can only work if it is assumed that social actors share a normative orientation to rationality, defined by Parsons largely in Weberian means-ends terms, since, as social actors, they must be able to understand one another, define objects and situations in the same way, draw similar conclusions, and so on. Such rationality becomes a methodologically necessary principle of the actor's action if the actor is to have factual knowledge of his or her situation. The theory, as we have just said, introduces this community of objects and shared expectations through the device of a shared culture: how understanding is achieved by actors on a day-to-day, moment-by-moment basis is not established as a problem for investigation.[54] By suspending judgement on the givenness of what Parsons and others assume and by reducing these categories further, Schutz and later Garfinkel make them 'visible' and investigable.

The major consequence of opting for Schutz's social philosophy as a set of theoretical elections, and which provides ethnomethodology with its overriding concerns, is to see social actions as mutually co-ordinated productions, as *work* done by the members of society. Whatever orderliness an activity might display is an accomplishment of members doing that activity and not the result, as it is in Parsons for example, of some disembodied systemic operation. Action is practical rather than rational or rule following, as it seems to be in most conventional sociological accounts. While rationality, as an efficient allocation of means to the realization of given ends, might adequately describe elements of the attitude of scientific investigation, it certainly fails to describe or account for conduct in daily life. For Schutz and Garfinkel, there is one paramount reason why common sense cannot conform to scientific rationality, since if everything is dubitable-in-principle, as under the scientific attitude, conduct will become senseless and 'multiply the disorganized features of the system of interaction'.[55] Also, since for Schutz experience is the fundamental category, then a science of social action should begin its theorizing with the activities in which actors are engaged. It is this which Garfinkel adopts as a methodological recommendation by proposing to treat all activities, all social actions, as the observable accomplishments of actors themselves. So, by adopting Schutz's social philosophy as a theoretical election we are in a position to ask how is it that actors accomplish the rational, factual, obvious characters of their activities in the course of doing them.[56] It is this which is the starting point for Garfinkel and ethnomethodology.

The first point we should reiterate is that Garfinkel's stance is methodological rather than philosophical.[57] For the purpose of doing sociology, his election, his recommended study policy, is to choose to treat activities as observable, methodic productions. Garfinkel's adoption of Schutz has the sociological implication that as a methodological principle he can suspend the use of fixed and permanent criteria for determining factuality, legality, rationality, femininity, tribal membership, mental illness, and so on, that will provide in a decontextualized manner what such characterizations are to mean, and, instead, pursue what for him is 'an awesome contingency' that factuality, legality, rationality, femininity, tribal membership, and so on, can be treated as members' accomplishments.[58] Garfinkel proposes 'paying to the most commonplace activities of daily life the attention normally accorded extraordinary events'.[59] As we saw in Chapter 1, Garfinkel's study of Agnes points out that any and all our inferences and findings about her 'feminity' are based on what Agnes herself says and does. It is her actions which we see as methodological practices for the accomplishment of her identity as a woman. Garfinkel is not concerned, as a detective or a lawyer might be, with the veracity or otherwise of Agnes' claims about herself, rather he is electing to treat her activities as a methodical attainment. So, in more general terms, Garfinkel's concern is with the investigation of members' methods for producing the world of everyday life.

But, as we saw earlier in this chapter, the so-called 'humanistic' sociologies have always laid claim to studying the ordinary, routine doings of social actors going about their business. Admittedly, many of these actors belonged to the exotic worlds of jazz, drug cultures, professional crime but, nevertheless, interactionism, for example, did and still does stress that sociology should investigate social life from the point of view of those who live in it and not from the detached comforts of an armchair. While such qualitative sociologies do share ethnomethology's concern with the exploration of social actions in their natural settings, it does, as we hope to have made clear, identify rather different phenomena and ways of investigating them. Garfinkel starts from the position that from the point of view of any actor, including ourselves, society is encountered as an external, given, pre-formed reality. This, if you like, is the emphasis provided by Schutz and other phenomenologists. The world is profoundly *there* as a world of everyday life, full of routine ways and familiar scenes. Garfinkel, following Schutz's recommendations, proposes to study this fact, avoiding the issues raised by the distinction between 'how the world really is' and 'how it appears to them', by examining the social-world-as-it-is-experienced.[60] The purpose of this is to produce a better understanding of the way in which daily life acquires its objectivity, factuality, and so on.

In this respect, Garfinkel's programme is concerned with that most pervasive of sociological questions: how is that actions recur and reproduce themselves? How is it that interaction displays properties of orderliness, stability and patterning? How does social life get organized? However, Garfinkel insists that this orderliness be looked at as arising from within activities themselves due to the work done by parties to that activity. He eschews the traditional sociological strategy of seeking to explain this orderliness and organization of social activities by attempting to identify conditions and causes 'outside' of the activities themselves; conditions and causes which include cultural, environmental, structural and personality elements.[61] Rather his overarching question, stated as a line of enquiry, is, how do actors, knowing what they know, produce the social activities they do produce? Action is practical. The actor, any actor, has to decide, at any point in time, what is the next thing to do. Though the circumstances may be less then ideal, actors do deal with them, do achieve their ends, and manage social organization for all practical purposes. In doing so they must make use of knowledge, common knowledge at that, of social structures, and in this important sense are very much practical sociologists. For the members of society, its orderliness is highly visible. They can, without special effort, strenuous enquiry, prolonged delay, undue hesitation, see what their life is like and what it is they have to do. Indeed, without this property, if the social order were not readily observable, it is hard to see how it could be further produced, how the patterns of daily life could be sustained and carried forward in any recognizable manner. Each member of society, then, must needs be a 'practical sociologist' determining how a social scene is organized, its regular features, the kind of persons involved, their typical motivations and actions, the distribution of rights and obligations, what the other persons are now doing and why, and so on. And it is this interest which unites both the professional and the lay sociologist.

Garfinkel's programme also provides an answer to a problem highlighted at the beginning of this chapter, namely, the problem of subjectivity and the inaccessibility of mind. Weber, for one, although recognizing the absolutely crucial role meaning, interpretation and other subjectivities played in social life and, hence, in its explanation, failed to pursue the problem he had identified deeply enough. The actor's subjective point of view remained largely inaccessible only to be glimpsed imperfectly through such methods as 'imaginative reconstruction' by the social scientist using such devices as the 'ideal type' and checking the findings produced against the strict canons of scientific enquiry. The symbolic interactionists, too, while holding meaning central in their conceptions of social life, argued that access to these largely private phenomena could only be gained by the researcher participating as an actor in the world being investigated and, in this way, vicariously gaining access to the meanings actors use through his or her own private vision. Schutz, however, and later Garfinkel, by focusing on the 'life-world' in which subjectivity is a problem that has to be solved by all of us as a routine, daily, and practical matter, provide for the social world as an inter-subjective phenomenon in which we all, in commonsense ways interpret and make sense of our actions and the actions of others. Our 'stocks of knowledge' include ways of imputing motives, inferring and stating reasons, gauging moods, seeing ourselves as others might see us, attributing attitudes, and more. In other words, mind and its variously attributed phenomena are not so much private and inaccessible but very much public, though not displayed in ways social scientists (and some philosophers) have conventionally thought. As social actors in the everyday world, we routinely, without difficulty, without hesitation, attribute motives, beliefs, attitudes to others as ways of making sense of the social world. How this is done and in what ways, and how subjective apprehensions of the world are made available through talk and conduct is one of Garfinkel's abiding interests. By making what we have called 'subjectivity' a routine problem for all social actors in the life world, Schutz and Garfinkel have opened to view what was hitherto private and largely inaccessible to investigation.

In the following chapters we intend to flesh out in more detail some of the further implications of Garfinkel's study policies. In what immediately follows, however, we shall pursue further, matters to do with traditional sociological research in order to, once again, effect some contrasts with ethnomethodology.

NOTES AND REFERENCES

1. M. B. Morris, *An Excursion into Creative Sociology*, Columbia University Press: New York 1977. Also J. D. Douglas et al., *Introduction to the Sociologies of Everyday Life*, Alwyn and Bacon: Boston 1980.
2. Morris, *op. cit.*, p. 8.

3. See R. Bendix, 'Two Sociological Traditions', in R. Bendix and G. Roth (eds), *Scholarship and Partisanship: Essay on Max Weber*, University of California Press: Berkeley, 1971, pp. 282–98. The distinction referred to here is, of course, a well worked one though by no means less important for all that. We are also aware that there are more subtleties to these issues than are indicated here.
4. See on this J. A. Hughes, *The Philosophy of Social Research*, Longman: London, 1980; A. Giddens, 'Positivism and its Critics', in his *Studies in Social and Political Theory*, Hutchinson; London, 1977; T. Benton, *Philosophical Foundations of the Three Sociologists*, Routledge & Kegan Paul: London, 1977.
5. The classical example of this is normally taken to be T. Parsons, *The Social System*, Tavistock: London, 1952. See also W. Buckley, *Sociology and Modern Systems Theory*, Prentice-Hall: Engelwood-Cliff, 1967. W. E. Connolly, *Appearance and Reality in Politics*, Cambridge University Press: Cambridge, 1981, esp. Ch. 2 has some interesting comments to make on why positivism has become the orthodox way of studying social and political life. Some people have argued that the tradition infuses the whole of Western culture from Aristotle onwards, and is not merely a feature of the social sciences. See, for example, D. Held, *Introduction to Critical Theory*, Hutchinson: London, 1980 for a discussion of some of those thinkers.
6. This conception owes much to the work of P. F. Lazarsfeld. See P. F. Lazarsfeld and M. Rosenberg, (eds), *The Language of Social Research*, The Free Press: New York, 1965, for a collection of work in this tradition.
7. H. S. Hughes, *Consciousness and Society*, MacGibbon and Kee: London, 1959.
8. See J. Freund, 'German Sociology in the Time of Max Weber', in T. Bottomore and R. Nisbet (eds), *A History of Sociological Analysis*, Heinemann: London, 1978, pp. 149–186.
9. See Z. Bauman, *Hermeneutics and Social Science*, Hutchinson: London, 1978, for a fuller discussion of the issues here. Also J. A. Hughes, *op. cit.*
10. It should be pointed out that this account of Weber is very much the one adopted by current sociology. Recent English publications of some Weber's essays suggest the need for a radical revision of this view. See, for example, M. Weber, *Roscher and Knies: The Logical Problems of Historical Economics*, (trans. G. Oakes), The Free Press: New York, 1975.

11. M. Weber. *The Methodology of the Social Sciences*, (trans, and ed. E. A. Shils and H. A. Finch), The Free Press: New York 1949.

12. T. Parsons, *The Structure of Social Action*, The Free Press: Glencoe, 137. It is perhaps unfortunate that Parsons was the one to make Weber's work accessible in English since he gives the impression that Weber was simply concerned to make a positivistic social science more complete and respectable. More recent commentators, however, place greater emphasis on the romantic strain in Weber's thought.

13. M. Weber, *Economy and Society*, (trans. and ed. G. Roth and C. Wittich), Bedminster: New York 1968, pp. 1, 12–18; Also R. Bendix, *op. cit.*

14. See P. Rock, *The Making of Symbolic Interactionism*, Macmillan: London, 1979 for an excellent account of the intellectual origins of symbolic interactionism. Also R. E. C. Faris, *Chicago Sociology, 1920–32*, University of Chicago Press: Chicago 1967; B. M. Fisher and A. Strauss, 'Interactionism', in T. Bottomore and R. Nisbet (eds), *op. cit.*, Ch. 12.

15. N. Anderson, *The Hobo*, University of Chicago Press: Chicago, 1961; F. M. Thrasher, *The Gang*, University of Chicago Press: Chicago, 1963; P. Cressey, *The Taxi Dance Hall*, University of Chicago Press: Chicago, 1932; also Faris, *op. cit.*

16. See, for example, A. M. Rose (ed.), *Human Behaviour and Social Processes*, Routledge & Kegan Paul: London, 1962; J. G. Morris and B. N. Meltzer (eds), *Symbolic Interaction*, Allyn and Bacon: Boston, 1967; N. J. Filstead (ed.), *Qualitative Methodology*, Markham: Chicago, 1970; G. H. Mead, *Mind, Self and Society*, University of Chicago Press: Chicago 1934, ed. C. W. Morris.

17. H. Blumer, *Symbolic Interactionism: Perspective and Method*, Prentice Hall: Englewood-Cliffs, 1969, p. 5.

18. For a more formal and detailed discussion of the notions of 'self' 'other' and related concepts of the 'I' and 'me' see A. Rose (ed.), *op. cit.*, Ch. 1.

19. H. Blumer, 'Sociological Analysis and the "Variable"', in Morris and Meltzer (eds), *op, cit.*, p. 93. Also, his 'What is wrong with social theory', *American Sociological Review*, **19**, 1954, is also worth attention.

20. Rock, *op. cit.*, p. 182. Not all interactionist theories conform to this characterization. See later in this chapter.

21. *ibid.*, p. 186.

22. H. Blumer, 'Sociological implications of the thought of George Herbert Mead', *American Journal of Sociological*, **71**, 1966, p. 539.

23. H. S. Becker, 'Problems of inference and proof in participant observation', *American Sociological Review*, **23**, 1958, pp. 682–90. See also his study *Boys in White*, University of Chicago Press: Chicago, 1961. There are signs in his later work that he has become less enthusiastic about a more positivistic conception of symbolic interactionism. See his *Outsiders: Studies in the Sociology of Deviance*, The Free Press: New York, 1963.

24. See B. J. Biddle and E. J. Thomas (eds), *Role Theory*, Wiley: New York, 1966; B. H. Stoodley (ed.), *Society and Self*, The Free Press: Glencoe, 1962; M. H. Kuhn, 'Major Trends in Symbolic Interaction Theory in the Past Twenty-five years', in Morris and Meltzer (eds), *op. cit.* pp. 46–47.

25. J. D. Douglas, 'Understanding Everyday Life', in his *Understanding Everyday Life*, Routledge & Kegan Paul: London 1974, p. 17. Arguably, 'behavioural interactionism' should, perhaps, be regarded as orthodox sociology in interactionist clothes.

26. D. Matza, *Becoming Deviant*, Prentice-Hall: Englewood-Cliffs, 1969, p. 5.

27. For a discussion of some of the problems and ambiguities in participant observation, see Rock, *op. cit.*; W. F. Whyte, *Street corner Society*, University of Chicago Press: Chicago, 1955, is still worth attention. Other relevant selections in Filstead (ed.), *op. cit.*

28. Bauman, *op. cit.*, p. 13. Of course even if two participant observers did come up with different findings, it would not be easy to decide whether this was due to variation in their perceptions or to real changes in the group or society.

29. For much fuller discussions, see K. Wolff. 'Phenomenology and Sociology', in Bottomore and Nisbet, *op. cit.*, pp. 499–556; R. J. Bernstein, *The Restructuring of Social and Political Theory*, Blackwell: Oxford, 1976; M. Phillipson, 'Phenomenological Philosophy and Sociology', in P. Filmer, et al., *New Directions in Sociological Theory*, Collier-MacMillan: London, 1972, pp. 119–64; T. Luckmann (ed.), *Phenomenology and Sociology*, Penguin: Harmondsworth 1978.

30. T. Luckmann, *ibid.*, p. 9. Italics in original.

31. E. Husserl, *The Crisis of European Sciences and Transcendental Phenomenology*, trans. D. Carr, Northwestern University Press:

Evanston, 1970, p. 48. Also A. Gurvitsch, 'Problems of the Life-World', in M. Natason (ed.), *Phenomenology and Social Reality*, Martinuus Nijhoff: The Hague, 1970, pp. 34–61.

32. See M. Natanson, 'Phenomenology as a Rigorous Science', in T. Luckmann (ed.), *op.cit.*, 181–99.

33. Translated by and quoted in K. Wolff, *op. cit.*, p. 515. A more idiomatic rendering is to be found in A. Schutz, *The Phenomenology of the Social World*, trans. G. Walsh and F. Lehnert, Northwestern University Press: Evanston, 1969, p. xxxi.

34. Baumann, *op. cit.*, p. 174.

35. A. Schutz, 'Phenomenology and the Social Sciences', in T. Luckmann (ed.), *op. cit.*, pp. 135–5. The whole essay is an important statement of Schutz's position.

36. A. Schutz, 'Concept and Theory Formation in the Social Sciences', in his *Collected Paper*, Vol. 1, Martinuus Nijhoff: The Hague, 1962, p. 53.

37. A. Schutz, 'Phenomenology and the Social Sciences', *op. cit.*, p. 139

38. A. Schutz, *Collected Papers*, vol. 1, *op. cit.*, p. 37. Here Schutz is attacking the dualism between the 'physical' and the 'mental' that has infected much of the ontological/epistemological discussion in the philosophy of the social sciences.

39. *ibid.*, p. 57.

40. *ibid.*, p. 59.

41. *ibid.*, p. 255.

42. *ibid.*, p. 248.

43. A. Schutz, *Collected Papers*, vol. 3, *op. cit.*

44. D. Zimmerman and M. Pollner, 'The Everyday World as a Phenomenon', in J. D. Douglas (ed.), *op. cit.*, p. 86.

45. A. V. Cicourel, 'Interpretative Procedures and Normative Rules: Negotiation of Status and Role', in his *Cognitive Sociology*, Penguin: Harmondsworth, 1973, p. 24.

46. Since many of Garfinkel's ideas are so central to ethnomethodology and will appear in many places throughout this book, in this chapter we will concentrate on the 'pretheoretical' elements of his work, leaving a detailed account of particular concepts for later.

47. See R. J. Hill and K. S. Crittenden (eds), *Proceedings of the Purdue Symposium on Ethnomethodology*, Institute for the Study of Social Change: Purdue, 1968.

48. *ibid.*, p. 8.

49. *ibid.*, p. 12.
50. The nearest he came to this was in one (unfortunately) unpublished, paper, 'A Comparison of Decisions made on Four 'pretheoretical' Problems by Talcott Parsons and Alfred Schutz', mimeo and one or two remarks in his *Studies in Ethnomethodology*, Prentice-Hall: Englewood-Cliffs, 1967. The discussion here owns a great deal to the excellent thesis by R. J. Anderson, 'A Sociological Analysis of Some Procedures for Discerning Membership', unpublished Ph.D. dissertation, University of Manchester, 1981. We have also made full use of Garfinkel's unpublished paper though have waived the usual practice of recording citation from it, largely in order to avoid burdening and frustrating the reader by indicating pages, etc., from a regrettably unpublished piece of work. Nor do we hold Garfinkel responsible for the interpretations we have drawn from it.
51. *ibid.*, p. 55.
52. H. Garfinkel, *Studies in Ethnomethodology*, p. 273.
53. Given this view, one anology we could draw of the way in which science maps the world is from the way in which children and others set up areas in which to play football. Sometimes coats are placed on the ground to represent goal posts, and natural features such as a school wall, stream or pavement can bound the domain of the playing area. In other places other natural features of the environment might be used to designate a goal, such as a wide barn door or the gap in an alley way. Similarly a street lamp can mark a corner post on the field of play. Wherever the game is played, the local terrain can be mapped by 'goal posts', 'goal lines', or whatever, and the game of football set up. Similarly science can be played anywhere regardless of the shape of terrain of the particular area in which it is played. The fact that the logic of scientific procedure maps the world, says nothing about the structure of any presupposed 'external' reality. God need not be a mathematician.
54. T. Parsons, *The Structure of Social Action*, The Free Press: Glencoe, 1949. See also, T. Parsons and E. Shils (eds), *Toward a General Theory of Action*, Harper and Row: New York, 1962; T. Parsons, *The Social System*, Tavistock: London, 1952, and essays in M. Black (ed.), *The Social Theories of Talcott Parsons*, Prentice-Hall: Englewood Cliffs, 1961.
55. Garfinkel, *op. cit.*, p. 283.
56. Anderson, *op. cit.*, p. 64.

57. The reason for stressing this is that, in our opinion, most commentators have seriously misrepresented what Garfinkel is about, often, on the one hand, portraying him as a traitor to sociology, on the other, that despite all Garfinkel is 'really' a conventional sociologist with a talent for writing incomprehensible jargon. Another favourite theme is to link him with linguistic philosophy. While, no doubt, there is something in all of these, they do not, in our mind, accurately portray Garfinkel's endeavour nor his achievement. See, for example, S. Mennell, 'Ethnomethodology and the New Methodenstreit', in D. C. Thorn (ed.), *New Directions in Sociology*, Rowman and Littlefield: New York, 1976, pp. 139–57; D. Gleeson and M. Erben, 'Meaning in context: notes toward a critique of ethnomethodology', *British Journal of Sociology*, 27, 1976, pp. 473–83; P. Attewell, 'Ethnomethodology; since Garfinkel', *Theory and Sociology*, 1, 1974, pp. 179–210; E. Gellner, 'Ethnomethodology; The re-enchantment industry or the Californian way of subjectivity', *Philosophy of Social Science*, 5, 1975, pp. 431–50.

58. Anderson, *op. cit.*, p. 66.

59. Garfinkel, *op. cit.*, p. 1.

60. W. W. Sharrock and R. Anderson, 'A Minimal Case for Ethnomethodology', mimeo.

61. Indeed, at one level at least, one can view Garfinkel's notorious 'experiments' as attempts to see how stock sociological theories can 'generate' the properties of everyday activities by turning them into 'production procedures' for the organization of routine activities. In other words, they represent an attempt to act out the implications of sociological theories. The disorganization they produce is some evidence that such theories fail to identify the basis of the organization of our daily life. This point was brought to our attention by Wes Sharrock and Bob Anderson.

Chapter three

SOCIOLOGICAL RESEARCH: PROBLEMS OF PHENOMENA AND THEIR DESCRIPTION

In the first chapter we illustrated some of the ways in which ethnomethodological enquiry differs from that of conventional sociology. The second chapter was concerned with the sociological traditions to which ethnomethodology belongs and the kind of issues that prompted its origin and growth. In this chapter we intend to pursue a number of themes already raised in the previous two chapters linking them this time to a discussion of the practice of sociological research. We have already identified as an important element in the 'humanistic' tradition the critique it advances of much of conventional sociology's wish to emulate the natural sciences, and there can be little doubt that ethnomethodology extends that critique but does so in rather unorthodox ways, as we shall see. So, while in the following we will have cause to question many of the methods currently used in sociological research, we do not do this in the spirit of seeking to expose the wicked excesses of conventional sociologies – they do this very well themselves, without our aid – but with the intention of illustrating, as a preliminary to closer discussion in the following chapter some of the features of practical reasoning, one of ethnomethodology's prime interests, which can and do arise in the doing of sociological investigations, whether lay or professional. In this respect, the discussion in this chapter is a preparation for a more formal account of a number of ethnomethodological concepts designed to handle the phenomena we will point to here. However, while we do admit that it is all too easy to disavow any vicious or seditious intent, it is rather less easy to persuade trained sociologists the ethnomethodology is not claiming to be a better way of doing sociology, especially since this is normally the first task any new approach to sociology sets itself. Ethnomethodology is not in the business of repairing the deficiencies of social science or claiming that unless one is studying common-sense rationalities and activities then one is not doing proper sociology. We shall argue, here and elsewhere, that the research and methodological problems conventional sociology faces and tries to overcome are, essentially identical to problems faced by all practical theorists, and for ethnomethodology this constitutes the phenomenon not a complaint. What we intend to do in this chapter is make some observations on the research practices of conventional sociology concentrating, in the main, on the interview and participant observation since these are the most well known of research methods already in use.

DESCRIBING SOCIAL ACTIVITIES

We concluded the last chapter by putting forward Garfinkel's programme for ethnomethodology as, among other things, concerned with the self-organizing properties of social activities; that is, to put it another way, with the kind of work members do to organize their activities in the ways that they do. This being so, one of the first tasks of such an investigative strategy is to describe what it is that members do. This requirement ethnomethodology shares with conventional sociology, though it is somewhat surprising that relatively little attention in sociology has been given to problems of description, certainly in comparison with the energy and devotion paid to grappling with the problems of 'theory' and 'explanation'.[1]

Describing what members do is an essentially important issue for one very obvious reason: sociology, like any other discipline, like any other activity, deals with phenomena which have to be specified, characterized, mapped or otherwise described. At its broadest, sociology sets out to explain the patterns found in social life, and unless it first of all describes that social life it will have little or nothing to explain. If, for example, an investigator is interested in explaining patterns of political violence, he or she will have to define, or otherwise specify, what is to count in the world as political violence.[2] Similarly, the factors used to explain such patterns, say social class, political and civic norms, relative deprivation, and so on, would all have to be described in some fashion. Broadly speaking, within conventional sociology two major questions constitute the framework within which solutions to the problem of sociological descriptions are to be found. The first concerns the formal, logical, and rational criteria to which such descriptions ought to conform, and the second, how much and in what ways sociological descriptions should correspond to descriptions made by social actors themselves? We emphasize the fairly obvious point that the decisions made on each of these questions are not unrelated. Indeed, to use a notion presented in the previous chapter, the decisions made on each of these constitute 'theoretical elections' which profoundly shape the nature of what is to be taken as an adequate sociology. They are also the methodological counterparts of the theoretical and philosophical discussions of the relative domains of the 'objective' and the 'subjective' in human affairs that were discussed in the previous chapter.

The first issue has to do with the kind of criteria which can be said to govern not only the constitution of a concept but also its adequacy. In this respect, the dominant view is that the concepts used for sociological explanation and description should conform to the criteria appropriate to scientific enquiry; that is, they should be precise, unambiguous, rigorous, objective, determinate and, if possible, measurable. One commentator refers to these as the conditions of 'literal description'. What this means is that the descriptions of the 'objects' entering into explanations, and, let us remind ourselves, in sociology such objects include attitudes, and beliefs as well as actions and behaviour, groups of various kinds, social relationships, structures, processes, and so on, have stable meanings independent of the circumstances and occasions which produce them.[3] A literal description amounts to asserting that on the basis of particular but determinate features this instance counts as belonging to a particular class of phenomena. For example, if we define, or describe, suicide as a death which is self-inflicted and that the victim knew that death would be the outcome of his action, then in classifying instances of death into the categories of 'suicide' and 'not-suicide' we have to be sure that the features of particular deaths unambiguously determine the class into which they are allocated.[4] Similarly, if we are interested in constructing an index which measures the degree of political violence within and across societies, we have to be sure that the items constituting the scale have stable meanings across the events so classified.[5] Without these requirements measurement becomes a dubious exercise, at least in the terms required by this view of scientific enquiry. Failure to meet this condition would, in measurement terms, amount to giving the same number, implying that they are equivalent, to what are, in fact, different things. Further, those description requirements are necessary for the construction of logically rigorous theory, since without them the strict canons of deductive inference cannot be met.

The second question recognizes the fact that the members of society are also able to offer descriptions and accounts of what they are doing; indeed, as we shall see, it is these accounts which constitute in some form or another, much of the raw data produced by sociological investigations. However, for our immediate purposes what is important about this particular issue is the status accorded to such members' descriptions. Many if not most sociological approaches accept that any viable sociological theory needs to make *some* reference to the fact that the members of society have a point of view on their society; the problem is how to handle it. At one extreme, Durkheim, while admitting that social actors are able to describe the 'social facts' of their world, argued in the strongest possible terms that these were too vague, ambiguous, rough and unclear for scientific usage.[6] He went further than this to argue that such 'subjective' phenomena were not the 'things' that were the special province of sociology. At the other extreme, as we saw in Chapter 2, the symbolic interactionists stress that it is the actors conception of the social world which is, about all else, the essential topic of sociological enquiry.

Nonetheless, as we suggested a moment ago, the decisions on each of these issues are not unrelated. It is possible, indeed Parsons whom we discussed in the previous chapter is a prime example, to argue that sociological theories should contain descriptions which are both scientific *and* pay some obeisance to the actor's point of view and the descriptions incorporated in this. However, which of these is to receive relative importance is another matter, and one which has fateful consequences for the practices of conventional sociological research.

THE ROLE OF RESEARCH METHODS IN CONVENTIONAL SOCIOLOGY

Conventional sociology tends to draw a more or less sharp distinction, as we noted in respect of Parsons, between theory and the empirical world. Theory explains the world and, as such, responsive to facts of the world. Theory is tested against the facts, or, more properly speaking, data, produced by investigations of the world. It is in this sense that systematic observations of the world have priority as far as the truth or adequacy of a particular theoretical explanation is concerned. It is further recognized, however, that the facts are not obviously available but must be gathered, in the form of data, from an often intractable world. To this end, conventional sociology has devised, borrowed, adopted, sometimes invented, a number of methods or techniques of empirical research. These are designed to produce data which conform to the criteria of objectivity required of a scientific discipline, namely reliability and validity. These methods of research and data analysis are generally regarded as standardized and neutral atheoretical techniques which render the investigator anonymous and are, in effect, rules which ensure that the data produced through their application are objective and uncontaminated by the personal views of the researcher. The choice of methods is based, in the main, on instrumental grounds, and provides, in advance, the conditions of proper sociological enquiry.

Another requirement is that theories and hypotheses should be formulated precisely, quantitatively if possible, so that they can be rigorously tested against data produced by research techniques. This further requires establishing some correspondence between the language of the theory and that used in describing the empirical world. And it is in respect of this particular issue that we can begin to discuss the interview method as a technique for transforming the ways in which the social world can be, and is, described by actors into scientifically acceptable descriptions.

THE INTERVIEW METHOD

As we have already indicated, methods of research can be seen as rules for instructing researchers on how to fashion data out of a complex, often 'messy', social world. It is recognized though not fully appreciated, that most sociological data is collected from social encounters of various kinds. Even secondary data, such as official statistics, begin with social encounters of some description, if only between a client and some recording officer, or more specifically, between an applicant for social security benefit and a civil servant, between an offender and a police official, between a death and a coroner, between a tax payer and an accountant, and so on. It is this fact which is seen as posing rather special problems for social research; problems which are clearly exemplified in the interview.

The interview is a social encounter in which the respondent, under the stimulus of questions put by an interviewer, provides verbal data which are later coded and processed, normally as part of a social survey. The data produced by interviews consist, then, of reports of what the respondent said on the occasion of the interview itself.[7] These reports can be about a multitude of topics, a claimed advantage of the method, such as attitudes, beliefs, opinions, past and intended actions, present activities, details of present circumstances, and so on. It is these replies which are later transformed into instances of norms, roles, relationships, values, etc., and thereby become ways of 'seeing the society that stands behind the reports'.[8] In other words, while the method acknowledges, indeed is predicated upon, the fact that social actors do have views, beliefs, values, in short, are able to give accounts of their lives in society, it does not go as far as to say that any old account will do. As a sociological instrument the method recognizes that respondents live in social worlds and, as a result, have perceptions shaped and moulded by their social experiences. It is these experiences which the interview intends to capture and record. Respondents, as social actors, can be ideologically motivated, see from only a partial perspective, hold irrational beliefs, have strange ideas about the cosmos, and more. Accordingly, the responses cannot, do not, stand on their own but are transformed into sociological data of the relevant kind; in other words, the responses stand as *indicators* of social facts and processes incorporated in and constituted by relevant sociological theories. The descriptions respondents offer about what it is they have done, are doing or are likely to do, what they believe in, the attitudes they express, the knowledge they exhibit, and so on, are merely the raw material out of which scientific descriptions are assembled. But, naturally enough, matters are not quite so simple as this might suggest. Even though it is taken as axiomatic that responses can be indicative of 'underlying' social processes, it is by no means always clear which of them are so indicative in any particular case, and one factor which can be responsible for this lack of clarity is the interview itself. Accordingly, although it is regarded as a method, and an artificial one at that, of glimpsing the ways in which social actors go about the business of reflecting and displaying sociologically conceived facts and processes, it is also recognized as a social encounter; a fact which, so it is argued, could seriously affect the kind of responses produced, and jeopardize their quality as scientific data. To overcome or control this possibility, a whole lore has been devised to enable the interviewer assess the impact of the interview itself on the data produced.

To put the matter bluntly, the interviewer's job is to make sure that the respondent tells the truth and expresses his views, attitudes or beliefs accurately. To achieve this, the interview schedule and the conduct of the interview itself are designed to conform to a body of rules which dictates the most efficacious way of ensuring that the research encounter does not, unknowingly, bias the replies of the respondent. Questions must avoid ambiguity, for example, not threaten the respondent's self-esteem, or give the impression that one kind of reply is more socially desirable than another. The replies must also conform to some criteria of rationality or consistency. The interviewer must also try to create an atmosphere that encourages the respondent to talk freely in the knowledge that what is said is a private and anonymous matter; that he can talk about the more private and intricate details of his life without consequence. The interviewer must also be sensitive to the effect of his manner on the frankness of the replies and, to put the issue more summarily, be able to evaluate the effects of the interview as a social encounter on the quality of the data gathered.[9]

In detail the rules interviewers need to follow are both more complex and varied depending, among other things, on the type of interview, whether, for example, it relies mainly on fixed-choice alternative type questions or open-ended ones, or whether it is a standardized or free-ranging interview, and so on. Nevertheless, the rules aim at providing the interviewer with instructions as to how to manipulate the social encounter between him and the respondent so that the latter is able to provide authentic data, 'something that springs from the soul of the respondent to the notebook of the interviewer without encountering any contaminating influences en route'.[10] To express the point in a slightly different way: the rules of interviewing embody theories of social encounters which, when 'correctly' applied, produce verbal responses which thereby qualify as data.[11] Such rules derive from and are supported by a huge body of research findings on the influences of various interviewer characteristics such as age, gender, social status, race, style, etc., on the replies given by different types of respondent, the influence of respondent characteristics of the perceptions of the interviewer, the variable impact of question order and content on replies, and so on: all designed to improve the ability of the interviewer to control, manipulate or evade the normal everyday properties of social encounters to produce 'unbiased' responses.

Although we do not intend to give a full blown and comprehensive critique of the interview, we can note one or two features about it, especially those to do with the presuppositions on which it is based as a method of social research.

For the sociologist, the basic unit of the interview is a question (or a statement) and its response. It is the response which stands as the index of some property of the actor or social world and through which the sociologist glimpses the society, as we have said. That is, the response is not only an answer to a question but an indicator, and means of describing the respondent's say, social class position, political views, marital status, aspirations, normative orientation and so on. In this respect, the interview is like 'a calibrated dipstick'. The sociologist presumes that what adheres to the stick itself is not important, except for what is indicates about something else.[12] The interviewer is not interested in the interview itself and the information gathered in it not seen as part of that particular interaction, but taken as standing on behalf of other activities the researcher never observes. By way of example, let us take the following fixed-choice question from a schedule used in a study of political change in Britain: If the Government has a choice between reducing taxes and spending more on social services, which should it do?'[13] Each respondent was noted to choose one of the alternatives indicated or expressing 'don't know' or 'no opinion'. On the face of it, this question and others like it constitute very powerful instruments for gathering sociological data. The data produced consist of a simple and easily recorded verbal report, is economically gathered from large numbers of people and, along with similar data, can be relatively easily analysed to produce quantitatively expressed associations between the distribution of replies on one item with that on others, and with respondent properties such as the level of education, type of occupation, newspaper readership, party support, and more. In this way, descriptions can be made of the social structure and the kind of people who inhabit it. By using verbal reports in this way, it is claimed that the researcher has potential access to a massive amount of information that is not directly accessible except at huge cost. Thus, in terms of the above example, we could say that 'X per cent of Labour supporters are in favour of spending more on social services', or, to be more sophisticated, use such an item as part of a scale measuring variables such as 'political ideology', 'degree of commitment of party policy', 'degree of political apathy', and so on. In other words, out of the respondent's description of him or herself as someone who believes that more should be spent on social services, and along with other responses, a description of a type of social actor is assembled as, say, a 'typical Labour Party supporter', 'a party ideologue', or whatever: descriptions intended as more suitable for a sociological theory.

So far so good. However, for us, that such questions are used in this way is merely a starting point. Our questions is, how do researchers get to this point starting as they do from *particular* interviewers with *particular* respondents? In other words, what we want to do is make visible the work being done to achieve the kind of results just described and to do this try to make clear some of the assumptions upon which the interview method depends.

Let us go back to the example question given earlier to see what some of these assumptions might be. For any indicated response to be taken as an answer to the question, the researcher must be satisfied that the respondent has correctly interpreted the meaning of the question and supplied an appropriate answer. Even though the answers in this example are pre-chosen, the point still holds since the interviewer must assume, if he is to take the response as an *answer* to the question, that the respondent has not randomly picked a response, is merely giving an answer to get the interview over with, etc. Further, in processing the material produced by a number of interviews, it must also be assumed that each respondent has understood the same question in the same way and provided replies which are also equivalent in meaning. As Cicourel puts it, 'Every interview... requires coding which assumes identicality or equivalence classes among widely differing acts, interpreted questions and responses.'[14] It is this assumption which enables the researcher to add responses in order to obtain statements such as 'X per cent of Y persons are in favour of increasing social service expenditure', and to be able to describe types of social actors in terms of their beliefs and distribution. Although this may well sound obvious, perhaps obvious to the point of banality, there still remains the question of how 'meaning equivalence', to call it that, is achieved within the various interview encounters. To get some purchase on this, let us look at what the questionnaire item does not explicitly state. It does not, for example, say by how much taxes should be reduced, what thresholds the respondent is prepared to accept in the trade-off between taxation and welfare spending, whether taxes can be reduced *and* welfare spending increased by reducing spending on other government services, such as defence, and so on. In other words, it presumes much that is left unstated and none of the possibilities we have just identified, and there are many others, are, we would suggest, outrageous or pernickety, but fairly routine queries anyone might raise on occasions when asked such a question. How, then, can a researcher ensure that A's reply to the question means the same as B's, C's, etc.?

Of course, in questionnaire research this issue of ensuring meaning equivalence has not exactly gone unnoticed, and a number of devices are recommended as ways of uncovering meanings more adequately by removing ambiguities in question design and detecting them in question responses. These include such things as funnelling, supplementary questions, probes, attitude-scales, open-ended items, and consistency checks. Using these techniques, it is claimed, the interviewer can explore the respondent's initial reply by asking for amplification, clarification, or whatever. Thus, to pursue imaginatively our present example a little further, if a respondent expressed uncertainty about whether or not expenditures should be increased on social services or whether taxes should be reduced, the interviewer might well ask for some further clarification of his doubt. Moreover, according to the lore of interviewing, this probe should be asked in such a way as to avoid threatening the respondent with his appalling ignorance about something he should know, avoid, too, leading him to state one preference or another for reasons of social desirability, or otherwise interfering with the respondent's true and accurate expression of his view. It might be that the respondent raises one of the possible queries we mentioned a moment ago, in which case the interviewer faces a further choice between encouraging a further discussion of the issue and run the risk of exceeding his very practical interest in getting the job done, or to avoid this, run the risk of appearing unsupportive. As anyone who has done interviewing will tell you, all of these are very real and very practical matters facing all interviewers, and in this respect can be seen as efforts to cope with the question facing all social actors throughout the moments of their daily lives, 'What do I do next?'

In the case of the interview this practical activity is directed toward the job of collecting valid data, including that of ensuring 'meaning equivalence' in the responses. Thus, in our imagined interview, the interviewer out of all the interchanges that occur has to select those which he is to take as a valid reply to the question asked, reject those which have little or nothing to do with the topic, whatever it might be, make judgements on the respondent's beliefs, decide which of the replies are consistent, which are inconsistent and evidence that, for whatever reasons, the respondent is not paying attention. To assist him, the researcher has available any number of devices to test for such things as consistency of replies, but these still have to be *applied* with respect to particular interview productions, and this application is interpretative work.

We are now beginning to get a glimpse of the interview as a very practical activity in which a particular interviewer interacts with a particular respondent in a particular place at a particular time.

And, though the trained interviewer may well have imbibed all the rules and theories of research interviewing until they are coming out of his ears, there still remains the very practical problem of applying such rules in particular occasions in order to get the job done in the way prescribed.[15] For example, achieving 'meaning equivalence' in questions and replies is not something formally guaranteed by standardizing questions across interviews, or programming the interviewer's behaviour in order to minimize the sources of variability, but has to be worked at. As Cicourel's study of the process of interviewing and coding in a study of fertility amply shows, the neat tables which are the end results of the empirical work conceal, or at least fail to display, the massive amount of interpretative work done by the interviewers, work which is not explicated in any procedures identified in the rules of interviewing , except in some general, abstracted and decontextualized fashion, and as we shall see in detail in the next chapter, the following of strict procedures involves the use of an indefinite set of practical considerations.

Cicourel illustrates, using transcripts of the interviews, how the interviewers 'resolved' ambiguities, let certain remarks pass, allowed propriety to constrain lines of questioning, how meanings were held in reserve, and so on.[16] What becomes clear from this is that it is impossible for the interviewer to programme questions, his own self conceptions and their presentation, or his relationship with the respondent in advance, but must manage the interview as it is happening. As Cicourel remarked in an earlier work:

The interviewer cannot precisely check out his own responses in detail and follow the testing of an hypothesis during an interview; he is forced to make snap judgements, extended inferences, reveal his views, overlook material, and the like, and may be able to show how they were made or even why they were made only after the fact. The interviewer cannot escape from the difficulties of everyday life interpretations and actions. The commonsense 'rules' compromise literal hypothesis testing, but they are necessary conditions for eliciting the desired information.[17]

Here Cicourel is pointing to an important ambiguity between the warrant upon which the method of interviewing is based and the facts or circumstances of its practice. On the one hand, it is prescribed as a set of rules of theories which, if correctly followed, will produce valid and objective data, to put it simply; yet, on the other hand, the practical circumstances in which interviewing is conducted means that the interviewer must necessarily pay at least as much attention to managing it as a social encounter to get the job done at all. While Cicoural himself sees no possibility of resolving this ambiguity through traditional research designs, what we can readily admit to is that the relationship between the rules of interviewing and their application in practical circumstances is something that is, at best, vague and unexplicated. We shall return to this point towards the end of the chapter.

There are a number of responses to these kinds of remarks on interviewing. One which is fairly common is to take it as a refutation of the scientific pretensions of the method itself. Even within conventional sociology, many commentators have expressed doubts about the presuppositions upon which the interview method depends, and condemn it for its artificiality and detachment from actual social situations, the often noted discrepancy between what respondents say and what they do, and the rather crude conception of language and meaning it presumes.[18] At one level this takes the form of a complaint against existing theories and rules of interviewing arguing that they too lightly dismiss or gloss problems arising from the social encounter between an interviewer and a respondent. What is needed, it is claimed, is more and better research on these kind of effects so that they can be more adequately evaluated. In other words, there is little fundamentally wrong with the interview; what is needed is to make it more effective.[19]

At another level, these criticisms can and do lead to a more positive condemnation of the method itself. This, in general terms, takes issue with one of its major justifications, namely, that by using respondents' verbal report the researcher gains access to events, behaviours, and other phenomena, it would be uneconomic to observe directly. It is argued against this that far from being a virtue, this research strategy results in manifold distortions of the very phenomena it is intended to study. Even though a respondent, candidly and completely, 'tells the truth', this is never a direct exhibition of the behaviours themselves. 'It is a gloss for them, a breaking down of the ongoing flow of life into a set of verbal categories.'[20] The interviewer, for example, by directing the interview, by using precoded categories, by presenting complex beliefs and attitudes in the form of rating scales, by supplying the topics of the talk, by controlling the questioning, eases his way to causal description of social phenomena that bear little relationship to the daily lives the respondents, as people, lead. Matters are made worse when the interview data is coded, analysed, and tabulated. In this process, the answers contained in the interview schedule are used as indicators of such things as 'economic position', 'attitudes toward the

EEC', 'political conservatism', and so on, and replaced by 'objective' numerals and presented in tabular fashion. This enables statistical and other mathematical operations to be used as ways of seeing whether or not the original theory 'fits' the data and, further, whether the reality constituted in the theory corresponds to the reality uncovered by the empirical research. Yet, this reality supposedly uncovered by the research would seem, in light of what was said earlier, to be more the creation of the method of investigation used than it is a reality independent and invariant of the ways it is made visible.

It might be thought that the methodological problems of the interview arise from the fact that, as a method, it aims at producing verbal reports about social phenomena rather than directly observing them. As a consequence, the descriptions it generates, though they may be rational and scientific according to the canons of scientific investigation, present a distorted or at least inadequate depiction of the description social actors use in the course of their daily lives.[21] Accordingly, before raising further issues of a more general nature, let us examine a method of research which explicitly rejects the interview and survey, on many of the grounds we have just sketched, in favour of a research strategy which aims at a fuller, more rounded, less abstracted, appreciation of the fact that social life is an ongoing process and, moreover, one constructed in and through the meanings social actors use to negotiate, often in subtle and delicate ways, their courses of action; ways which the interview and survey method, because of their crudeness and inflexibility, cannot but fail to capture. This alternative strategy we refer to as participant observation.

PARTICIPANT OBSERVATION

Proponents of this method argue that the only way to discover the meanings actors use to construct social reality is through a direct involvement in their activities. Only in this way can a researcher escape the constraints of the interview and avoid producing a lifeless 'scientized' conception of the social actor.[22] The task participant observation sets itself is to discover the values, norms, categories, rules and so on, that typify a society, from the 'inside' by participating, in some fashion, in the way of life of the social actors concerned. Only in this way, it is argued, can the sociological researcher affect a more adequate relationship between the accounts and descriptions offered by social actors themselves and those produced by sociological theories. In other words, compared with the interview method, participant observation proponents argue that descriptions of social phenomena should be more securely grounded in the point of view of the actor rather than the researcher.[23] However, problems to do with the scientific nature of sociological descriptions are not ignored. Involvement must be tempered by a disinterested and objective stance otherwise the result of such research would fail to reach the standards of objective scientific investigation. There is, then, something of a dilemma here. On the one hand, the participant observer needs to become involved in the group in order to learn the values, norms and outlook of its members, yet, on the other hand, he must remain sufficiently detached to relate what he learns to relevant social scientific theories. In trying to meet both of these aims he runs major kinds of risk. He may become so involved that any claim to detachment and objectivity is lost; a process aptly termed 'going native'. The result of this, if any, is that the researcher merely describes the social world in lay rather than scientific and sociological terms. The opposite of this risk is maintaining detachment to such a degree that little or no significant insight is gained. As with interviewing, researchers are not unaware of these and other problems of the method, and much thought has gone into the consideration of the appropriate role a participant observer may adopt.[24]

As in the case of the interview, let us examine participant observation as a research encounter. Depending on the choice of research role, the researcher, for example, has to decide what kind of relationships he should cultivate, what types of person he should contact, how these contacts should be effected, how maintained, how they might influence the data obtained, etc.

During the course of the research, which may well extend over many months and even years, the fieldworker has to assemble what is seen, heard and reported into data. Unlike the interview, in participant observation, theoretical categories are normally intended to emerge through the course of the research. Indeed, one of the claimed strengths of the method is the way in which theoretical insights are the direct consequence of participation in the setting and, thereby, less open to the criticism levelled against much of sociological theory that it is too detached and abstracted from real social life as it is lived by social actors.

Typically, a fieldworker will observe sequences of activities, hear the ways in which group members talk about their activities, collect reports from members, some of them possibly informants, on what it is they are doing, and why. It is through these formulations that the final picture of the group's life is assembled. These reports and formulations are, of course, gathered during the course of the fieldworker's interactions with those he is studying, and, as such, are occasioned matters which, in the final report, become instances of norms, values, beliefs and rules of conduct, that constitute the social order of the group concerned. One cannot discuss fieldwork of this kind without mention of the notion of culture. It is a characterization of the culture belonging to a group of social actors that the fieldworker seeks. It is this which serves to explain patterns of action observed and, further, provides the dispositions, through socialization into the culture, which motivate and predispose actors to behave in such a way as to produce the patterns of action. It is this kind of model which guides the fieldworker's perceptions and analysis as he works up his material into a portrayal of the life of the group from their point of view.

By way of illustration let us take Suttles' excellent study of the organization of slum neighbourhoods in a district of Chicago.[25] Suttles makes use of the notion of ethnic ecology to account for the patterns of behaviour he observed. He discovered that the 'Addams area' of Chicago was segmented into distinct ethnic districts in which streets were considered to belong to a particular ethnic group or, alternatively, were neutral zones between districts. Buildings, parks and shops were also closely identified with ethnic territories. This framework enabled Suttles to categorize and describe incidents and actions as instances of easily recognizable occurrences within this normal ethnic ecology. Even actions and events which had earlier puzzled him, or which he had understood differently, could now be seen as instances of normal behaviour within an ethnically differentiated social order. The cultural order organized around the theme of ethnicity provided the inhabitants of the area with rules of conduct which constrained them and which, at the same time, furnished them and Suttles with ways of seeing, describing and explaining occurrences of behaviour as instances of actions of a particular kind. Thus, the model, in keeping with much of the ethnographic tradition, places considerable emphasis on the ways in which social actors see their world and go about constructing their daily lives; indeed, one could say that since it is largely assembled from the reports of actors it could hardly do otherwise. In other words, by using instances from what he observed during his stay in the community, what people said, what they did, when, how they dealt with each other, and all the other small details of their lives. Suttles was able to construct the cultural rules which governed the social ecology of the district. For example, one of the patterns of action Suttles accounts for using the model, and one which is presented as 'evidence for' the model, is the use of Taylor Street. This street ran through part of the Mexican section of Addams forming a boundary between groups of hostile Mexican gangs. Suttles reports that while adults were allowed free passage in and across the street on the assumption that they wished to make use of the shops and homes, adolescents from other sections were suspected of more serious intentions. That is, seeing an adolescent cross over from one territory into another was sufficient grounds for supposing that he was out to 'cause trouble'.[26] In this way the model is not merely a sociologist's construction but is assumed to be one used by members in order to 'see' what they and others are doing on the street. In other words, the ethnic normative order is not simply a set of externalized rules but also internalized ways of attributing meanings to actions and their environment; in this case 'causing trouble', 'threatening another gang', an 'invasion of territory', and so on.

Interviewing and participant observation share at least one feature in common. Both involve the researcher making inferences about collectivities of social actors from occasioned encounters between the investigator and social actors as subjects. On the one hand, the interview seeks deliberately to establish a relationship between an actor and an investigator and manage this relationship in order to encourage the social actor to produce the data required. Participant observation, on the other hand, is rarely so overtly deliberate as this. The participant observer's encounters are likely to be sporadic, often accidental, sometimes covert, sometimes involving intimacy as well as instrumentality, and highly varied. It is out of encounters such as these that the sociological picture is assembled. However, there is one immediately obvious difference between the two methods. From the point of view of those who subscribe to the interview, participant observation is far too haphazard a method to produce objective data as a means of effecting adequate scientific description. The whole thrust of the interview method is designed to increase the anonymity of the interviewer, whereas in participant observation there is no clear guide as to whether the researcher, in his wanderings and casual chats with those he is studying, has successfully suspended his own view and produced objective findings. How, for example, can we be sure that Suttles' account is both scientific and from the point of view of those who live there, an accurate portrayal of life in Addams. Would another observer produce the same findings? What is clear is that compared with the interview, participant observation has few clear rules guiding the researcher as to how to go about the business of research.

There are, broadly speaking, two kinds of response to this and other charges against participant observation. One is to deny that it does, in fact, lack adequate rules of procedure.[27] While these may not be the same rules as those said to be employed in interviewing, they do, nonetheless, make participant observation rigorous and, what is more, enable such a researcher to observe the 'real stuff' of social life. Another response is to accept that participant observation is not a scientific method in the way interviewing seems to be, but is a rather different sort of enterprise altogether. Producing descriptions of social life from the actor's point of view requires rather different capacities, such as an ability to empathize, interpret, and otherwise 'see' the society as a native of that society. But these kind of capacities are not exactly routinizable, nor subject to rigorous elucidation, and in the absence of any of these qualities how are we to judge whether a researcher has produced a valid account of the culture of the group concerned? How can we be sure that our own cultural viewpoint has not distorted that of the social actor? How can we be sure, especially when dealing with peoples who belong to a different culture and who speak a language very different to our own, that in recording their lives for sociological posterity we do not inadvertently portray them as less than knowledgeable, or less than rational, as stupid and ignorant savages rather than as authentic human beings?

Put this way, of course, the task of participant observation becomes all but impossible, especially so with regard to societies and cultures very different to our own.[28] Moreover, producing a set of rules showing how one could go about knowing a society from within as a native would know it is tantamount to producing rules to show how to live a life: no easy task.

The problems we are pointing to here arise mainly from the issue we identified at the beginning of this chapter, namely that of producing descriptions of social activities from the point of view of social actors which are, at the same time and in some sense, objective, not to say scientific. As far as participant observation is concerned, this boils down to the task of accurately reproducing, if only as a starting point, descriptions of social activities that actors actually use in the course of constructing their social order; a problem that becomes particularly acute, though it is by no means absent in other situations, when dealing with social actors who, it can be said, belong to a culture very different from that of the researcher. It is from this standpoint that the relative lack of explicitly formulated procedures for research becomes at worst a total condemnation of the method as unscientific, subjective and arbitrary, or, at best, simply embarrassing.

FINDING ORDER

We said at the beginning of this chapter that our interest in discussing these examples of social research methods is not so much to complain about or condemn them, but to highlight some of the features of practical reasoning they display; features which, to anticipate a little of what follows, are exhibited in both professional and lay sociological practices. The first point we want to make is that interviewing and participant observation are *done*; that is, merely as a recordable fact, many millions of social research interviews have been conducted, and that many participant observation studies have been carried out. What is more, both methods have been employed satisfactorily, at least as judged by those whose business it is to judge these things. As we have said, our issue is not the possibility or impossibility, the validity or invalidity, of such procedures as methods of social research, but rather with *how* they are done as social activities. That is, following Garfinkel's recommendations, we intend to look at these methods as practical achievements, as mutually co-ordinated productions, by those who engage in them. Or, to put it slightly differently, as social devices for accomplishing sociological descriptions.

Both participant observation and the interview, however else they may be held to differ, share the axiomatically held belief of most of conventional sociology, that social life is patterned, regular and orderly, but that this orderliness, this regularity, this patterning, is concealed and obscured and can only be revealed by means of the correct method of investigation. Sharrock and Anderson propose the analogy of a jigsaw to express this point. The picture, the pattern is present in the pieces but not recognizable in any of them until they have been assembled, piece by piece, to make the whole visible.[29] Assembling the overall picture by inferring from the fragmented and dispersed pieces, some of which may be missing, are what the methods of research are intended to achieve. Thus, from the answers given in an interview to a few questions on a questionnaire, the researcher, by applying the accredited rules, is able to build up a pattern that characterizes the collectivity he is studying. Equally, by observing and becoming involved in the various doings of the members of a group, the fieldworker is able to construct and provide evidence for the cultural rule which guide and shape their social life. It is the methods, as relatively systemic and standardized procedures, which bring the pattern, the orderliness, the regularity of social life to view.

One rather important presupposition in all this is that the methods bring out patterns which are undetected by the social actors themselves. They only have a partial view of matters, views which may also be ideologically expressed interests, views which betray a 'false consciousness', views which are irrationally based; in any event, views and beliefs which are seen as the product, direct or indirect, of the external social forces which shape, propel, confuse, cause, direct, social actors and their actions. Associated closely with this presupposition is a conception of the 'world of everyday life' as disorderly and fragmented; isolated bits that can only be seen to fit into a pattern when they have been reconstituted by proper scientific procedure. By way of example, we have only to look back to the rules governing interviewing which, above all else, are designed to either eliminate or control the 'irritations' of everyday life, such as the tendency of some people to wander off the point, to digress about their aches and pains when they should be answering questions about public policy, to rush through the interview because the pubs close in half an hour, to fail to understand the point of a question. It is these all too present features of social encounters that probably provoked one eminent social researcher to remark, 'If is were possible [to get information from a respondent] without asking him any questions, and without the respondent having to "respond" that would be so much the better . . . '[30] In other words, the organization of daily life creates obstacles to the proper execution of research method and further seems to conceal the patterns, processes and structures which are the proper concern of sociology.[31]

In the assembly of sociological descriptions, the researcher, while making use of descriptions done, in some form or another, by social actors seeks to render these scientifically useful by transforming them into descriptions which are clear, determinate and invariant. This is achieved by treating the particulars as instances of a general class. For example, the very particular happenings in and around Taylor Street in Addams, the hostility expressed, the remarks made, the identification of types of persons, and more, all done by the inhabitants in very routine, matter-of-course ways, were classified by Suttles as instances of a general class of behaviour to do with the ethnic culture of the area. A snub, a joke, a passing remark, a story told on a street corner, a reluctance to go into certain areas, friendship patterns, were all parts of the jigsaw which, when fitted together, provided evidence for and were seen as cultural rules guiding the patterns of interaction between the various ethnic groups in Addams. Similarly, out of all the talk that transpires in the interview, the researcher 'selects' those elements which he deems to be relevant, and the coder, often faced with 'inadequate' information, makes sense of the replies and fits them into classes of actions, beliefs, types, or whatever.

The point is, however, that the work done by researchers to make the correspondence between, or to justify the inference from, the concrete instances of talk, actions, and so forth, that transpire in the data collection setting, and the general theoretical categories is unexplicated. And this is as true both for participant observation and interviewing, as well as for other methods of professional and lay sociological enquiry. A body of knowledge of social structures is assembled, but we are not told how this is done. In this connection Garfinkel points out that there are

innumerable situations of sociological inquiry in which the investigator – whether he be a professional sociologist or a person undertaking an inquiry about social structures in the interest of managing his practical everyday affairs – can assign witnessed actual appearances to the status of an event of conduct only by imputing biography and prospects to the appearances. This he does by embedding the appearance in his presupposed knowledge of social structures.[32]

What Garfinkel is drawing our attention to here is that for an investigator to decide what he is looking at now, he must, on innumerable occasions, wait for future developments which, in their turn, may well qualify or alter what he had previously seen. Thus, Suttles' initial collection of the various and variegated doings in Addams were, later, transformed into instances of the ethnic ecology of the area by relating them, seeing them, through the sense and conception of social structure which emerged later. Similarly, the intended sense of an answer to a question is often later, through probings, the replies to other questions, and so on, prospectively revealed as an instance of a view belonging to a 'type of social actor'. For Garfinkel, an 'approximate description' of the process that best fits how professional and lay sociological researchers actually go about their work as a practical activity is the 'documentary method of interpretation'.[33]

THE DOCUMENTARY METHOD OF INTERPRETATION

By the concept of documentary interpretation Garfinkel is pointing to one of the ways in which members, both lay and professional, make sense of their environment. It is a process which

consists in identifying an underlying pattern behind a series of appearances such that each appearance is seen as referring to, an expression of, or a 'document of', the underlying pattern. However, the underlying pattern itself is identified through its individual concrete appearances, so that the appearances reflecting the pattern and the pattern itself mutually determine one another . . .[34]

In somewhat less abstract terms, the documentary interpretation of action is a process in which participants see each other's actions as expressions of patterns, the patterns enabling them to see what the actions are. So that 'on any occasion in the course of the interaction, the actions that the participants see each other performing are seen as such in terms of the meaning of the context, and the context in turn is understood to be what it is through these same actions'.[35] A central feature of documentary interpretation is that later appearances, later actions, may provoke a reinterpretation of the perceived pattern which, in turn, results in a reinterpretation of what the previous appearances 'really were'. So, not only 'is the underlying pattern derived from its individual documentary evidences, but the individual documentary evidences, in their turn, are interpreted on the basis of "what is known" about the underlying pattern. Each is used to elaborate the other.'[36]

Garfinkel claims that the method is recognizable as a way of getting to know what a person is 'talking about', given that the person does not say exactly what he means, as a way of recognizing common occurrences and objects such as postmen, friendly gestures, promises, answers to questionnaires, displays of ethnic geography. It is recognizable, too, in deciding such sociologically analysed events as, to use his own examples once again, Goffman's strategies for the management of impressions, Erikson's identity crises, Riesman's types of conformity, Parson's value systems, Malinowski's magical practices, Bales' interaction counts, Merton's types of deviance, Lazarsfeld's latent structure of attitudes, and the occupational categories used in the census.[37] In short, Garfinkel in trying to throw some light on an issue we have been raising throughout this chapter, namely, how, as a practical activity, does a researcher do the work of finding, say, a respondent's attitude from replies to questionnaire items, and ethnic ecology from talks with and observations of the inhabitants of Addams, the extent of real crime from crimes known to the police, and the type of mental illness from the instances of behaviour. What, in Garfinkel's words, 'is the work whereby the investigator sets the observed occurrence and the intended occurrence into a correspondence of meaning, such that the investigator finds it reasonable to treat witnessed actual appearances as evidences of the event the means to be studying?'[38] Garfinkel provides us with a demonstration of the method at work; an attempt, as he puts it, 'to catch the work of "fact production" in flight'.[39] Work, let us stress, done by both lay and professional sociological enquirers.

Ten undergraduates were asked to take part in research being done to explore alternatives to psychotherapy as a way of giving persons advice on their personal problems.[40] Each volunteer was seen by an experimenter masquerading as a trainee student counsellor. After this preliminary discussion in which the volunteer was asked to give some background to a serious problem on which he would like advice, he was then asked to address a 'counsellor' through a series of questions which would permit a 'yes' or a 'no' answer. The experimenter-counsellor heard the questions and gave the answers from an adjoining room via an intercom system. These answers were predetermined by a table of random numbers, each subject asking the same number of questions being administered the same series of yes or no answers. After each answer the subject was asked to evaluate and tape record his comments.

From the protocols it is clear that none of the subjects had any difficulty getting through the exchange. The answers, though randomly chosen, were typically heard as 'answers-to-questions' and subjects saw directly what was meant by the answer. All reported that they had been given 'advice' and addressed their criticism and appreciation to this fact. What was also a feature of the protocols was that there were no pre-programmed questions and that present answers altered the sense of previous exchanges. In other words, over the course of the exchange the assumption seemed to operate that there was an answer to be obtained, and if the sense of the answer was not immediately obvious, then its meaning could be determined by active search, such as asking another question to find out what the adviser 'had in mind'. The underlying pattern was elaborated over the series of exchanges and accommodated to each present 'answer' so as to sustain the 'course of advice', to elaborate what had 'really been advised' previously, and to look for new possibilities as emerging patterns of the occasion itself. Where answers were unsatisfying or incomplete, the subjects were willing to wait for later answers to decide the sense of the previous ones. Incomplete answers were often treated as incomplete because of 'deficiencies' in the method of counselling. That is, incomplete and ambiguous answers were so for 'a reason', and resolved by imputing knowledge and intent to the counsellor. Even those subjects who had suspicions were reluctant to act on this belief in the adviser's untrustworthiness. Such subjects found this suspicion difficult to sustain.

Throughout there was a search for a pattern. Indeed, a pattern was likely to be seen in the first appearance of 'advice'. Even where the possibility of deception occurred, the counsellor's utterance was seen as a pattern of deceit, thus preserving the utterance as a document of a pattern, though, in this case, one of deceit rather than advice. Subjects also made specific reference to various social structures in deciding upon the sensible and warranted character of the counsellor's advice. These references were to social structures treated as actually or potentially known in common with the adviser, such as motivations people might have for giving advice, categories of persons and typical modes of behaviour in which such people might engage, including what attitudes parents, friends, fellow students might take to the need for advice, and more. These social structures consisted of normative features of the social system as seen from within, and which, for the subject, were definitive of his memberships in the various collectivities with which he had to deal as conditions of his decision. Subjects, that is, presupposed known-in-common features of the collectivity as a body of common-sense knowledge subscribed to by both parties. They drew upon these presupposed patterns in determining what it was that the counsellor was talking about, as documentary evidence of the normative features of the collectivity setting, whether it was the experiment, the family, the school, occupation, and so on, to which the subject's interests were directed. These evidences and the features of the collectivities concerned were referred back and forth, each elaborating upon and being elaborated by one another. Finally, through a retrospective-prospective review, the subjects justified the 'reasonable' sense of the advice as grounds for the managing of their affairs, and its 'reasonable' character consisted in an accomplished compatibility with the normative social structures presumed to be known in common. The position of the subject required him to use his knowledge of the ordinary 'typical' grounds of human behaviour and of the ordinary motivated 'typified' courses of action that people undertake, to come to some sort of determination as to where he was in the course of the interview thus far. And he must use that 'now determined' position as a basis for further actions and interpretations of other people's actions. These further actions themselves act on the past actions and interpretations, and possibly modify them. In regard to as yet future actions, current actions, then, have an open 'horizon of meaning'. Where we are now we know in that way; where we will have come to have been is not yet known. In this way it could be said that in any strict calculable sense the subjects did not know the position they were in. This resonates with the position Agnes was in, having to use current appearances as a resource to interpret past actions and also to discover new meanings.

It is Garfinkel's claim that this process of documentary interpretation better describes the features of practical reasoning employed in the production of sociological accounts, both lay and professional. It is not his claim that this thereby makes them 'unscientific'. Rather, his concern is to explore how it is that the scientifically warrantable status of accounts is achieved as a practical accomplishment. How is a fact established? How is validity established? How are disputes resolved? How are arguments warranted? In short, the procedures which establish science as an activity in the world. After all, much of the work in producing natural scientific accounts has to be done in and through processes of this kind, making use of and ducumenting knowledge known in common, a retrospective-prospective assembly of a pattern, making sense of previous signs through subsequent ones, and so on. Before moving to the next chapter in which we shall deal with some of the issues raised here in more detail, let us try to summarize so far.

CONCLUSION

In this discussion of conventional methods of professional sociological investigation we have pointed to some of the ways and means that ethnomethodology employs in approaching the analysis of reasoning as a practical matter. In Chapter 2, we presented Garfinkel's programme as one of looking at the determination of sense, of facticity, of reasonableness, etc., as essentially involving work done by members motivated by a practical interest. In this chapter what we have done is indicate what difference this viewpoint could make to our conception of professional sociological investigation. Among the features we pointed to was the unavoidably practical nature of much of sociological enquiry, making use, as it does in order to get the job done at all, of taken-for-granted and presumed-to-be-held-in-common knowledge. This included such things as determining that replies were 'replies to the questions asked', deciding what a respondent 'had in mind', using excerpts from protocols to describe complex scenes like industrial organizations, communities, and others, documenting actions or utterances, as signs or indications of cultural behaviour, and more. All moves, and unavoidable ones at that, in the game of making sense of occasional features of very particular circumstances by relating them to a pattern which purports to describe the whole.

We presented these observations in the context of discussing a core, but too much neglected, issue in conventional sociology, namely, that of the nature of sociological descriptions. We suggested that, as far as much of conventional sociology is concerned, this issue boils down to one of description having to satisfy two criteria: first, that of being scientific, and, second, that of accurately portraying the society from the members' point of view. Although we have not by any means dealt with all the ramifications this task entails, we did indicate that attempts to satisfy both led to an incompatible emphasis on either 'objectivity' or 'realism' with all the methodological heart searching this produces.[41] However, from Garfinkel's point of view, what is of interest is not the methodological and philosophical issues raised, but how we can describe what sociologists do as practical activities. In this respect, professional sociologists are in the same position as coroners, friends in a relationship, canteen ladies, and all of us, in having to use the same procedures to find out what is going on. What these procedures are is another matter and although we can propose that traditional treatments of the task of sociological description have resulted in various kinds of infelicitous conceptions of the social actor and the nature of social activities – infelicities which have been accused of amounting to gross distortions – we are not yet in a position to say what a more adequate kind of description might consist of. What we have strongly hinted at, however, is that sociological description is itself a social activity engaged in by both lay and professional social investigators.

In the next chapter we will deal with some of these matters in more detail and introduce two important concepts in ethnomethodology, namely indexicality and reflexivity. What these two concepts do is to bring to the fore an important idea, one implicit in much of the discussion of this chapter, that much of social life is constituted through language. Language not as written up for us by grammarians, linguists and others, as a formalized and idealized structure, but language as used by members in the naturally occurring circumstances of their lives. People talk to each other, give orders, answer questionnaires, talk to fieldworkers, ask for a cup of coffee, debate in parliaments, sing songs, pretend to be other than they are, fill in forms, lie and cheat, buy and sell, foment rebellion, get married, write letters, and more and more; all activities inseparable from natural language. In view of this, then, the character of natural language would seem to be of some importance in the understanding of social life, and it is to ethnomethodology's stance on this which we now turn.

NOTES AND REFERENCES

1. This observation is owed to Wes Sharrock and Bob Anderson.
2. See, on this particular issue, P. Drew, 'Domestic political violence: some problems of measurement', Sociological Review, 22, 1974, pp. 5–26.
3. T. P. Wilson, 'Normative and Interpretative Paradigms in Sociology', in J. D. Douglas (ed.), *Understanding Everyday life*, Routledge & Kegan Paul: London, 1974, p. 71.
4. See, for example, J. M. Atkinson, *Discovering Suicide*, MacMillan: London, 1978. The definition, of course, is from Durkheim, *Suicide*, Routledge & Kegan Paul: London, 1952, p. 44.
5. See Drew, *op. cit.*
6. For a discussion on this see J. A. Hughes, *The Philosophy of Social Research*, Longman: London, 1980.
7. These reports can be verbatim of checklists, but the point still stands.
8. D. Zimmerman and M. Pollner, 'The Everyday World as a Phenomenon', in J. D. Douglas (ed.), *Understanding Everyday Life*, Routledge & Kegan Paul, London, 1974, p. 91.
9. Any good text on research methods will provide a full discussion of the principles of interviewing. Specific texts on inter-

viewing include H. Hyman, et al., *Interviewing in Social Research*, University of Chicago Press: Chicago 1954; R. L. Kahn and C. F. Cannell, *The Dynamics of Interviewing*, Wiley: New York, 1952; J. M. Converse and H. Schuman, *Conversations at Random*, Wiley: New York, 1974.

10. Kahn and Cannell, *op. cit.*, p. 59.
11. Familiarity with available literature suggests that these theories are not always consistent with one another. See A. V. Cicourel, *Method and Measurement in Sociology*, The Free Press: New York, 1964, Ch. 3. One might also note the theories embodied in police interviewing of suspects, job interviewing, debriefing spies, etc., as well as those in social research.
12. H. Mehan and H. Wood, *The Reality of Ethnomethodology*, Wiley: New York, 1975, p. 49.
13. D. Butler and D. Stokes, *Political Change in Britain: Forces Shaping Electoral Choice*, Penguin: Harmondsworth, 1969, p. 561. We are not, of course, singling this out as a poor question in a terrible study. It is merely a convenient and typical example.
14. *op. cit.*, p. 101.
15. When we refer to the 'practical' constraints of interviewing, such as time, money, concern to get the job done, it is not to be understood that these could be removed by an additional input of money, researchers or greater directorial control. They are the 'practical' concerns which invade all human actions. See next chapter.
16. A. V. Cicourel, *Theory and Method in a Study of Argentine Fertility*, Wiley: New York, 1973.
17. A. V. Cicourel, *Method and Measurement*, op. cit., p. 100.
18. See, for example, D. L. Phillips, *Knowledge From What?*, Rand McNally: Chicago, 1971, pp. 39–47; I. Deutscher, 'Asking Questions Cross-culturally: Some Problems of Linguistic Comparability', in H. S. Becker et al. (eds), *Institutions and the Person*, Aldine: Chicago, 1968, pp. 318–41, and his selection *What We Say, What We Do*, Scott, Foresman and Co.: Glenview, 1973.
19. There is no false modesty nor hypocrisy in saying that the critique of the interview amounts to negative criticism in that it could or ought to be improved. Rather, the critique attempts to show that being a social encounter, the interview is on a par with other styles of interviewing, such as job interviewing, police questioning, psychiatric diagnosis, student counselling.

They are all varieties of practical reasoning. The sociologist need only have concern if he is misled into thinking he is doing something other than practical reasoning.

20. Mehan and Wood, *op. cit.*, p. 49.

21. Of course, it may be argued that the aim of sociology is not to replicate the descriptions members use. Nevertheless, to the extent that the interview method relies on reports given by respondents, the point stands.

22. See A. Rose (ed.), *Human Behaviour and Social Processes*, Houghton Mifflin: Boston, 1962; S. Bruyn, *The Human Perspective in Sociology*, Prentice-Hall: Englewood Cliffs, 1966; J. Lofland, *Analysing Social Settings*, Wadsworth: Belmont, 1971; H. S. Becker, *Sociological Work: Method and Substance*, Aldine: Chicago, 1970; P. Rock, *The Making of Symbolic Interactionism*, London, MacMillan: 1979. Also remarks in Ch. 2 of this volume.

23. H. S. Becker and B. Geer, 'Participant Observation and Interviewing: A Comparison', in W. J. Filstead (ed.), *Qualitative Methodology*, Markham: Chicago, 1970, pp. 133–42.

24. There is an extensive literature on this and other problems of participant observation. See, for example, selections in Filstead (ed.), *op. cit.*, E. Bittner, 'objectivity and Realism in Sociology', in G. Psathas (ed.), *Phenomenological Sociology*, Wiley: New York, 1973, pp. 109–25, suggested that this tension between realism and objectivity has been evident in sociology from its beginnings.

25. G. D. Suttles, *The Social Order of the Slum: Ethnicity and Territory in the Inner city*, University of Chicago Press: Chicago, 1968. We are indebted to P. Drew's unpublished Ph.D. dissertation, 'Some Moral and Inferential Aspects of Descriptions of Violent Events in Northern Ireland', University of Lancaster, 1977, for a discussion of Suttles' study.

26. Suttles, op. cit., pp. 142–3. For making types of actors 'visible' on the street see Ch. 5 of this book for a discussion of police methods and the detection of suspicious persons. Also, D. Sudnow, 'Temporal Parameters of Interpersonal Observation', in D. Sudnow (ed.), *Studies in Social Interaction*, The Free Press: New York, 1972. pp. 259–79.

27. One attempt to produce a set of such rules in H. S. Becker, 'Problems of inference and proof in participant observation', *American Sociological Review*, 23, 1958, pp. 682–90. Reprinted in Filstead (ed.), *op. cit.*, pp. 189–201.

28. This particular aspect raises all kinds of philosophical and quasi-philosophical issues beyond the scope of this book. See, for example, G. McCall and J. Simmons, *Issues In Participant Observation*, Addison-Wesley: Reading, 1969; R. Beehler and son (eds), *The Philosophy of Society*, Methuen: London, 1978; C. Geertz, 'From the Native's Point of View', in J. L. Dolgelin, et al., (eds), *Symbolic Anthropology*, Columbia University Press: New York, 1977; and the provocative paper by W. W. Sharrock and R. J. Anderson, 'On the Demise of the Native', *Occasional Paper No. 5*, Department of Sociology, University of Manchester, 1980.

29. W. W. Sharrock and R. J. Anderson, 'Conceptions of Orderliness and their Implementation', mimeo, Department of Sociology, University of Manchester. Paper prepared for SSRC workshop on Ethnography held at University of Birmingham, Sept. 1979.

30. A. N. Oppenheim, *Questionnaire Design and Attitude Measurement*, Heinemann: London, 1966, p. 49.

31. Sharrock and Anderson, 'Conceptions of Orderliness and their Implementation', *op. cit.*, pp. 11–12.

32. H. Garfinkel, *Studies in Ethnomethodology*, Prentice-Hall: Englewood Cliffs, 1967, p. 72.

33. *ibid.*, pp. 76–103. The original formulation from which Garfinkel borrows this conception is K. Mannheim, 'On the Interpretation of Weltanschauung', in his *Essays on the Sociology of Knowledge*, Routledge & Kegan Paul: London, 1959, pp. 53–63.

34. Wilson, *op. cit.*, p. 68.

35. *ibid.*, p. 69 and P. McHugh, *Defining the Situation*, Bobbs-Merrill: New York, 1968.

36. Garfinkel, *op. cit.*, p. 78.

37. *ibid.*, pp. 78–9.

38. *ibid.*, p. 79.

39. *ibid.*

40. This is reported in Garfinkel, *ibid.*, pp. 79–94 and P. McHugh, *op. cit.*

41. E. Bittner, *op. cit.*

Chapter four

INDEXICALITY AND THE REFLEXIVITY OF ACCOUNTS

Sociological research, as we have just seen, continually encounters problems in its attempts to satisfy the twin conditions of its aim: to be both scientific and, in some respects at least, faithful to the world as seen from the actor's point of view. One of the problems identified was the tendency to idealize away the identifying characteristics of daily life, even though the knowledge of these is often used as a tacit resource. Sociological research is apt to idealize away the actor's practical involvement and, given this, the production of the social order as a practical accomplishment. But before dealing with this aspect further, it is worth looking at one diagnosis of the 'trouble' besetting conventional sociology.

Despite the considerable efforts that have gone into trying to emulate the achievements of the natural sciences with their formally constructed theories of wide generality, sociology constantly seems to fall short of even a modest approximation to this standard. Although many reasons are offered for this state of affairs one is especially interesting for us. Blumer suggests that much of the failure of sociology is due to the lack of clarity of its concepts.[1] For example, concepts such as personality, attitude, norm, culture, institution, and so on, are unclear. Even the production of a precise definition is of little help; in fact it compounds the difficulty, since it still leaves problematic what is to stand as an example to fit the definition in any particular case: an issue we discussed in the preceding chapter in respect of research investigations. However, Blumer is interesting in that he rejects a fairly common solution to this problem, namely, that of operationally defining a concept. Using the example of intelligence testing, Blumer argues that if a hard-line operationalizing approach is adopted, whereby intelligence is defined as that which IQ tests measure, this results in theoretic aridity in that what constitutes IQ scores as a class comprises merely the methods whereby they were measured and *nothing else*. Hence, no linkages could logically and legitimately be made to other concepts. Intelligence under this procedure would simply be an artefact of the measuring procedures employed and have no connection whatsoever with other concepts dealing with the social world. Nor is Blumer satisfied with a more modest operationalism in which, to use the example again, intelligence tests are seen as indicators of some factor, intelligence, which we cannot directly observe. In this case the test, as a performance, is indicative, stands for, the phenomenon 'lying behind' and producing in some way, the indicator itself. But, as Blumer recognizes and as we have indicated previously, that which 'stands behind' the indicators, the underlying pattern, to put it this way, is still constituted by general and common-sense understandings in the manner suggested by the documentary model of interpretation. The indicators, in other words, bear all the features of contextual determination. The conclusion to which Blumer is led is that the concepts in sociological theory should be regarded as 'sensitizing concepts' which, 'by means of exposition . . . yield a meaningful picture, abetted by apt illustrations which enable one to grasp the reference in terms of one's own experience' since 'what we infer does not express itself in the same fixed way, we are not able to rely on fixed objective expressions to make the inference'.[2]

Since we have met the kind of problem Blumer is addressing before, it is as well to look at whether and in what sense 'clear' concepts fit the social world, whatever 'clear concepts' might turn out to be.

Blumer here seems to have identified an important problem with respect to social scientific concepts but is not quite sure how consequential a problem it is, nor indeed, whether it is a problem peculiar to sociology and the social sciences, or one which has a wider relevance. Garfinkel, however, is in no doubt. To the extent that professional and lay sociologists use natural language as a resource for their enquiries, these enquiries will, perforce, seek to 'remedy the indexical properties of practical discourse'.[3] It is to a discussion of the concept of indexicality to which we now turn.

INDEXICALITY

Indexicality bids to be one of the central concepts of ethnomethodology. Indexical expressions, that is, expressions which derive their sense and meaning from the occasions on which they are used, such as 'this', 'that', 'you', 'I', and so on, have been the concern of logicians for centuries. For Garfinkel, however, the characteristics of indexical expressions extend to the whole of language and, thereby, furnish ethnomethodology with its particular concerns.

The traditional philosophical concern with expressions such as 'I', 'you', 'here', 'now', arose out of the observation that the meaning of such words, and the truth-value of expressions containing them, depended on such things as who was uttering them, when, where, and other contextual particularities. In short, their meaning depended crucially upon the circumstances in which they were uttered. The sentence 'I am drunk', for example, depends for its truth or falsity upon who is uttering it, when, and where. Such expressions have no fixed truth value, no fixed meaning. To avoid this vagueness, philosophers sought to repair indexical expressions by replacing them with objective ones with fixed meanings. Thus, 'I am drunk' could be transformed into an objective expression by replacing 'I' with a proper name with a time and date. In which case it is claimed to be a relatively simple matter to determine its truth value by seeing if, in fact, Bill Bloggs is drunk at 10.25 p.m. on 29 July 1982.

Garfinkel's claim, however, is that natural language as a whole is profoundly indexical in that, for members, the meaning of their everyday talk is dependent on the context in which the talk occurs: an idea embodied in the notion of documentary interpretation discussed in the previous chapter. That is, to understand an utterance members must also know something about the particular circumstances in which the utterance was made, who the speaker was, the previous course of the talk, the relationship between the user and auditor, what is said subsequently, and so on. In this sense members may attend to the utterance 'I am drunk' with a concern to such matters as whether it is a complaint being made prior to exiting from a party, an apology to the host for unseemly behaviour, or the boast of a novice drinker, among many others. Whatever it turns out to be, whatever it is taken as, is dependent upon its location in the stream of interaction. Each and every repetition of the utterance is not to be taken as 'doing' the same thing and, importantly for members, the questions of its *truth* value may be of no consideration.[4] Members are interested in the particular not in idealized, standardized or typical meanings as such.[5] They want to know what that guy meant then by that particular remark; what that gesture was I made to you yesterday; what that notice on the common room door means, and so on. And to make sense of these and other communications members pay artful attention to the available contextual features to achieve an interpretation. These aspects of situations attended to, whether they be a word, story, event, action, or whatever, Garfinkel refers to as 'indexical particulars'. Far from being a philosophical notion, Garfinkel stresses that 'indexicality' is a property of the ways in which members interpret actions, talk, and events, and meaning is no longer a philosophical issue about words but embraces the various motives, implications, nuances, prospects, etc., that members see in a particular.[6] He does not talk as if 'meaning', 'context', 'objects', 'particulars' are discrete things which generate philosophical problems about their relationship to each other, but as members' creations constantly collapsing, shifting expanding like a swarm of bees.

So, for Garfinkel, the significance and the sense of any symbolic form, whether it be speech, writing, an act, a gesture, a mathemaical formulae, or whatever, is dependent upon the context in which it appears. By the notion of indexicality he is drawing attention to another property of social experience, namely, reflexivity.

REFLEXIVITY

All sociology axiomatically holds to the view that society provides its members with the opportunities, the motives and the methods for describing and analysing it. For ethnomethodology, the facts about society are features accomplished by the members of society using practical reasoning and common-sense knowledge in the course of their everyday lives. In this way, the accounts about society and its workings become constituent parts of the very thing they describe. They are, in short, reflexive. As Garfinkel puts it: 'Not only does commonsense knowledge portray a real society for members, but in the manner of a self-fulfilling prophecy the features of the real society are produced by persons' motivated compliance with these background expectancies.'[7] As was noted in the case of Agnes, the features of femininity which she portrayed and produced were portrayed and produced through attending to 'seen but unnoticed' elements of the setting in which she was in (which included her own behaviour) thereby constructing her femininity. Agnes' talk, gestures, and other 'symbolic behaviour' was embedded in tacit assumptions concerning 'the-fact-that-she-was-a-woman' which operated as an interpretative device for other's seeing Agnes' behaviour, and as something which stood in need of construction by Agnes. Garfinkel argues that since this is the case in all settings and on all occasions, there being no 'time out', then the 'reflexivity of accounting practices' pervade the social order. By this notion, Garfinkel collapses the distinction so essential to conventional sociology between the social order, structure, or society and the various methods of seeing and knowing about it: a distinction which, as we have suggested previously, provides conventional sociology with many of its methodological and theoretical problems to do with the relationship between a society and depictions of it.

However, in the course of acting, members do not attend to the reflexive features of their actions and accounts. As Garfinkel suggests in his discussion of the determination of suicide, an attention to the fact by the persons involved that they were engaged in 'constructing' motivations, 'selecting' features of surrounding circumstances, and the like, would deflect them from their *practical activities*. Yet, although reflexivity is unattended, members do, nevertheless, encounter its pervasiveness through the indexical properties of natural language. In other words, and to repeat an earlier point, the sense, rationality, reasonableness, understanding, significance of any talk or action is embedded, reflexively, in the setting of which it itself is a feature.

INDEXICALITY, REFLEXIVITY AND THE USE OF RULES

One way to illuminate the above ideas is to examine a variety of topics to do with rules. Although much of conventional sociology regards rules and rule-following behaviour as one of its central ideas, through such concepts as norms, culture, role, and so on, we do not wish to accord any theoretical primacy to rules or presume that an appeal to rules is somehow fundamental to an understanding of social behaviour.[8] Nevertheless, it is the case that appeals to rules are often made in an attempt to eradicate some of the practical problems that people face when dealing with the 'vagueness' or 'looseness of fit' of concepts, definitions, recipes, maps, musical scores, experimental protocols, coding practices and so on. One of the uses of rules seems to be, then, the clarification of meaning.

Garfinkel points to the indexicality of rule use when discussing how members' accounts of ordinary activities are invariably experienced as having only 'loose' connections with comparable activities which they are intended to 'locate, to identify, to analyze, to make recognizable'.[9] That is, the rule does not exhaustively specify all the conditions under which it is to be applied. This feature, we may note, is observable in respect of scientific laws and with so-called laws of history. As Helmer and Rescher note in regard of the latter: 'since the conditions delimiting the area of application of the law are often not exhaustively articulated, a supposed violation of the law may be explicable by showing that a legitimate but as yet unformulated, precondition of the law's applicability is not fulfilled in the case under consideration.'[10] But, rather than deal with scientific laws or candidates for such, let us look at a set of rules of rather more direct consequence to social life, namely, the law.

In law, in order to constitute an act or the omission of an act as a crime, the physical or 'behavioural' element of the act must be accompanied by a specific mental state. This mental state is termed *mens rea*. The nature or type of *mens rea* required necessarily varies with the class of offence and is commonly to be found in the definition of the particular offence. For example, with the act of murder, part of the *mens rea* is contained in the phrase, 'with malice aforethought'. It could be proposed then that *mens rea* is an essential ingredient in every crime. Indeed legal pronouncements of just a principle have been made. Thus:

R-v. *Tolson*
The full definition of every crime contains expressly or by implication a proposition as to a state of mind. Therefore if the mental element of any conduct alleged to be a crime is proved to have been absent in any given case, the crime as so defined is not committed.[11]

However, there is an opposing principle at work in the formulation of some crimes: a principle of 'absolute prohibition'. The following is a case in point.

Cundy v. *Le Cocq*
Charge – Licensee selling liquor to drunken person.
Defence – no knowledge that person was drunk.
Stephen T: 'The words of the section amount to an "absolute prohibition" of the sale of intoxicants to a drunken person. The clause says nothing about the knowledge of the state of the person served. The existence of a mistake, though *bona fide*, as to the condition of the person served is not an answer to the charge, but is a matter only for the mitigation of penalty.'[12]

The judges ruling in this case asserts that, at least with regard to this particular law which does not specify any *mens rea*, then the statute prohibits the action of selling liquor to drunks 'absolutely', regardless of time, place and personnel involved. However, even the cases which fall under statutes decreeing absolute prohibition are themselves subject to practical exigencies. In another case, *Sherras* v. *De Rutzen*, the offence described was one of supplying liquor to a constable on duty which, according to statute, was an offence under absolute prohibition, there being no specification of *mens rea*. Here, however, it was held that knowledge on the part of the licensee was necessary otherwise he could not defend himself and no defence could possibly save him.

Thus application of law to particular instances involves the selection of specific features of the case at hand in order to determine the relationship of the law to this instance in question. This remains so even when dealing with things less 'tricky' than the state of mind of the putative offender.

Within that branch of sociology which deals with the police there has been a good deal of work relating to the law and the actual practices and day-to-day activities in which the police engage. One of the ways in which sociologists have attempted to formulate their interest in police activities has been to note that not only are the police agents of the law, but that their activities are also subject to the law. Accordingly, the question arises as to the extent to which members of the police conform with the law circumscribing their activities. Not surprisingly perhaps, some 'discrepancy' has been found between the actual activities of the police and the legal procedures which are supposed to 'govern' their actions. An explanation as to why such 'discrepancies' occur is often couched in terms of a dichotomy between the concern of the police with 'being legal' and following the law 'by the book' and a concern, not always compatible with 'being legal', of maintaining public order.[13] A common observation made by the police themselves about their activities is that, 'you can't play it by the book. You'd never get anywhere in a job like this.'[14] Much play is made of the situational factors or pressures which force the police to deviate from legal rule. However, what is of interest to us is the presumption that there is an obvious and clear sense to the law, or the rules of procedure, and to instances of such violations of the law that occur. As one researcher of police behaviour notes:

Some of the most common felonies, such as burglary, and auto theft generally involve stealth and occur when the victim is absent; by the time the crime is discovered the offender has parted. . . . It remains noteworthy that the police officially disregard one-fourth of the felonies they handle in encounters with complainants. These are not referred to the detective division for investigation; offenders in these cases receive a pardon of sorts.[15]

Here the author is not only suggesting that the police are doing something wrong in not recording all complaints about burglary and theft, but doing so in a way that presumes that the facticity of the crime, to put it this way, is easily determinable. But is this necessarily the case? Could it not be suggested, for example, that for particular cases there could be good grounds for not officially recording an offence? As one ex-policeman put it to one of the authors:

Sometimes we'll get a person say, well for instance a holiday-maker at Morecambe, he parked his car in a street and he goes and has a few jars. And he comes out and he can't find his bloody car, in other words he doesn't know where he's left it. So he reports it to the police an' they go on searching and in the next two streets away they find the bloody car. It's a crime that's been reported and yet in actual fact it's not a crime. So then we in anticipation of the Chief Constable's approval we suggest that this is no crime.[16]

Similarly goods which are reported as 'stolen' may indeed never have been stolen at all but merely 'mislaid' or 'lost'. There are, that is, in many cases 'good reasons' for not recording all complaints as crimes.

What this suggests is that the relationship between police procedure, the law and other rules circumscribing their behaviour, and what they actually do is not something that is adequately described always as a clear issue of conformity or nonconformity. Even in the supposedly simple matter of determining whether or not a crime has been committed and, hence, whether it is recordable as such, requires a massive amount of interpretative work, by the police personnel, in relating 'what has happened' to any rule which may be deemed relevant as a description of what 'in fact' happened.

The police, of course, are not the only body of people whose conduct is governed by rules. Garfinkel noted features similar to those mentioned above when examining the records of the Out-Patient Psychiatric Clinic at the UCLA Medical Centre.[17] The research was conducted in order to answer the question: by what criteria were applicants selected for treatment? Graduate research students were selected and trained to search diligently among the records in order to extract as much information as possible from the files. Unfortunately much of the necessary information was missing. A patient's sex was discoverable in most cases, marital status in 75 per cent, ethnic background, education, religion, and annual income in less than one third of the cases, and so on. On details about the history of the contacts between patients and clinic personnel, wide discrepancies in the amount of information were discovered. Garfinkel and his co-workers, after a frustrating year, reoriented the study by taking the 'shortcomings' of the records as a product of the attempt to seek information from a self-reporting system that had to be 'reconciled with the routine ways in which the clinic operated' so tying the 'unavailable information to the theme of "good" organisational reasons for "bad" records'.[18] In this way, the 'missing information' was recast as being itself the phenomenon of interest and not, as many researchers working with records and files regard it, a trouble, irritation, or inadequacy of the data base and something to be remedied, if possible.

The way in which Garfinkel and his students eventually began to think about the 'gaps' in the records and the troubles they had in obtaining information from them, was that these troubles were 'normal, natural troubles'. They were not to be seen as troubles that arose because, after all, what can you expect from organizational personnel except laziness, incompetence, inefficiency and the like, but rather because the personnel making entries in the hospital records did so on the basis of taken-for-granted understandings of the correct procedures prevalent in the hospital. Garfinkel went on to propose that if an investigator were to try to remedy the shortcomings of the records, he would quickly find that they were 'persistent, reproduced from one clinic's file to the next, they are standard and occur with great uniformity . . . and, above all, they have the flavor of inevitability'.[19] All of which strongly suggests that the records are deeply embedded in the organization's activities and practices and tied to other routinized and valued practices of the clinic. 'Reporting procedures, their results, and the uses of those results are integral features of the same social orders they describe . . . There is an organisational rationale to the investigator's difficulties.'[20]

This suggests that there is an economic factor at work here. It could be argued that there is a marginal utility to the incremental increase of information, which places some limitation upon the incentive to collect certain kinds of information. Some information, such as age and sex, can be had easily, at a mere glance one could say, whereas information on the educational and occupational history of the patient is more difficult and time consuming to acquire, and may well compete with the time the nurse might better spend doing other things. Also, while an administrator and a researcher might request staff to provide full and consistent information, there is a need also to provide motivation given that the 'full and consistent information' may be used for purposes as yet unknown; purposes which may vary 'from benign to irrelevant to ominous, and for reasons that have little to do with the archives'.[21]

The attempt to provide complete information runs into conflict with other sets of practical constraints to do with the operation of the organization and the various preferences which motivate the clinic's personnel. It would be a mistake, however, to think of the 'troubles' associated with the clinic records as consisting in the inability of administrators to design and impose a recording system which will be 'properly' completed by the staff. For if the 'rules of reporting', as provided for in the contents of the recording form, are strictly adhered to, there is the risk that the structure of the form itself will provide a description of the events it purports to describe which owes more to the manner of reporting than it does to the events themselves. We have noted this problem with respect of the interview and questionnaire. One way in which the Clinic Staff attempted to cope with the fact that by following the form 'to the letter', as it were, they ran the risk of providing distorted information, was by writing in marginal notes to the record entries. However, as a device to ensure more adequate information by making suitable qualifications where the record itself might distort, it failed to provide a determinate solution.

Unless the several staff members who produced these records had in mind all of the signs that anybody subsequently brings up, we have no assurance that they were looked for or noted. Anyone who has done file research knows the frustration of having no basis for deciding when the lack of mention of a symptom indicates its absence.[22]

The relevance of these remarks for our current concern is that taking the record form as a template into which a description of the event is to be fitted, and given that there are known 'discrepancies' between the structure provided by the form and the structure of the event being described, then even if 'marginal notes' are used to supplement the form this would still not aid later users. The fact that in some instances there are no marginal notes, cannot be taken as necessarily indicating that certain supplementary features of the event were not present. This suggests that the lacunae, so often noticed in records and files, form almost an 'essential' aspect of them. To expect that the file or records be 'complete' is to propose that an event, person, illness, crime, etc. can be described and recorded in a manner that would be relevant for all possible purposes and future requirements of those records. Since certain features of events only have relevance for *some* practical purposes then we could not be expected to provide a description of those features which would be required for *all* possible practical purposes.

So, when we speak of certain social activities as being done according to specific rules, whether it be policing, coding, interviewing, recording, and so on, we also have to speak of the purposes for which the rules are *invoked*, and the 'ad hoc' use of rules to accomplish many and varied social activities. To see what is involved here let us look at coding practices as an illustration of 'ad hocing'.

'AD HOCING'

The activity of coding consists, among other things, of the researcher acting in accordance with certain rules laid down for the particular study. These rules state in which categories particular responses should be placed. For example, a rule may state what theoretical category of social class a report on what the respondent does for a living should be placed, and in addition to this, detail the machine readable code for this theoretical category. Of course, as is fairly routine, more than one person is involved in the coding; in order to ensure standardization, training of coders is an essential requirement so that they can agree on how to code the sometimes ambiguous responses. The level of agreement or the 'concordance rate' is then taken as a measure of the validity of the coding. Taking Bales' analysis as an example, if the coders agree that the question 'what time is it?', is a 'request for information', then this is evidence for the fact that what was said *was* a request for information.[23] Given the rules of coding and the training of the coders, it should be expected that coding is a relatively unproblematic activity. Is this the case?

Garfinkel, at a different stage of the research into the clinic, reported above, gave his graduate students the task of coding the information from 1,582 clinic folders onto a Coding Sheet.[24] A reliability procedure was used to gauge the level of agreement between the coders, this being assessed in terms of agreement in the end result, that is, that the item was coded in the same category.

As we might begin to suspect by now, the actual coding practices followed by the students did not accord with any simple actuarial procedure as defined by the coding rules, no matter how 'precise' such rules might be. Instead, what was observed in the behaviour of the researchers going about the task of sensibly coding the information was that they necessarily utilized their knowledge of the supposed ways in which clinic personnel operated in carrying out their tasks. Knowledge of the social structure which, let us note, had been derived from elsewhere, was being used in completing the work of coding. More interestingly, such presupposed knowledge seemed necessary and was most deliberately consulted whenever, and for whatever reasons, the coders needed to be satisfied that they had coded 'what really happened'. However else one might describe the procedures being used to do the coding, what is certain was that such procedures were not just a matter of following the coding rules. Some other procedures, yet to be described, were being utilized. Naturally, since the data extracted by the coding practice was in part the outcome of this, as yet undescribed procedure, any analysis of the data would be unavoidably 'contaminated'.

In an effort to identify the features of the actual methods used by the coders, Garfinkel shifted the focus of interest to one of discovering how, as a practical matter, the 'reliability' of coded results was produced. Instead of being interested in the production of reliable coding techniques as a way of more adequately producing the records in order to provide a better account of the hospital's intake practices, a matter of lending credence to the inferences made from the data to the real social world, his concern was with the activity involved in placing items from the forms to the coding sheet.

Let us pause for a moment to consider the general interest that such a study might have. Garfinkel is not proposing that the study of coding practices is an area of enquiry hitherto neglected by sociologists, nor that an understanding of the way in which coders actually perform their task is an indispensable necessity for interpreting findings relating to data gleaned from hospital and other clinic folders, interviews, questionnaires, and the like. We have already seen that the practices of the police are often described as divergent from the actual rules of procedure as evidenced in the law, and we have also seen how personnel in clinics produce clinic records which exhibit wide 'gaps' in the information they provide despite the fact that the records contain categories which act as instructions about the kind of information the clinic staff need to collect. What we have now is coding where coders are doing something else other than making reference to the coding rules. All these instances can be seen as examples of 'following instructions', where 'following instructions' is a gloss for an unknown, or at least undescribed, set of procedures.[25] For Garfinkel, the problem is a general one because 'following instructions' is a generic social practice and one that stands in need of description. How then did the coders 'follow instructions' in order to produce the particular results they did?

For the coders the 'reliability' problem was a matter of moving from the clinic folders to the code items in such a way that they were satisfied that the coded items represented real events that took place within the clinic. That is, to decide the relevance of the coding instructions to the organized activities of the clinic, in their work of interrogating the folder contents for answers to their questions the coders paid attention to what Garfinkel refers to as 'ad hoc' considerations. It was these considerations which the coders used to decide the relevance of, and satisfy themselves about, whether the coding instructions analysed actually encountered folder contents so as to allow the coders to treat the folder contents as reports of 'real events'.

As we pointed out in relation to the 'gaps' in the folder contents, which Garfinkel saw as essential to the records, 'ad hocing' practices are also essential features of 'following instructions': they are not avoidable by extending the scope and detail of the rules through which the coding is conducted. This is because in order to see the relevance of particular instructions for a particular case, it is necessary to 'fill in' the instructions in order to bring that case under the relevant rule, since one cannot formulate rules of relevance in advance of knowledge of the case in question. In 'following instructions' what the coders were doing was bringing the particular case under the auspices of the coding instruction via 'etcetera', 'let it pass', 'unless', and 'factum valet', as 'ad hoc' considerations.[26] The use of these 'ad hocing' practices enabled the coders to maintain the relevance of what they were doing by using their knowledge of the presumed ways in which the clinic operated and was organized, and provided the rational grounds for the interpretations of the coding instructions necessary for bringing them into alignment with the folder contents. In short, 'ad hocing' practices are used in order to recognize what the instructions are definitely talking about'. They are 'consulted by coders in order to recognize coding instructions as "operational definitions"' of coding categories'.[27]

Although conventional research procedures treat 'ad hocing' as a nuisance not to say an embarrassment, for Garfinkel this is tantamount to complaining that if the walls of the building were removed one could better see what held the roof up.[28] 'Ad hocing' is an essential feature of coding procedures if the researcher is to grasp the relevance of the instructions to the particular and actual situations they are intended to analyse. They operate as the grounds for, and as methods to advance and secure, the investigator's claims to have coded in accordance with the instructions. There are some further important consequences of this discussion of 'ad hocing' which we shall deal with towards the end of this chapter. Meanwhile, we want to move onto other aspects of indexicality.

THE UBIQUITY OF INDEXICALITY

One of the ways in which social science justifies itself is through the manner in which its descriptions and accounts of social life are an improvement on the accounts provided by ordinary or lay members of society. As we pointed out in Chapter 3, it views the ordinary, visible, mundane world as mere appearance, a veil which has to be drawn aside to reveal the 'real' structure underlying the surface features. Ordinary people are bemused by the differing surface appearances of the society and, accordingly, put forward false or at least partial views on the nature of social life and the causes of human actions. The ordinary member, not being versed in the ways of science, presents 'evidence' and 'theories' which are easily rendered untenable when subjected to critical scrutiny. For Durkheim, to use an example mentioned in Chapter 1, suicide, as it appears in the world of everyday activities as a phenomenon and the subject of talk and lay inquiry, is a flawed conception compared with that which is the result of proper scientific definition and investigation.[29] Indeed, for Durkheim it is the task of social science to improve upon lay versions of the workings of the social order which, in this case, produces suicide as one of its outputs. Some of the common ways in which these scientific accounts are produced we have already discussed in the previous chapter. But there are two additional facets of that discussion which we want to emphasize here.

First, and perhaps obviously, the social scientist is not attempting to provide a descriptive and explanatory scheme totally removed from the lived experiences of people in society. The very objects that are of concern of the members of society are also the very objects that are the concern of social scientists; what are the causes of suicide? How do periods of both high inflation and high unemployment arise? What are the effects of increasing specialization in education? And so on. The social scientist asking these questions is, thus, constrained in his choice and construction of theoretical objects by the need to align them, in some way, to the social objects as known by members. While, in principle, the social scientist may be free to define, say, suicide in any manner he so desires, if the research is to speak to the reality of ordinary members' experiences then it must connect with common understandings. As Durkheim put it:

Although we set out primarily to study reality, it does not follow that we do not wish to improve it; we should judge our researches to have no worth at all if they were to have only a speculative interest. If we separate carefully the theoretical from the practical problems, it is not to the neglect of the latter; but, on the contrary, to be in a better position to solve them.[30]

The theoretical concerns of sociology are, in this sense, firmly wedded to the same common-sense order as that of the ordinary member in society. There is an additional twist in all this. Recalling Blumer's remarks, quoted earlier on the subject of operational definitions, what we have just said seems to imply that sociological conceptions tacitly rely for their ready comprehension on the variegated conceptualizations, normally regarded as vague, used by ordinary members. Thus, one of the considerations which prompted the need to develop a more precise social scientific vocabulary, namely the vagueness of ordinary language, is tacitly retained as a necessary 'ad hoc' feature of this precise vocabulary, in order to relate it to the concerns of the ordinary member.

The second matter we want to emphasize relates to the investigative procedures used by social scientists. Again as we saw in the previous chapter, many of these procedures involve researchers talking to people and trying to evaluate the accuracy, validity and relevance of what was said. They do this in face of the fact that not only might people lie but also that they may never have thought about or been concerned with the topic under investigation. The researcher, much less than 'tapping' an opinion, belief or attitude held by the respondent, might better be seen as creating that recorded belief *in situ*, as Cicourel suggests in the discussion of interviewing we reported in Chapter one. Further, researchers also engage in arguments about their data and their findings; arguments concerning, for example, what is to count as an instance of a suicide? How to assess and use data drawn from a wide variety of materials, including newspaper reports, papers published by colleagues many years before, official figures, questionnaires, and so on. The researcher cites authorities, argues against rivals, travels to conferences and presents work that will do 'for the job in hand'. In other words, engages in the self-same practical activities that belong to the world of the everyday. Once again, the problems and concerns which motivated the scientific study of society, that is, the partial and atheoretical versions provided by members, are retained, again tacitly and invisibly, in the practical activity of scientific research. The findings of different pieces of research on the 'same' topic differ, a fact which can be located in the differing ways in which the data was collected, the different features of the respective research sites, the different theoretical considerations which might have led to research designs at odds with each other, the difference in time which might have passed between the studies, and so on. The ordinary everyday practical considerations such as time, place, personnel, who talked to whom, how the topic was handled, resolved and analysed, etc., come into play in a consideration of the 'meaning' of the research results. The indexical 'dirt' which was found to reside in our everyday world reappears in the supposedly sanitized world of the social scientist.

Of course, it is the task of methodology to 'clean up' research techniques, improve them and generally increase the scientific respectability of social investigation. And, as we saw in the previous chapter, there is no shortage of advice on how to improve the objectivity of interviewing, increase the reliability of coding, check out initial hunches in participant observation, devise more plausible statistical testing, and so on. But, whatever the 'advice' given, as Garfinkel found with coding, it is fairly clear that such advice rests once again upon the unexplicated bedrock of common-sense understandings regarding truthful replies, relaxing settings, interviewer rapport, sampling adequacy, and the like. Once again the vagaries of time, place, and personnel intrude. While these vagaries, at the methodological level, are treated as nuisances, troubles to be got around, they also appear at the philosophical level. One of the aims of the philosophy of the social sciences is to provide firmly grounded principles to govern the investigation and explanation of social life. The pragmatic interest a researcher might have in improving the ability to predict aggregated behaviour from attitude scale scores has its philosophical parallel in discussions about the relationship between what people say and what they do, about the nature of action, whether reasons are causes, and so on. But, as Weber pointed out, arguments like this proliferate like a 'plague of frogs' suggesting that not only are they unresolved but unsolvable, *except for all practical purposes.*

The features of indexical expressions, their inherent 'vagueness' and the 'local' character of their meaning, reappear as problems at each level of inquiry: at the everyday, at the sociological, at the methodological and at the philosophical. This ubiquitous fact of indexicality and the need it generates in any researchers, lay or professional, to clarify the meanings of their terms, is the starting point for ethnomethodology. As Garfinkel and Sacks put it in the following homespun way:

If, whenever housewives were let into a room, each one on her own went to some same spot and started to clean it, one might conclude that the spot surely needed cleaning. On the other hand, one might conclude that there is something about the spot and about the housewives that makes the encounter of one by the other an occasion for cleaning, in which case the fact of the cleaning, instead of being evidence of dirt, would be itself a phenomenon.[31]

The attempt to 'clean' the world of indexical expressions, which is the attempt to substitute 'objective' expressions for indexical ones, becomes a topic for description and analysis rather than an effort to solve a problem. And, further, this becomes nothing more nor less than the ways in which persons assemble the appearances of a stable, rational and organized social setting.

REFLEXIVITY OF ACCOUNTS

We can now further elaborate the idea of reflexivity, and connect it to the discussion of indexicality The indexicality of expressions and actions are ways in which, Garfinkel and Sacks argue, members encounter the reflexivity of accounts. They propose that, 'the fact that natural language serves persons doing sociology – whether they are laymen or professionals – as circumstances, as topics, and as resources of their inquiries, furnishes to the technology of their inquiries and to their practical sociological reasoning *its* circumstances, *its* topics, and *its* resources'.[32] The ubiquity of indexical expressions and the fact that members encounter them as 'problems', 'troubles', 'things to be remedied', not only when doing science, but in conversation, assembling reports, ordering books, and other more mundane activities, arises from what Garfinkel terms, 'the reflexivity of accounts', or the way in which accounts and accountable actions structure the experience of the social order. This can be seen, for example, in the way a description is a 'constituent part of the circumstances it describes, endlessly and unavoidably elaborates these circumstances and is elaborated by them'.[33] Take two people sitting around a coal fire on a winter's evening, the rain and wind rattling the windows; one of them remarks, 'The fire's going out.' This is obviously not a mere distinterested objective description of the fire, but, depending on other contextual matters, can be heard as a request to put some more coal on the fire, an expression of resignation at the thought of having to leave the warmth of the room to get some more fuel, a comment on the fact that a long day is now drawing to a close and it is time to go to bed, etc. The expression, 'The fire's going out', is not only a descriptive comment on the scene but is also part of the very setting it describes, and is thus a *feature of its own circumstances*. As we pointed out in our earlier discussion of reflexivity, in the ordinary run of affairs people do not attend to the fact that, for example in the course of a conversation, they are 'constructing' the sense, the flow the orderliness, the rationality, and so on, of what they are engaged in. In other words, the reflexivity of accounts is not available to members as they do it.[34] How they do encounter this reflexivity, however, is in the occurrence of indexicals.

For Garfinkel there is no remedy to this reflexivity even though members, when engaged in sociological reasoning, continually seek one. Indexical expressions, as we have seen, are troubles, they can be named, and techniques devised for eliminating or controlling them. Moreover, such efforts are successful in clearing up the indexical 'dirt', at least for all practical purposes. So, by studying how members repair, replace, remedy, handle indexicality gives Garfinkel, and ethnomethodology, a way to locate and investigate the procedures members use in practical reasoning.

To illustrate further some of these points and to relate them more directly to ways in which the social order may be studied from an ethnomethodological viewpoint, let us look at Weider's study of the convict code as used in a half-way house for convicts recently parolled.[35]

Many of the studies of prisons reveal the existence of an inmate culture often described as the convict code. Rather like Suttles' ethnic culture, discussed in the previous chapter, the code consists of a set of rules which, it is claimed, governs the behaviour of prisoners toward staff and toward other inmates. Sociologists, prison officials and convicts concur in the view that it is the very existence of the convict code which normally hampers the efforts of personnel to 'reform' the prisoners, and which generally interferes with the official way in which the prison should operate. Aspects of the code include such injunctions as 'Above all else, do not snitch', 'Do not trust staff – staff is heat', 'Do not take advantage of other residents', and so on. Such a code of behaviour explains the whys and wherefores of the actions of the inmates. The fact that the inmates did not sit down and eat with the staff at the same table during mealtime could be explained quite simply by a reference to the code, indicating that the code said staff were not to be trusted. The code in this way is viewed as both an explanatory and a descriptive device which is external to the setting and the actions which the code organizes. It also provides ways of interpreting actions, for example, it is not a case of David disliking John, but rather an instance of the conflict between inmates and staff. Weider likens this kind of account to a travelogue in which the code is used and seen in a similar manner to a commentary accompanying a travel film organizing the scenes and activities on the film for an unknown audience.

Weider, however, suggests an alternative way of seeing the convict code. First, the code is not simply a construction invented by sociologists after intensive investigation. Both staff and inmates know about the code. Second, for them the code constitutes some of the ways in which they see and act in the setting of the hostel and, thereby, provides for the appearance of rational and consistent behaviour across varying and particular situations.[36] Third, the code is not something external to the settings it describes, but, reflexively, part of the seamless fabric of action which make up the activities in the half-way house. Fourth, instances of 'telling the code' are not merely instances of reciting rules to someone who is not concerned with nor able to act in the environment of the hostel, 'instead the code was being "told" about matters which were critical to hearer and listener, because "the telling" fed into their joint actions'.[37]

Weider illustrates the complex resonances occasioned by instances of 'telling the code'. On many occasions he had observed and noted that often friendly conversations with inmates had been terminated by one of them producing the remark, 'You know I won't snitch.' This utterance, Weider suggests, formulated the local setting, the surrounding social organization and the relations between the two.[38] Among other things, the utterance performed the following functions:

1. It told what had just happened, for example, 'You just asked me to snitch.'

2. It formulated what the resident was doing in saying the phrase, for ex-

ample, 'I am saying that this is my answer to your question. My answer is not to answer.'

3. It formulated the resident's motive for saying what he was saying and doing, what he was doing, for example, 'I'm not answering to avoid snitching.'

4. It formulated . . . the immediate relationship between the listener and teller . . . by re-locating the conversation in the context of the persisting role relationships between the parties.[39]

In addition to the formulating work done by the utterance, it also had consequences for the course of the conversation after that point. The utterance was not merely a comment in a conversation on a part of that conversation, for example, 'your previous talk asked me to snitch' but was also itself part of that self-same conversation and, as such, had consequences for how the conversation was to develop after that point, in this case the cessation of that particular line of talk. The formulation is thus inextricably part of the stream of interaction it elaborates: it 'elaborates' on features of the scene and is in turn elaborated by those features. The formulation is *reflexively* tied to the setting, as Garfinkel has it, and it is this reflexivity which members experience as the indexical properties of language. Let us consider this further.

REFLEXIVITY AND FORMULATIONS

One of the activities in which members of society engage is the production of accounts which describe that society or actions which take place in it. The use of records in a hospital, for example, are accounts of activities in that hospital, and professional sociological 'explanations' are also in this way to be taken as accounts of aspects of society. Similarly the comments or formulations Weider found, such as 'you know I can't snitch' are also to be seen as accounts in that they are describing, or making comments upon, or *formulating* some aspect of the prior talk.

Among conversationalists it is an immensely commonplace feature of conversations that a conversation exhibits *for its parties* its own familiar features of a 'self-explicating colloquoy'. A member may treat some part of the conversation as an occasion to describe that conversation, to explain it, or characterize it, or explicate, or translate, or summarize, or furnish the gist of it, or take note of its accordance with rules, or remark on its departure from rules. That is to say, a member may use some part of the conversation as an occasion to *formulate* the conversation . . .[40]

Two of the examples Garfinkel and Sacks offer of formulations is as follows:

J. H.   Isn't it nice that there's such a crowd of you in the office?

S. M.   (You're asking us to leave, not telling us, right.)

H. G.   I need some exhibits of persons evading questions. Will you do me a favour and evade some questions for me?

N. W.   (Oh, dear, I'm not very good at evading questions.)[41]

What formulations consist of, then, is a practice amongst conversationalists of 'saying-in-so-many-words-what-we-are-doing'. The practice is one of doing 'definitive talk' in the way that professional sociologists are doing 'definitive talk' when they engage in practices which are taken as remedying the indexical properties of language. It is an attempt at producing a substitute 'objective' expression for the 'defective' indexical item or items. How, do these formulations operate as claimed objective expressions?

Consider the formulation 'You're asking us to leave, not telling us to leave, right?' One of the actions of this particular formulation is to propose itself as a proper description of a prior piece of the talk, namely, that it was a request to leave. Members are skilled at providing descriptions of the actions that people can perform, both in talk and in their other behaviour, and being requested to leave the room is one. But of what is 'being requested to leave the room' a proper description? What actions, words, movements, say, were enacted such that 'being requested to leave the room' is its proper *gloss*?[42] There are, clearly, many varied ways in which members can produce something for which 'being requested to leave the room' is a proper description. It can be done as above, with a finger pointing toward the door, with the index finger and its partner set in a V-shape, with a nod of the head, with a verbal request, and so on. Similarly, to recall the earlier discussion on coding, there are many ways of producing something for which 'following the coding instructions' is a proper gloss.

It would appear, then, that for formulations, the actions which they gloss are not recoverable through inspection of the formulation itself: one is unable to move from the formulation to produce the items and tokens of behaviour for which the utterance is the formulation. This would mean, then, that not every repetition of a formulation can be considered as indexing the same phenomenon, *nor* that the activity performed by a formulation is the same activity on each occasion of the formulation's use. They are not freely available to be repeated anywhere in a stream of talk and be taken as being the identical action upon each and every occasion. As glosses, formulations are as much dependent upon the circumstances in which they are uttered as the very items for which they were introduced as a 'remedy'. The remedy, the attempt to produce 'accountably definitive talk' retains all the features for which they were to be seen as the cure. The very resources of natural language assure that 'formulating is itself for members a routine source of complaints, faults, troubles, and recommended remedies, *essentially*'.[43]

Here then, from a different direction, we have the same features as were noted earlier in our discussion of the attempt to move from a lay sociology, flawed empirically and theoretically, to a professional sociology which we discover contains comparable troubles and flaws which then need to be dealt with at the methodological and philosophical level. The pervasiveness of indexically is as pervasive as natural language.

In light of all this, what are we to make of the accounts produced by organizations of their own actions? What we can say is that, in the way a formulation is not only a comment on the conversation but is also part of the unfolding conversation in which it takes place, it is reflexively tied to it, then accounts of organizational behaviour (such as the records kept in a hospital on admissions), are also part of the unfolding processes of the organization. The accounts of the organization's workings are, like formulations, reflexively tied to the setting in which they are produced and of which they are a part. But are these accounts, of which professional sociological accounts are merely another instance, to be seen as 'doing' something rather than as 'merely descriptive' of the way in which the organization works. Do these accounts, that is, 'do' things of an order similar to 'ending a line of conversation'? Garfinkel suggests that this is so. Writing of his researches and findings in connection with coding, Garfinkel says that the results as furnished by the coding were typically *treated* as though they were 'disinterested descriptions' of events in the clinic. But given the necessary involvement of 'ad hocing' practices in order to produce these results, practices requiring that a version of the clinic's activities be used in actual instances of coding, then all that the coding results consist of is a 'persuasive version' of the clinic's activities. This is because the coding is conducted independently of what the *actual* order of clinic activities might be: 'the account may be argued to consist of a socially invented, persuasive, and proper way of talking about the clinic as an orderly enterprise since "after all" the account was produced by "scientific procedures".... *The actual order remains undescribed.*'[44]

Further, the account of the clinic's activities provided by the coding instructions furnished members with a 'social science' grammar of rhetoric, reconciling, for members with different interests, their talk about clinic affairs in an impersonal way. Nevertheless, the matters being talked *about* retain their sense for the 'discussants' as 'a legitimate, or illegitimate, a desirable or undesirable, an advantageous or disadvantageous state of affairs for the "discussants" in their "occupational lives" '.[45] That is, the 'social scientific' description of the clinic, as exemplified in the coding instructions, provides members of that organization with a way of talking about events, occurences, etc., in that organization, which is 'apparently' disinterested and neutral. However, *what* is being talked about, be it decisions to reduce nursing staff on a ward, allocate more resources to administration, redistribute parking spaces, and more, retain all the 'vested interests' particular persons might have in those issues 'under cover' of a disinterested vocabulary.[46] It is this which exhibits the inextricably moral nature of accounts and is, incidentally, another way of expressing the point that social science is through and through a practical enterprise.

These remarks also put some ethnomethodological flesh on some of the bones of ideas we hinted at in the first chapter, especially to do with the way in which conventional sociology normally treats the officially produced crime statistics, and the way in which the records on which they are based are an inextricable part of the organization which produces them. Similarly, the ideas of indexicality and the reflexivity of accounts have more than a passing relevance for the use made of such methods as questionnaires, interviews, and participant observation discussed in Chapter 3. Not only do accounts, as analyses of social settings have features which parallel those of formulations, they are also like formulations in that they gloss the circumstances which they are taken to describe; that is, they mean other than what they can say in so many words.

GLOSSING PRACTICES: AN EXAMPLE

One of the most illuminating ways we have seen of illustrating 'glossing practices' is the image Garfinkel and Sacks use of a 'mock up'.[47] The particular 'mock up' to which they allude is a plastic model of an engine with facsimile pistons, crankshaft, etc., used to demonstrate the workings of internal combustion engines. A relevant feature of this model is that in order to make it 'work' the user has to turn the fly-wheel with his finger. The plastic machine can be considered as an account of some real state of affairs, that is, of actual types of internal combustion engines. In comparing the model, the account, with the real state of affairs it describes, the 'mock up' with the real engine, the sociological account with the real world, we can notice some important properties of accounts as glosses.

First, in the very way that the 'mock up', the account, provides for an accurate representation of some features of the actual situation, it also makes specifically and deliberately false provision for some of the *essential* features of that situation. Just as accounts of, say, working-class families, jazz clubs, public houses, bowling alleys, and so on, can be said to describe features of those settings, then, for any given working-class family, club or pub, those accounts will provide an accurate description of only some of their features. Some of their essential features will either be missing or wrongly represented. With the 'mock up' engine, the finger has to turn the flywheel. How one plays bowls is missing from Whyte's account of a bowling alley.[48] How one plays and recognizes jazz is missing from Becker's account of jazz musicians.[49] And, accounts of factory life generally exclude descriptions of what it is to 'work' in the factory.

Second, the deliberately 'false provisions' in the account must be there for the account to be seen as an account of an actual situation or occasion. This leads onto, third, the way in which the account is said by the user to 'resemble' the situation which it is being used to represent. This is, of course, the way in which sociology treats its generalized accounts of social phenomena as relating to particular instances in which it is interested.

Fourth, that accounts do make 'false provision' and leave out features of actual occasions means that persons using the accounts also use knowledge of the way in which the accounts are false as ways of seeing that the accounts *do* analyse any particular setting. That is, the fact that the flywheel on the 'mock up' is moved by the finger, which is knowably a 'false provision', means that the model can be used as a way of analysing a real engine that uses petrol.

Fifth, the adequacy of the account depends 'exclusively' upon what the person wants to use the account for. It is understood throughout by the user that it is a guide to practical actions in an actual situation. In other words, the relevance or otherwise of accounts depends upon the practical circumstances and practical actions to be accomplished. Whyte's account of ten pin bowling might not be of much use if one wanted to use it as a guide on how to become a gang leader, for example.

Finally, use of the 'mock up', the account, is accompanied by the user's willingness, whenever he encounters a 'false provision', to pay 'full authority' to the actual situation without feeling it necessary to correct the 'mock up'.

Garfinkel and Sacks intend this analogy only as a 'thematic' characterization of what is a pervasive feature of social life, namely 'glossing practices' as one of the methods members have for doing 'observable-reportable understanding'. As such, it further illuminates, and makes available for enquiry, the indexicality of natural language and the way in which the reflexivity of accounts is experienced by both members and those who do professional sociology. For both, it identifies the pervasive practice of 'doing accountable understanding'.

In this chapter we have been concerned to display the fact that the world of everyday activities has a structure that is not adequately described by what we have been calling 'conventional' sociology. This could be expressed by saying that the phenomenon with which ethnomethodology is concerned is *unavailable* to *constructive analysis*.[50] It is unavailable in that, members in the world, engaged in the practical activities of cooking, deciding upon economic policy, constructing a horoscope, measuring the social mobility of women, making contact with a drug ring, organizing a conference, or writing up research notes, cannot attend to the phenomenon of 'practical reasoning' as a topic and still conduct the practical activities with which they are concerned. If one is a coroner attempting to find the causes of death then one literally can have no theoretic interest in *how* one is using features of the dead body in order to construct the possible courses of action and motivations which led to the body being found in the condition in which it was discovered. The coroner cannot have that interest and still be engaged in the very serious business of classifying the death, constrained as he is by time, money, the interest of relatives, the police and insurance companies, and other practical exigencies of life. In phenomenological terms one cannot at one and the same time suspend the natural attitude and have the natural attitude.

Constructive analysis cannot have ethnomethodology's phenomena given its policies in regard to indexical expressions which it seeks, by its variety of practices, to repair, and where, for each subject of study, the attempt to repair indexicals gives each subject its characteristic methodological problems. Ethnomethodology proposes that given the all-pervasive nature of indexical expressions it must seriously be entertained that indexicals do not need saving or, to use an image of Garfinkel and Sacks, they are not illiterate relatives who need to go to college to become educated.

We have just seen that accounts of phenomena as glosses upon the activities they describe necessarily leave out essential features of any given particular scene which these accounts might be used to analyse. We have also seen how coding practice, following a rule, formulating a conversation – *as examples of practical activities* – all gloss the circumstances of their production and are embedded in these circumstances.

Central, then, to all these matters is the way in which one goes about attempting to describe social phenomena, the way in which for example, social scientists attempt to produce general descriptions of social actors and activities in order to analyse these activities. It is to this we now move, discussing how one of the major figures in ethnomethodology, Harvey Sacks, both posed the problem and sought ways of producing literal descriptions.[51]

NOTES AND REFERENCES

1. H. Blumer, 'What is Wrong with Social Theory', in W. J. Filstead (ed.) *Qualitative Methodology*, Markham: New York, 1970, pp. 52–61.
2. *ibid.*, pp. 59–60.
3. H. Garfinkel and H. Sacks, 'On the Formal Structures of Practical Actions', in J. C. McKinney and E. Tiryakian (eds), *Theoretical Sociology*, Appleton-Century-Crofts: New York, 1970, p. 339.
4. J. L. Austin, *How to Do Things with Words*, Oxford University Press: Oxford, 1965, ed. J. D. Urmson, where he draws the distinction between 'constatives' and 'performatives', and makes the point that, especially in the latter case, it is not quite sensible to talk of the 'truth-value' of an expression such as 'I promise'.
5. H. Schwartz and J. Jacobs, *Qualitative Sociology: a Method to the Madness*, The Free Press: New York, 1979, p. 220.
6. Schwartz and Jacobs, *op. cit.*, pp. 220–1.
7. H. Garfinkel, *Studies in Ethnomethodology*, Prentice Hall: Englewood Cliffs, 1967, p. 53.

8. Most traditional textbooks on sociology discuss social behaviour as, at least among other things, rule-following. A particularly salient example of this view is P. Winch, *The Idea of a Social Science*, Routledge & Kegan Paul, London, 1963, although he does draw some untypical conclusions from the idea.

9. *op. cit.*, p. 2.

10. O. Helmer and N. Rescher, *On the Epistemology of the Inexact Sciences*, P–1513, Rand Corporation: Santa Monica, 1958, quoted in Garfinkel, *ibid.*, p. 2.

11. R. R. Baker, *Police Promotions Handbook, No. 1: Criminal Law*, Butterworth, London, 1969, p. 7.

12. *ibid.*, p. 8.

13. See, for example, J. Skolnick, *Justice without Trial: Law enforcement in a Democratic Society*, Wiley: New York, 1966 and see Ch. 6 of this book.

14. A policeman's view quoted in M. Cain, 'On the Beat', in S. Cohen (ed.), *Images of Deviance*, Penguin: Harmondsworth, 1971, pp. 62–97.

15. D. J. Black, 'Production of crime rates', *American Sociological Review*, 35, 1970, pp. 737–8.

16. Interview conducted by D. Benson during SSRC financed project, 'Community Reactions to Deviance', Director Dr M. Atkinson.

17. *op. cit.*, Ch. 6.

18. *ibid.*, p. 187.

19. *ibid.*, p. 191–2.

20. *ibid.*, p. 192.

21. *ibid.*, p. 193.

22. P. E. Meehl, 'When shall we use our heads instead of the formula', in *Minnesota Studies in the Philosophy of Science*, 2, 1958, p. 502.

23. Concordance cannot, of course, legitimately be used in this way. The fact that two teachers can agree on a mark for an essay does not mean that that mark is what the essay really is? One can only say that two teachers given a range of categories into which to place objects can agree on the conventional placement of such objects. Similarly two (or more), psychiatrists might agree that a patient be diagnosed as schizophrenic, but that does not mean that the person so diagnosed *really is* a schizophrenic.

24. H. Garfinkel, *op. cit.*, pp. 18–24.
25. On 'gloss' and 'glossing practices' see H. Garfinkel and H. Sacks, 'On Formal structures of Practical Actions', *op. cit.*, and later on in this chapter.
26. 'Factum valet' refers to the case of an action, prohibited by a rule, which is taken as being a correct action once it is performed.
27. Garfinkel, *ibid.*, p. 22.
28. *ibid.*, p. 22.
29. E. Durkheim, *Suicide*, Routledge & Kegan Paul: London, 1952, p. 41. Quoted in Ch. 1 of this volume p. 5.
30. E. Durkheim, *The Division of Labour in Society*, Free Press: New York, 1947, p. 33.
31. H. Garfinkel and H. Sacks, *op. cit.*, p. 347.
32. ibid., p. 338.
33. *ibid.*, p. 357.
34. Here we refer the reader back to the discussion of Agnes in Ch. 1 where the disclosure of the fact that she had been taking hormone tablets revealed how Garfinkel's account in his *Studies* was itself reflexively tied to circumstances of its production.
35. D. L. Weider, *Language and Social Reality*, Mouton: The Hague, 1974. An excerpt is to be found in Turner (ed.), *Ethnomethodology*, Penguin: Harmondsworth, 1974. The citations are to the latter.
36. *That* social action is regular, routine, organized and transituational is one of the starting points for sociology. *How* it comes to be so produced is one of ethnomethodology's prime concerns.
37. Weider, *op. cit.*, pp. 152–3.
38. For the moment we can understand 'formulating' as 'saying in so many words' what one is doing or saying. See J. Heritage and R. Watson, 'Formulations as Conversational Objects', in G. Psathas (ed.), *Everyday Language*, Irvington: New York, 1979, pp. 123–62.
39. Weider, *op. cit.*, p. 153.
40. Garfinkel and Sacks, *op. cit.*, p. 350. Italics in original.
41. *ibid.*, p. 350. The formulations are in brackets.
42. *ibid.*, p. 362.
43. *ibid.*, p. 353. Italics in original.
44. Garfinkel, *op. cit.*, pp. 23–24. The strong persuasive force of this scientizing of the clinic's activities is evidenced by the fact

that the coding frame came to be used by members of the organization as a proper way for *them* to record their actions.

45. Garfinkel, *op. cit.*, p. 24.
46. This point by Garfinkel parallels, in some respects, the 'technological veil' as discussed by writers known as the Frankfurt School. See, for example, D. Held, *Introduction to Critical Theory*, Hutchinson: London, 1980.
47. Garfinkel and Sacks, *op. cit.*, p. 363.
48. W. F. Whyte, *Street Corner Society*, University of Chicago Press: Chicago, 1955, (2nd ed).
49. H. Becker, *Outsiders*, Collier-Macmillan: New York, 1963.
50. Garfinkel and Sacks, *op. cit.*
51. Note that a literal description of an object does not equate with 'exhaustive'. The stop light on a traffic light is 'red', and to describe it as 'red' is to describe it literally. It is not *all* that one could say about it, nor would that description be appropriate for *all* purposes. Similarly the attempt by ethnomethodologists to produce literal descriptions of a phenomenon does not mean that a description proffered is *the* description let alone the *only* literal description. Its import as a description resides in the extent to which it is capable of describing interesting structures of practical action.

Chapter five
THE USE OF CATEGORIES AND THE DISPLAY OF CULTURE

The concepts discussed in the previous chapter, indexicality and re-flexivity, are the two main concepts which have been orchestrated in much of the debate concerning the scientific status of ethnomethodology and its relationship to sociology. Much of this debate, as we have seen, has been pitched at the philosophical level.[1] However, ethnomethodologists generally find such debates unhelpful and do not engage in them for very long, the main reason being that they are time-consuming and unproductive of empirical work. Nor are the terms in which such debates are conducted of much use when it comes to confronting materials for study. For ethnomethodology, the issue of indexicality does not turn on such matters as, for example: are all expressions equally indexical or are there gradations? Can indexicality be resolved by analysing express-ions into their primitive parts? Can they be controlled by the use of a careful pilot study prior to the main survey? And so on. For ethnomethodologists, indexicality is a fact of life, just as it is for members. Accordingly, it is not a matter of holding up one's hands in horror at the indexical properties of natural language and refus-ing to commit a social science ever again, but to recognize that all descriptions, including those produced by ethnomethodological analysis are 'for all practical purpose descriptions' not, as con-ventional social science maintains, 'descriptions for *all* theoretic purposes'. So, the ethnomethodologist in trying to describe the com-ponent features of the materials at hand, whether they be ethno-graphic field notes, video or audio tape recordings, newspaper cut-tings, texts, or whatever, is trying to produce 'practical purpose descriptions' of members' activities; ways of describing the structure and organization of those activities and social practices as work done by members in accomplishing the scenes of daily life.

In this chapter we intend to illustrate some of the ways in which ethnomethodologists, especially Harvey Sacks, have gone about the task of describing the procedures members themselves use to describe and categorize their social life. As Garfinkel's policy recommendation for ethnomethodology has it, the aim is to describe the work members do and the procedures they use to construct a *sense* of social order. Although there is little in this prescription which tells us how to go about investigating this phenomenon, nevertheless, Garfinkel does stress the importance of paying close attention to the smallest detail of social life and attempt to describe how it is produced. In contrast to conventional sociology, ethnomethodology does not drift inexorably toward the large scale and sweep of social systems regarding the minutiae of daily life as just so much irrelevant dross. Rather, it starts from the presupposition that all the instances of daily life are orderly and its task to describe that orderliness. Hence, the smallest fragment of material can be the starting point for the analysis of cultural phenomena. Just as it has been argued that the understanding of a single sentence implies the resources of a language, so it could be said that an understanding of a small fragment of culture implicates whole segments of cultural knowledge. In what follows we look at some examples of cultural analysis, as developed mainly by Harvey Sacks, of the categories and procedures used to describe and identify members, to engage in disputes over membership within cultural groups, and to identify actors and actions in public settings. To begin, however, we will proceed by discussing the way in which Sacks faced the problem of sociological description since his work can be seen as flowing from his proposed reorientation of the problem.

SOCIOLOGICAL DESCRIPTIONS

Sacks' major concern in his early paper is to make the current way in which sociology approaches its subject-matter appear 'strange'.[2] He endeavours to show that what is taken for granted by sociologists as a normal and natural way of approaching their subject matter is, in fact, inappropriate for the development of a *science* of social life. In making this point, Sacks is concerned to distinguish between sociology as currently practised, which he regards as a practical activity like any other, and a science. If the sociologist is content with the former status, then the problem of description is identical to that faced by members in the course of their daily life.[3] Descriptions and accounts produced under this auspice are simply practical purpose descriptions and accounts, and are to be dealt with as adequate to the purposes at hand until such time as their inadequacy is manifest, in which case further descriptive and accounting work becomes necessary. This is another way of stating the point that the problem of the indexical nature of natural language is not a theoretical problem for members since their practices are able to deal with the various issues that arise *as* they arise. Sociology, then, as currently practised, and the domain upon which it is practised, is just another set of ways for providing descriptions and accounts of social behaviour on a par with other folk disciplines.[4]

By contrast, if one aims at making sociology scientific then the task is to produce literal descriptions of social phenomena. Yet, as we have seen in previous chapters, as far as sociology is concerned this looks to be an elusive goal. Briefly, the point is that for any particular social object or action, any description of it could always be extended or filled out but not merely by extrapolating from the account at hand. Given, for example, Morris' account of working-class child-rearing patterns that we discussed in Chapter 1, the 'sensible' and 'reasonable' character it has for describing a particular family or set of families could be provided by extending and filling out the account by bringing in additional knowledge. But *what* is added to the account is not a simple extrapolation from the original one. It is yet another gloss and only the worse for that if the intention was to produce a scientific description. Hence, each and every description can be read as flawed, inadequate or synecdocal. Conversely, a shorter description could be assessed as concise, terse, to the point, and the like. There would appear, then, to be no clear and definitive way in which to claim that one description is better than another, no way of achieving literal and exhaustive description; a difficulty compounded by the impossibility of holding the description up to reality to assess its correspondence or representativeness.

One solution to this problem, proposed by conventional sociology, is to assess a description in terms of its method of production, namely, the research methods employed to furnish the material out of which a description of some phenomenon can be assembled.[5] These we discussed in Chapter 3. Associated with this is the effort to produce generalized descriptions which, on the face of it, appear to handle many instances of the subject matter being described. Examples of such general descriptions might be 'the working class', 'adolescents', 'technological society', 'men', 'friendship patterns', and more colloquially, 'public opinion', 'the silent majority', 'British people', 'football supporters' and 'taxpayers'. These can give an air of abstraction without, in fact, being abstract, at least in the sense provided by mathematics.[6] In mathematics the abstract description retains the features of any particular instance, a particular equation for example, and hence, mathematical transformations of the abstract description allow the manipulation of the equation. The general descriptions produced by sociology so far do not have this quality. They do not allow the researcher to find or recover in any formal way the particular instance from the general description itself. In which case it is unclear as to what is gained by a generalized description over and above a description of any given instance, 'since any description that purports to be about a particular case can be read as about "such cases", it is quite obscure what a purportedly generalized description gains'.[7] Even if the sociologists were to claim that they merely describe typical features of a collection of items, this represents little or no gain over ordinary everyday common-sense descriptions.

So far, Sacks' argument can be summarized as follows: to the extent that social science has a concern with producing abstract generalized descriptions of its subject matter, then it is no gain to produce general descriptions through the process of aggregating a collection of items and reducing them to their 'typical' features. Nor is there any more gain in the Weberian tactic of constructing ideal types by the theoretical selection and emphasis of certain features of some complex phenomenon. There is little to gain in both cases since the relationship between the general description and particular instances remains to be decided. While, formally speaking, such descriptions might provide some grounds for the exclusion of certain phenomena from being covered by the description, such as support for a football team not being taken as an instance of religious belief, they do not determine what is to be included. Although we could provide a general description of the family, for example, which could be used to decide that the group of people who work in the office do not constitute a family, it would not provide definitively for whether an unmarried mother living in a house along with a single male, having separate beds but sharing meals, constituted a family. Merely altering the definition of family to include the latter instance would shift the problem to other cases.

Sacks' own pragmatic stance toward the problem of sociological description is to suggest, in the spirit of Garfinkel, that since sociology is predicated upon and incorporates, in an unreflective way, common-sense descriptions and accounting practices, then the place to begin a rigorous scientific sociology might be through an examination of these common-sense practices.[8] Examining, in short, descriptive practices and assumptions that are, to date, unexamined resources shared by both sociology and mundane reasoning. So, although sociologists do not produce abstract descriptions in the sense discussed above, they do produce descriptions which are adequate for practical purposes, and which work for them as they use them in the same manner as the members of society do. In this sense, describing is not only a gloss for a variety of ways of talking, but is itself an activity like 'making a complaint', 'asking directions', 'telling a story', and so on. As an activity it is not something that stands in need of, say clarification or criticism, but rather needs to be described and analysed. Moreover, since sociological descriptions and accounts are based on those of members, then elucidating a set of procedures for describing members' descriptions is, for Sacks, the first step to be taken.[9]

MEMBERSHIP CATEGORIZATION DEVICES

The notion of Membership Categorization Device (MCD) was developed by Sacks to describe the organized ways in which social actors both produce and understand descriptions of people and their activities. His starting point was a story told by a young child, 'The baby cried. The mommy picked it up.'[10]

There are a number of observations which can be made about the ways in which a member of the culture may understand the story embodied in the two sentences, 'The baby cried. The mommy picked it up.' Included among these are, first, the mother in the story is the mother of the baby; second, the baby cried and *then* the mother picked it up; third, and importantly, a member of the culture could provide an account of why it should be the mother who picks up the baby, perhaps citing such things as the normative ties between mothers and their babies. All of these, and more, could be offered by a member without ever having actually seen or heard any more about the mother involved. In other words, one of the things members can do is fill in a story by providing accounts of typical courses of action tied to types of persons.

What we seem to have here, then, is the fact that the members of a culture can listen to what is said to them in such a way as to see that what is being said to them stands as a 'possible description', recognizable and usable by members, by people who belong to the culture. The task of the analyst is to provide a description of the apparatus which enables members to do the activity, and which they do recognizably, of producing 'possible descriptions'. So how does the notion of MCD help us to analyse this aspect of 'describing' and, at the same time, deal with the particulars of the story before us?

A membership categorization device is 'any collection of membership categories, containing at least a category, which may be applied to some population containing at least a member, so as to provide, by the use of some rules of application, for the pairing of at least a population member and a categorization device member. A device is then a collection plus rules of applications.'[11] An example of a categorization device is 'sex' which includes two categories, 'male' and 'female'. Another is the device 'family' which includes such categories as 'mother', 'father', 'baby'... They are collections of categories which 'go together'. Often a single category from a device can be an adequate reference to a person. 'Colleague', 'baby', for example, can be sufficient to refer to a person without the need to employ any further categorizations. This Sacks refers to as 'the economy rule' which holds simply that a single category from any device can be referentially adequate.

A second rule of application is 'the consistency rule' which states that 'if some population of persons is being categorized, and if a category from some device's collection has been used to categorize a first member of the population, then that category or other categories of the same collection *may* be used to categorize further members of the population'.[12] Taking these two rules as hearer's maxims, we can begin to give some description of the machinery involved in hearing that the 'mommy' in the story is the baby's mommy given that there is no genitive in the second sentence establishing this fact. The economy rule provides for the adequate reference of 'baby', and the consistency rule tells us that if the first person has been categorized as 'baby' then others may be referred to by other categories from the same device, 'family'. Thus, 'mommy', 'daddy', 'brother'... but not 'centre forward' could be relevant given the use of 'baby'. However, in the weak form as stated, the consistency rule excludes no category of a device. Yet there is a corollary noted by Sacks which holds 'that if two or more categories are used to categorize two or more members of the same population, and those categories can be heard as categories from the same collection, then: hear them that way'.[13] This corollary is extremely useful in dealing with ambiguities since some categories occur in several devices and have quite different references. For example, 'baby' occurs not only in the device 'family' but also in 'stage of life' whose categories include 'baby', 'child' . . . 'adult'. Similarly, lovers may be 'babies' to each other, and grown men, who should know better, 'babies' to their wives. With cases like this in mind, the consistency rule can be modified as follows:

If a first person has been categorized as 'baby', the further persons may be referred to by categories from either the device 'family' or from the device 'stage of life'. However, if a hearer has a second category which can be heard as consistent with one locus of a first, then the first is to be heard as *at least* consistent with the second.[14]

In short, if 'mommy' and 'baby' can be heard as consistent with the device 'family', then hear them that way. Moreover, some devices, and 'family' is one, belong to a series of devices which are 'duplicatively organized'; that is, when such a device is used on a population, the categories are treated as a unit and members of the population regarded as cases of the unit. They are, as it were, treated as if they were members of a team, and the various persons involved seen as co-incumbents of the unit. Thus, the mommy and the baby in the story are not merely heard as members of families but as members of the same family.

Sacks develops another important notion out of the child's story in answer to the question: 'How is it that "baby" can be heard in a combined form as belonging to the devices "family" and "stage of life"?' The notion is that of 'category-bound activities'. These are activities which can be understood by members to be performed by persons belonging to a certain category or set of categories. For example, the activity 'giving medical advice' is tied to the category 'doctor' while that of 'passing sentence' is tied to the category 'judge'. Put very simply, and this is an observation anyone could make, 'crying' as an activity is tied to the category 'baby' in the 'stage of life' device. However, the connection between crying and babies is not merely on the basis that babies can regularly be observed to cry; the boundedness is much stronger than this. Sacks notes that categorization devices contain categories which are positioned, and for some of these this positioning is hierarchical such that category A can be said to be higher than category B, and so on. In these cases, there might well be activities that are tied to a high position, A, such that if a member of a lower category position, C, performed these activities, then this would be an occasion for praise and approval. We can see this in the case of children who refrain from crying after a serious fall and are praised for being 'a big boy'.

Conversely, a person can be degraded by asserting that although he is a member of category A, he is performing activities appropriate to incumbents of category C. When adults cry, for example, sometimes they are accused of 'acting like a baby'.[15]

This procedure then warrants the candidacy of 'crying' as a member of the class 'category-bound activities' and one bound to 'baby' as a member of the 'stage of life' collection. It gives us, too, another hearer's maxim to account for the way in which 'the baby' in the story is heard as a combined reference to two devices, namely, 'if a category-bound activity is asserted to have been done by a member of some category where, if that category is ambiguous . . . but where, at least for one of those devices, the activity is category-bound to the given category, then hear that *at least* the category from the device to which it is bound is being asserted to hold'.[16] The provides for hearing 'The baby cried', as at least coming from the 'stage of life' device, and the results obtained from the consistency rule corollary, being independent of this, are combinable with it. The consistency rule corollary gave that at least 'the baby' was from the device 'family' while the combination gives us both.

We have spent some time discussing an analysis of two simple sentences, 'The baby cried. The mommy picked it up.' But it must be remembered that the goal is to find a machinery, an analytically descriptive procedure, which will not only deal with the particular details of just these two sentences, but will have wider generality. Accordingly, let us see what further uses can be made of MCDs and the notion of category-bound activities.

One issue which might, at first sight, appear to be far removed from the considerations we have made so far, is how does one categorize an individual person given that, on any occasion, many potential categories are available for use? An example of this might be when one person asks another about a third party, 'Who's that?' We have already seen that for some population of persons, if a first one is categorized using a term from a given MCD, then any next member can also be categorized from the same MCD. This gives consistency in the use of categories to describe the members of some population, since for any next member a consistent category can be used. For example, having begun to categorize persons in a store as 'customers/sales assistants' we can continue using the device to categorize any next person. This does not, however, afford any solution to the problem of identifying one person in the sense intended above. There is no unique solution.

Nevertheless, what is regularly found is that members handle the single individual problem by converting it to a two-person problem. This can be seen in the following data:

A: Who's that?

B: That's Rita. Remember last week when you went to the party and met Una? Well Rita is Una's mother.[17]

In this instance Sacks proposes that the solution to the problem of categorizing a single individual is resolved through turning the issue into a two-person problem, in which what he calls, 'a relational pair', is used. Relational pairs (R), such as husband/wife, friend/friend, father/son, can be used to categorize two people and, thus, also used to solve the categorization of one person.[18]

The notion of relational pairs is not simply confined to the fact that these terms are regularly used in conjunction with one another, but also that they are standardized pairs which constitute domains of rights and duties and which can be appealed to for help, for example. Friends owe each other help in times of trouble and even strangers, on occasion, can be obligated to do things for each other. What is important here is that not only is this known by members of the relational pair, but can also be known by any third party. If it is known that A and B are husband and wife, then the expected rights and obligations that hold between that pair are known also by other members of the culture. We can see, then, that the notion of relational pair has a much wider import and usage than the categorization of a single individual. Indeed, Sacks has used the notion to analyse some actions of suicidal persons by treating their activities as being organized by the collection R, the set of relational pairs, which shapes the propriety of the 'search for help' by suicidal persons. Let us expand on this.

An observation we can all make is that in times of trouble we sometimes feel the need to turn to another person for help or advice, or just simply for a sympathetic ear. Is there any organization or order to the set of people to whom we can turn? Given that R involves rights and obligations, then a person who is, say, suicidal has the right to search for help from those people who are in a category relationship with him such that they are *obliged* to give help, such as spouse/spouse, friend/friend, child/parent. The rules of R then provide that there are two subsets of R: those to whom one may properly turn to for help, Rp; those from whom it would be improper to seek help, Ri. Thus far it would seem that in searching for help a person could choose 'anyone' from the set Rp and, indeed, in the talk people make about seeking help the question as to whether there is 'anyone' who can help, 'anyone' is understood as belonging to Rp. That is, although customer/shop assistant is a relational pair, and a member of set R, it is not a member of Rp. Hence, the claim by someone that he had 'no one' to turn to could not sensibly be countered by asserting that as a 'customer' he was in a relational pair with a 'shop assistant' to whom he was obligated to tell his troubles and from whom he could expect help. However, in addition to Rp providing the set of categories from whom one might seek help, regardless of whether there are any actual incumbents of these categories, Rp is organized in such a way that 'no one' as in 'no one to turn to' does not necessarily mean that there are no actual incumbents of the relational pair categories in Rp. That is, there might actually be friends and parents, even a spouse, around in Rp and yet there be 'no one to turn to'. To deal with this Sacks suggests that Rp has some sort of hierarchical arrangement to its proper use and that persons orient to and expect to use the relational pairs within the subset in an orderly manner. In other words, locating someone to tell one's troubles to does not mean talking to the first member of Rp one comes across or flicking though the telephone directory to find someone to call. Sacks proposes that we regard the categories in such a way that for any given individual, X, there is a 'first-position' or priority relational pair category. For example, if X is a husband then the relevant 'first-position' category related to that would be 'wife'. The proper way in which a husband should use Rp in a search for help would be the incumbent, if any, of the appropriate 'first-position category', namely, 'wife'. Any incumbent of a first-position category takes precedence over any second-position category.[19]

One consequence of this is as follows. It may well be the case that the problem facing the suicidal person is one which could not be talked about with the incumbent of the first-position category. The example Sacks gives, based on a suicide note, concerns a married woman who had been having an affair with one of her husband's acquaintances. Her husband, as the incumbent of the wife's first-position category, might well, on disclosure, provide help or, alternatively, end their relationship. As Sacks puts it, 'He is there (perhaps) so long as she does not speak; once she does, he may no longer be there.'[20] This kind of possibility does not mean that the suicidal person is then able to turn to some other member of Rp and relate the troubles to them. Or, rather, though such people may be turned to, they may not feel obliged to provide help and may, indeed, engage in efforts to locate first-position category incumbents to deal with the matter.[21] For example,

C1:   I wonder if you could give me a little bit of advice. Last Saturday I had a neighbor and friend who came over. She was very desperate about a family situation, and she told me that she just didn't want to live any more, and I really didn't take her seriously, but while she was here she took 18 sleeping pills.

S1:   At your home?

C2:   Yes. This was on Saturday – oh, about 5 o'clock, I'd say, and so I have advised her to – I didn't know that she did this, you know, because it was when I went out of the room. And I had advised her to go and see a relative. I thought it could give her more help than I could. You know, to stay with, everything . . .[22]

Thus, one consequence of the rules governing Rp and access to the incumbents of the categories in Rp might entail that if those in the first position do not, or can not, give help, then others in Rp are not to be expected to do so. In the midst of friends we can still be alone.

Our interest in the foregoing is not merely that it concerns an issue, namely, suicide and suicidal intent, that has been the close concern of sociology for many years, but that it illustrates a way in which ethnomethodology studies 'practical reasoning'; that is, the ways in which members themselves structure and make sense of the world in which they live. MCDs, relational pairs, categories, the economy and consistency rules, duplicative organization, and more, are all the results of Sacks' initial investigative programme into practical reasoning. And, to this end, they are to be regarded as an analytical machinery which describes the organization of category usage among members and the basis upon which they made routine inferences. The system and rules of category usage so revealed has a preferential character that provides for its inferential quality. Failures to apply the rules normally, for example in the case of MCDs and the rules embedded in the usage of relational pairs, are noticeable to members and grounds for making all kinds of inferences. What these formal descriptions do, to put it another way, is portray the logic of common-sense reasoning.[23]

Of course, not all category use is done for the purposes of 'categorization', as it were. Members use categories in many different ways and it would be premature, to say the least, to think that describing these ways in terms of MCDs would be the last, or even the first, thing one could say about them. People can use categories 'wrongly', so to speak, in order to achieve humour or 'put down' another speaker. A person who has just been given some unwanted and unasked for advice, for example, can reply with, 'Thank you, mommy', where the 'mommy' so addressed is neither mother, adult nor female. This particular fragment might lead an analyst to consider other uses of misidentification and, hence, move away from the idea of 'mommy' as a simple categorization device. In the following section we move on to consider another example of Sacks' work exploring the way in which categories can be used to display membership in cultural groups.

CATEGORIES AND THE MEMBERSHIP OF CULTURAL GROUPS

In the following data we can detect a 'battle' between two teenagers over how to name a car.[24] One refers to it as a Bonneville, the other as a Pontiac Estate; the same vehicle, two different names. Why?

> Ken: In that Bonneville of mine. I c'd take that thing out, an' if I've gotta *tie* an' a sweater on, an' I look clean? (1.0) Ninety nine percent the time a guy c'd pull up to me, in the *same* car, same colour, same year the whole bit, (1.0) roar up his pipes (1.0) an he's inna dirty grubby tee shirt, an' the guy'll pick the guy up in the dirty grubby *tee* shirt before uh he'll pick *me* up.
>
> (2.0)
>
> ( ): hheh
>
> Ken: Just – just for uh-
>
> Al: [but] not many people get picked up in a Pontiac station wagon.

The teenagers are discussing 'hotrodding' and 'drag racing' on the roads where the issue is how to get into a race with another 'hotrodder' and yet avoid trouble with the police. As we see from the extract, one of the discussants claims that when he goes out to drag race on the streets in his 'Bonneville' car, he wears a tie and a sweater and generally looks 'clean', and in this way hopes to avoid trouble if the police hear the roar of the engines. On the other hand, his grubbier looking opponent is likely to be the one the police pick on. Later in the conversation one of the other participants undercuts Ken's posture with the claim that not many people get arrested driving 'Pontiac station wagons', an alternative description for a 'Bonneville'. 'Bonneville' is a hotrodder description and 'Pontiac station wagon' one used by the manufacturer and a 'conventional' way of characterizing the vehicle.

Although there are a number of issues that can be raised about the way in which people choose to characterize the 'same' vehicle, here we want to focus on what it suggests about the ways in which members go about the business of assigning membership to cultural groups. Implicit in the remark made by Al, that not many people get arrested driving Pontiac station wagons, is that a Pontiac is not the sort of car a 'hotrodder' would drive but is, rather, the type of car an adult or parent would travel about in: in short, a 'mummy's car'. Sacks suggests that the differences involved in the use of two alternative terms to refer to the same vehicle has to do with the different accounting schemes implied by the two categories of 'hotrodder' and 'teenager'. Although, on the surface, there is a sense in which a 'hotrodder' could also correctly be seen as a 'teenager', this latter characterization is of a type an 'outsider' might give. Adults are people who use the term 'teenager' while 'hotrodder' is one generated among and used by 'kids' themselves. Sacks suggests that this has parallels with the way in which anthropologists go about naming a new tribe. Often the name is provided by what other tribes call them and, in many cases, this name means something similar to 'outsider' or 'stranger'. By analogy, 'teenager' is an 'outsider's' or adult's way of characterizing people of a certain age. It is a category known and administered by adults and, most importantly, this 'knowledge' about 'teenagers' is something that can be used to know about any given individual who is seen as a teenager. A 'teenager' is a 'sociological dope', to use Garfinkel's expression, who behaves in ways to produce the patterns of, say, adult-teenager relationships where it is 'known' that teenagers are 'naive', 'idealistic' and otherwise flawed versions of the real thing they will become when they 'grow up'.

Teenagers are not only seen as unformed adults but also as to a greater or lesser extent dependent upon adults. This dependence takes many forms varying from the legal constraints bearing upon the age at which one may legally drive a car, marry, vote or serve in the armed forces, to such things as dating, choosing friends, beliefs and political attitudes. This is not simply a matter of, say, being under the gaze of the law when the police are around, or being able to have parties because the parents are away; rather, the problem for teenagers is that, in one way or another, they are under surveillance by the whole adult population. In this case, one could say that routinely for teenagers one important issue for them is their independence *vis à vis* adults. The conventional way for teenagers to achieve independence, such as going to school, working hard, making and keeping the right friends, staying out of trouble and generally not ruining future chances, is achieved only at a price. This price is that the independence is achieved individually and by conforming to the adult view of social reality. Adults have fixed the game and if one wants to have any autonomy whatsoever, then one has to learn what the game is and play it according to 'their' rules.[25]

'Hotrodder', by contrast, is a category which is not only used by kids themselves but its *correct* use and a person's movement into that category is also controlled by them. It is hotrodders themselves who administer it. It is they who have the leverage on this reality and they who are in a position to assess whether or not a person is worthy of being categorized as a member of the category. Admission is at a price. A person does not simply become a 'hotrodder' by going out and buying a customized drag car 'off the peg', any more than tagging 'man' at the end of an utterance gives one free entry into counter-cultures. The fact that persons can assess others as to correct membership is known by members and can be used to monitor other persons for their legitimate membership is such groups, even where 'hotrodders', 'hippies', 'new romantics', or whatever, are not groups whose members necessarily know each other personally or who have any kind of formal corporate identity. Each member of the group takes it as his or her duty to be a guardian of admission. As an example Sacks remarks on the practice of sports car drivers to flash their lights at each other when they pass on the road. The drivers of any other type of car who tried to emulate this habit would be completely ignored. It is sports car drivers on behalf of other, unknown, sports car drivers who defend their collective membership and concerns.

This neatly parallels one issue faced by drag racers, namely, how do they get into a race with another car? It is not simply a matter of pulling alongside another car at traffic lights and noisily revving the engine. For it is known that any other 'dragster' could assess a challenger as to whether or not he or she is a *bona fide* 'hotrodder' and, if the assessment is negative, the challenge legitimately refused on these grounds.

From all of this we can begin to see some of the matters involved in the niceties of the discussion excerpted above. Ken is claiming that beneath his clean-cut image of an ordinary kid driving an ordinary car he is really a 'hotrodder'. He merely looks like a 'teenager' loyal to the adult version of reality, whereas in actuality he sides with the 'hotrodders'. But this is known to be a front, as Al's comment shows. For Al, Ken is really siding with the adult version aligning himself with the category of 'teenager' and subject to all that is known about that category. The 'hotrodder', by contrast, is attempting to launch attacks upon that conventional way of looking at the world. The general conflict residing behind this particular confrontation is the situation of the dependence of children upon adults in which any particular child is under their control, and the overriding issue for such dependents is the question of how to attain liberation from such domination. Or, perhaps more accurately, how is a version of independence proposed and achieved which is opposed to that currently accepted and enforced? Sacks suggests that the enforced notion of independence is one in which independence is achieved individually. A child becomes emancipated by conforming with current adult conceptions of behaviour and this is something which he or she does on one's own; a situation not unlike that facing blacks and women. In other words, it is not a question of the whole group being liberated from the constraints of the dominant culture. For this to happen what is required is a change in what people can claim to 'know' or 'see' when they see a 'teenager', 'black', 'woman', etc.

Are there ways to aim at this? Are there ways in which what is known about a member of some collection can be controlled by that collection? In other words, can 'kids', in this instance, control what is independence? 'Hotrodders' are one such group, among 'beats', 'hippies', 'punks', and more, who attempt to do just this by trying to get everyone else to see them in terms of their own evaluations. And, as Sacks notes, it is remarkable the number of attempts that 'kids' have made to achieve this independence, given the odds against such a 'revolution' due to the high turnover of personnel in such groups. It is important to remember here that Sacks is talking about categories and not groups as one might normally conceive of them. What the members are trying to change is what is known about the category for what is 'known' about the category is 'known' about any member of that category, and any action a member of that category does can be 'known' as about other members. In this respect one can note the concern shown by minority groups about the ethnic status of the assassinators of President Kennedy, for example, and about the gunman who attempted to kill President Reagan.

All of this is a far cry from the initial discussion about how a car should be named. Sacks' analysis suggests that 'kids' do not reclassify and rename cars which already have perfectly usable ones because they are more interested in cars, but rather that these new classifications are one of the major ways in which they can make attacks upon a conventional reality; a reality that only has substance, order and stability through everyone agreeing, so to speak, to see it that way and not recognizing that it could be changed. It is also a reality that is accepted without regard to any moral evaluations that might be made as to its justice, fairness, or pleasure-ability. 'Hotrodder' is a revolutionary category is this sense. Hotrodders are attempting to subvert the adult version of reality.

In the preceding discussion we have been concerned with the way in which 'hotrodders', as members of a particular cultural group or collectivity, have a concern with who is entitled to belong to that category. One way in which this concern is displayed is in the fragment of talk we quoted where a dispute involving the appropriate name to be used in describing a vehicle is evident. We also noted that membership turned on such matters as with whom to drag race and how to 'see' whether a person is or is not what is claimed. The visibility or otherwise of persons' membership is another topic which has somewhat wider relevance. How do persons, to put the issue as a question, deal with the appearances others present? For example, 'gays' have the problem of identifying others in that category while, at the same time, avoiding recognition by the police, colleagues at work, and others. Drug users have to locate other users in order to 'score', yet avoid detection by the authorities. Given that such groups, and others, can have a concern with displaying themselves as 'normal', 'not suspicious', 'going about their legitimate business', then by what means can membership in these groups be located?

ASSESSING MORAL CHARACTER

Once again what follows is based upon a further suggestive piece by Sacks which also deals with 'practical reasoning' and the ways in which its structures can be abstracted from what are often very particular and fragmentary items of human activities.[26] His theme this time is one which much concerned Goffman as well as Garfinkel and has to do with the types of inference that are made from presented appearances and the 'cover' such appearances can provide, for example, in the committing of offences of various kinds. Paralleling the argument presented earlier in connection with hotrodders, where it was suggested that one way in which 'kids' can achieve freedom from domination by adults is through conformity with an accepted view of the world, Sacks suggests that 'privacy', which can be glossed as freedom from interference by others, can be retained only to the extent that one 'conforms'; indeed, it is a matter of more than simply 'just conforming', but of 'naive conformity'.[27] Actions must not be, as it were, 'studied' but done with ease. A difference exemplified in those occasions when, having committed some minor infraction, we try to act 'normally' to others and feel ourselves to be 'at a distance' from our own actions.[28] Sacks uses a quotation from Emerson to dramatize this point:

> 'Commit a crime, and the earth is made of glass.
> Commit a crime and it seems as if a coat of snow fell
> on the ground, such as reveals in the woods the track
> of every partridge and fox and squirrel.'[29]

People, then, have some considerable concern for the appearances they present to others, for it is on the basis of these appearances that other persons can make inferences about such matters as character and moral status, and the grounds for these inferences are some conception of what 'typical' appearances are. That is, whatever might stand as the claimed actual basis for the appearance presented, the inferences can legitimately be grounded in the typical, usual routine conception of such appearances. So, although one might claim that the reason for choosing the cheapest meal on the menu is the fact that it is one's favourite dish, others can infer and 'see' that the grounds for selection had to do with price.

Inferences that others can make about oneself depend on a great deal upon the usual or 'typical' basis for the appearances one presents. This being the case 'deviants' can have as one way of hiding their activities, an interest in displaying ordinary appearances to lessen their visibility and possible apprehension by control agencies, such as the police. Posing as a gas meter reader is one way in which access can be gained to other people's homes. In the ordinary course of events we treat people, and expect them to treat us, as though the apparent basis of our behaviour and appearance is, in fact, the actual basis. Trying on clothes for size in a shop and being suspected of shoplifting is 'rightly' a cause for offence.[30] In this sense it can be said that we are 'naive observers' of other people's behaviour; that is, we take as actual the appearances before us.

However, there is one group of people whose job it is *not* to regard others' actions so innocently. These are the police. It is not being suggested that they are a special group of people who have access to esoteric knowledge about human behaviour that others do not, but that they do have a special concern with the location and apprehension of criminals and, accordingly, some interest in developing ways of looking at the world so as to locate those criminals. Clearly, criminals have a great concern to hide the fact that they are engaged in criminal activities and so tend to make full use of 'normal appearances' so as to rely, for concealment, on the typical inferences made upon these appearances. The police are, therefore, in the position of having to look at 'normal appearances' in such a way as to locate criminals and their activities.[31] According to Sacks the method they use is an 'incongruity procedure'. That is, they learn to view the world in such a way that the appearances presented to them become 'questionable' but under the constraint that appearances-in-general are not to be doubted. The police have to view the citizens who pass them by so that they notice the nuances and other fine details which suggest a 'lack of fit' in the presented appearances. This 'lack of fit', then, becomes the reason for making further enquiries and investigations but the evidence of 'lack of fit' has to be such that a court of law can see it as a warrantable basis for the policeman's suspicions. This latter constraint has important consequences as we shall see later. But the point is that what the policeman sees as suspicious is grounded in what 'anybody' could come to see as suspicious.

The policeman learns how to detect the 'lack of fit' between the presented appearances and the actuality on the beat by becoming familiar with the normal, everyday, routine course of events which take place, by knowing the timing of these normal activities, and the normal passage ways persons use in the area. And, of course, they learn it by patrolling with more experienced officers. What they initially see as a girl friend waiting for her date gradually becomes a 'hooker' plying her trade; the milkman, a dealer in illicit gambling; a man lighting another's cigarette, a dealer passing on his dope. These and other activities come to stand out against the background features of the environment in which they take place, and the police become accustomed to collecting seemingly trivial little details about personages and places because, of course, it is not known when and whether such details might be important.[32] The policeman eventually becomes sensitized to the appearances persons present on his 'patch' and in this way can be said to develop specialized knowledge regarding suspicious circumstances he might witness.

As we said earlier, there is, however, a constraint placed upon the policeman's ability to use this special knowledge to secure convictions. He must be able to present a description of what aroused his suspicions and present these in such a way that 'anybody' could see that he had 'good grounds' for following them through. Conversely, when the policeman has been 'fixed' or is covering up for a failure to apprehend a criminal, he must be able to show that 'no one' could have been suspicious of the presented appearances. Here, one might say, the policeman and the criminal connive at maintaining appearances to their mutual benefit. In any event, there seems to be a disjunction between the procedures a policeman uses to get to know about some nefarious activity, and those he needs to demonstrate to others that 'anybody' would have been suspicious. This disjunction suggests that the policeman may be put into a position where he has to 'rationally reconstruct' his description of what had occurred; more strongly, the evidence becomes manipulated. Many writers have noted the 'pressures' on the police which cause some of them to become corrupt or many more of them to bend or twist the regulations concerning evidence. Occasionally this has been put down to the nature of the crime involved as, for example, in the case of many drug offences which are notoriously 'invisible', and which, as a result, make the temptation to 'plant' evidence almost irresistable. Others have argued that such factors as desire for promotion and the need to accumulate a certain number of convictions, also increase the pressures on the police to 'manipulate' evidence. Sacks' analysis, however, puts another and rather interesting gloss on this. Although, no doubt, the kind of factors we have just mentioned do play their part, also involved is the more general feature of the local determination of what is to count as an instance of 'suspicious appearances' given that, in the normal course of events, persons' presented appearances are to be accepted unquestioningly. The 'rational reconstruction' of evidence may occur, then, not for any specific personal reasons such as greed, malice, the desire for promotion, or whatever, but as a way of resolving the disjunction between the procedures used for recognizing deviant activities and the methods by which 'good grounds' have to be shown for the initial suspicion.

CONCLUSION

Analyzing the way in which a culture operates has been, and still is, no easy task. From the ethnomethodological standpoint the local production and display of culture is something done by members. Giving greetings, telling stories, doing 'put downs', changing the names of cars, assigning group memberships, locating suspicious persons, and much more, are all cultural phenomena produced by members through the procedures they have for generating and interpreting social life. The analytic task is to describe these procedures, and in this chapter we have discussed merely a few of the ways in which this may be done. The traditional concept of culture prevalent in social science, as we saw in connection with Suttles' work in Chapter 3, refers both to a body of knowledge and to a set of practices. Moreover, it is taken as axiomatic that groups who share a culture can be distinguished from other such groups. People who belong to a separate culture know and do the same things: it is this which transforms them from a set of individuals to a community. This conception of culture parallels very closely that held by the members of society. Members repeatedly identify themselves as belonging to a particular cultural group and point to distinctive features of their lives and activities which mark themselves off from others. They also evince a ready surprise when they discover similarities between 'us' and 'them'. Unfortunately, efforts by ethnographers, sociologists and anthropologists to formulate criteria by which one cultural group can be distinguished from another, whether it be a tribe or a larger scale society, have rarely met with much unequivocal success.[33] The features identified rarely, if ever, amount to literal criteria sufficient to enable a researcher clearly and unambiguously to demarcate one cultural group from another. What is found is that different groups share some traits, do not share others, but not in any distinctive and systematic manner. Although the features often pointed to, such as beliefs in democracy, friendship norms, artistic styles, marriage patterns, drinking patterns, religions, and so on, may stand as criteria for members, they do so because they are already embedded in the notion of a cultural community and, in view of this, anything could be pointed to as marking the culture's distinctiveness as a manifestation of that distinctiveness. Members' theory of culture, to put it this way, is not constructed as a scientific idealization but as a practical activity to distinguish, for practical reasons, those who have identities, rights and obligations in common.

One of the consequences of the ethnomethodological programme is the requirement to suspend the idea of an overarching culture of shared expectations and mutual understanding as a method of accounting for action. Instead it asks that we demonstrate how mutual understanding and shared expectations are achieved through work done by members. In this respect, the member, too, is an investigator of his or her culture and is, moreover, equipped with the methods for doing so. It is these methods which form the interest of the topics we have discussed in this chapter. The idea of shared understandings and meanings is the point of departure, not something presupposed before analysis can begin. Shared understandings have to be shown as the outcome of interpretative actions, the outcome of the methods members use to resolve 'the contingency of meaning'.[34]

The topics we have discussed in this chapter reflect, in various ways, this endeavour. However, the procedures used and the styles they adopt do vary, showing once again, the seriously taken view of ethnomethodology that where the data and the questions they pose will lead is not known in advance. In this sense, the work of analysis is not only just beginning but is in a continuous state of development. What the efforts have in common is a concern to develop descriptions of the machinery of 'practical reasoning' which have both analytic generality and are formulated in rigorous terms. They also share a view, to hark back to a point made a moment ago, that culture, as represented by and reflected in the categories members use, is not some disembodied set of principles lying above the small-scale interactions of daily life and which constitutes the 'objective' conditions of that life. For ethnomethodology, culture is not 'a corpus of member's knowledge, skill, and belief standing prior to and independent of any actual occasion in which such knowledge, skill, and belief is displayed or recognized', as it is for most of conventional sociology. On the contrary, it is an 'occasioned corpus' in which 'the features of socially organized activities are particular, contingent accomplishments of the production and recognition work of parties to that activity'.[35] What the work discussed in this chapter represents is an examination of some of the ways in which members transform this 'occasioned corpus' into the orderly, regular, objective, recalcitrant, invariant state of affairs it appears to them. In the first section of the chapter we discussed the MCD machinery as an attempt to describe aspects of the logic of common sense and the way in which it operates to produce a particular 'hearing' of a child's story. In the second section we focused on how membership assignments can be done and, finally, how the matter of appearances can be handled by those whose task is to question presented appearances as a condition of 'doing their job'. In all this, we have been concerned to show how culture, to use this concept, is made possible through the work done and the methods employed by members to make it visible. Of course, the notion of culture is, thereby, transformed and relocated in the very doings of members, in their talk, their descriptions, their formulations, their disputes, their searches for help, and more, fragmentary and contingent as they may be, and no longer as a *deus ex societate*.

One direction in which some of the work of this kind has gone, has been partly motivated by a desire to work on materials which are reproduceable, capable of re-examination, and out of which alternative analyses can be developed. This is conspicuously the case with conversation analysis which makes use of the transcripts of audio, and occasionally video, recordings of interaction. Aspects of this work are the focus of the next chapter.

NOTES AND REFERENCES

1. See, for example, J. Goldthorpe, 'A revolution in sociology: A review', *Sociology*, 7, 1973, pp. 449–62, and reply by D. Benson, *Sociology*, 8, 1974, pp. 124–33; B. Barnes and J. Law, 'Whatever should be done with indexical expressions?', *Theory and Society*, 3, 1976, pp. 223–37.

2. H. Sacks, 'Sociological description', *Berkeley Journal of Sociology*, 8, 1963, pp. 1–19.

3. 'It is only given the concern to produce a science of social life that the stance of the discipline needs to shift. For anyone not intending to produce a science the current stance need not be conceived as radically problematic', *ibid.*, p. 15n. And again, 'The emergence of sociology will take a different course (when it emerges) from that of other sciences because sociology, to emerge, must free itself not from philosophy but from the common-sense perspective. Its predecessors are not such as Galileo had to deal with, but persons concerned with practical problems like maintaining peace or reducing crime.' *Ibid.*, pp. 10–11.

4. D. Zimmerman and M. Pollner, 'The Everyday World as Phenomenon', in J. D. Douglas (ed.), *Understanding Everyday Life*, Routledge & Kegan Paul: London, 1971, p. 82.

5. This, we suggest, is partly responsible for the bizarre position in which sociology finds itself compared with the natural sciences, of developing separate course on research methods. In the natural sciences one does not learn a set of techniques independent of and in advance of any and every subject-matter. Instead, research strategies and techniques are developed as suitable for the subject-matter at hand.

6. See on this D. and J. Willer, *Systematic Empiricism*, Prentice-Hall: Englewood Cliffs, 1973.
7. Sacks, *op. cit.*, p. 14.
8. See Ch. 2 for a discussion of Garfinkel's phenomenological conception of science and its application to sociology.
9. Sacks also makes the point elsewhere that it is not known in advance what sociological description should be like to be satisfactory, 'that is not an available phenomenon'. K. Hill and R. Crittenden (eds), *The Purdue Symposium on Ethnomethodology*, Institute for the Study of Social Change: Purdue, 1968.
10. H. Sacks. 'On the Analyzability of Stories by Children', in R. Turner (ed.), *Ethnomethodology*, Penguin: Harmondsworth, 1974, pp. 216–32.
11. *ibid.*, pp. 218–9.
12. *ibid.*, p. 219.
13. *ibid.*, p. 219–20.
14. *ibid.*, p. 220.
15. In his unpublished lectures, Sacks refers to the way in which both blacks and children are commonly asserted to be good mimics. Regardless of whether or not this is the case, he notes that the very observation relies upon the notion of category-bound activities where a mimic is someone who can perform actions which properly belong to another category.
16. *op. cit.*, p. 224.
17. Data given by Sacks in Hill and Crittenden, *op. cit.*, p. 30.
18. See H. Sacks, 'The Search for Help: No One to Turn To', in E. Schneidman (ed.), *Essays in Self Destruction*, Aronson: New York, 1967, p. 203. This is a much condensed version of Sacks' unpublished Ph.D. thesis. A lengthier version is to be found in D. Sudnow (ed.), *Studies in Social Interaction*, The Free Press: New York, 1972, pp. 31–74. It is to be noted that when we say that categorizing an individual person is a 'problem', we do not intend to imply that people consciously give thought to the matter. The problem is an analytical one generated from the analyst's stance and the data for which he is trying to produce an account. See H. Sacks and E. Schegloff, 'Opening Up Closings', in R. Turner (ed.), *op. cit.*, pp. 233–64.
19. The notion of 'first', 'second-position' category is not intended to imply that it would be sensible to arrange categories to some nth level of ordering. As Sudnow argues in respect of nurses,

while giving her first injection is remarkable, the nth is not. D. Sudnow, *Passing On*, Prentice-Hall: Englewood Cliffs, 1967. And consider the following in this light:

S1: Have you ever been married, Miss G___?

C1: No.

S2: And you're out here kind of on your own and things not going well?

C2: That's it.

S3: You have no one out here?

C3: Well, I have cousins, but you know they're cousins. They're third or fourth cousins . . .

From Sacks, 'An Initial Investigation of the Usability of Conversational Data for Doing Sociology', a shorter version of his Ph.D., in Sudnow (ed.), *op. cit.*, p. 64.

20. Sacks, 'The Search for Help', in Schneidman (ed.), *op. cit.*, p. 214.
21. Sacks also points out that first-position incumbents are routinely sought out by the police and coroners for evidence concerning suicidal intent in cases of sudden death.
22. Sacks quoted in Sudnow (ed.), *op. cit.*, pp. 68–9. A friend of the suicidal is the Caller (C).
23. One might think that the formal machinery of the MCD is rather overbuilt to deal with such apparently trivial matters as discussed. But, it is as well to reflect that the machinery used to power our understanding of how a baby cries and a 'mommy' picks it up, also provides us with the means of generating an understanding of the practical procedures used by suicidal persons to decide they have 'no one to turn to'. Also, one might reflect on the fact that understanding such simple sentences as told by a two to three year-old child, is illustrative of the cultural control language has in shaping our thoughts, deeds and motivations.
24. H. Sacks, 'Hotrodder: A Revolutionary Category', G. Psathas (ed.), *Everyday Language*, Irvington: New York, 1979, pp. 7–14. This is a lecture condensed and edited by Gail Jefferson. The transcript has been simplified. Note: the numbers in parenthesis indicate the pauses in seconds between utterances.
25. Similar arguments have been advanced by Foucault and Donzelot, among others, who suggest that with the rise of welfare

agencies and the interpenetration of medical ideology, among other factors, into the family, has led to an increasingly observable society which exerts strong control over its members. Of course, the issue of observability as a way of controlling the moral behaviour of citizens is older than capitalism. See, J. Donzelot, *The Policing of Families*, Hutchinson: London, 1979, and M. Foucault, *Discipline and Punish: The Birth of the Prison*, Allen Lane: London, 1975.

26. H. Sacks, 'Notes on Police Assessment of Moral Character', in D. Sudnow (ed.), *op. cit.*, pp. 280–93.

27. *ibid.* p. 281.

28. Laing talks about this kind of experience which many people have as 'typically schizoid' and can occur in very routine situations such as walking past a long cinema queue feeling that all eyes are looking at you, with the result that walking becomes 'studied'. On Laing, see his *The Self and Others*, Penguin: Harmondsworth, 1965.

29. Sacks, 'Notes on the Police Assessment of Moral Character', *op. cit.*, p. 281n.

30. There is a nice aspect to this which can also result in embarrassment and confusion arising from those situations in which one is accused of doing something wrong even though one is perfectly innocent. The embarrassment arises because one can see the possible warrant for the accusation. Being 'discovered' with someone else's wife is a common example.

31. Although not important here, it is of interest to note that not anybody can walk around the world and view it as a policeman. Being 'over observant' of others' actions and talk can be a cause of complaint, to say the least. Also, the 'public spirited citizen' who is constantly reporting offences to the police can find himself the subject of police scrutiny.

32. The possible incidental relevance of this for sociological theories of deviance is contained in the following: 'While in a sense these facts are obvious, it is obvious as well that sociological theories of deviance are not now constructed to deal with them. Yet even for demographic analysis such facts may be of real importance. For example, given the use of learned normal appearances as the groups of locating suspect persons, we would expect that territories in transition will have higher crime rates than stabler territories simply because the policeman geared to the normal appearances of a beat may, not adjusting exactly to the rate and character of transition, be ready

to see newer arrivals as suspicious for the beat seen as an area in which they are not normal features.' Sacks, in Sudnow (ed.) *op. cit.*, p. 286.

33. See, for example, M. Moerman, 'Being Lue: Uses and Abuses of Ethnic Identification', in J. Helm (ed.), *Essays in the Problem of Tribe*, University of Washington Press: Washington, 1968, also reprinted in R. Turner (ed.), *op. cit.*, pp. 54–68; W. W. Sharrock, 'On Owning Knowledge', in R. Turner, *ibid.*, pp. 45–52; W. W. Sharrock and R. J. Anderson, 'On the Demise of the Native', *Occasional Paper No. 5*, Department of Sociology, University of Manchester, 1980.

34. Sharrock and Anderson, *ibid.*, p. 23.

35. Zimmerman and Pollner, *op. cit.*, p. 94.

Conversation analysis is currently the most productive and prolific form of analysis which has been developed with ethnomethodological concerns in mind. In the relatively short period in which the discipline has evolved it has become increasingly technical, developing its own styles of work and methods of analysis. In the space of this chapter it is not possible to do full justice to all the complexities and all the niceties that are involved in the *doing* of conversation analysis. Instead, our more modest aim is to communicate a little of its flavour by briefly discussing some of its more salient aspects. We shall do this by concentrating upon the following areas: first, a discussion of the aims of conversation analysis and the kind of descriptions it seeks to provide of conversational interaction; second, examination of some aspects of the overall structural level of conversation, especially how conversations open and are brought to a close. The third aspect deals with the very important phenomenon of adjacency pairs, such as question-answer, summons-answer, which illustrates the way in which conversations are organized utterance by utterance. The fourth aspect concerns the notion of 'topic' and its organization in conversation. It cannot be stressed too strongly that what follows can only illustrate the kind of work done under the label of conversation analysis: to do more would require another volume. Nonetheless, it is to be hoped that we have at least established the point of conversation analysis and given some idea of what the enterprise entails. Now to some background and some methodological considerations.

Whatever else a martian social scientist might observe about the activities in which people on this earth engage, surely one paramount observation would be that people talk to each other. In families, in schools, in bars, on trains, in factories and even in bed people talk to each other. Imagine tape recording all the conversations that take place in the next five minutes – starting off with the 800 million Chinese. Manifestly, there is an awful lot of talk in the world. And yet, by and large, most sociologists, and social scientists in general, have found it possible to ignore talk. Or, rather, to set the record slightly straighter, while talk has been used by social scientists to obtain their data, *how* people talk, what its possible structure and formal properties might be, has been largely untouched. Conversation analysis is the study of such structures.

The motivation for the study of conversation no doubt derives from a wide variety of sources. We have seen in earlier chapters how the failure to understand and produce descriptions of the way in which people talk vitiates many of the 'findings' of questionnaire and interview studies which form the basis of much of social science. Garfinkel in his early writing had depicted the 'reflexivity of accounts' in such a way as to show that the talk which takes place within a setting is constitutive of the very features of that setting, as evidenced, for example, in the way that Agnes' accounts of her earlier life constituted and furnished features of the relationship with Garfinkel. Phenomenology, more generally, has an interest in language as being both the repository of cultural stocks of knowledge and the stuff from which the 'reality' of the social world is made incarnate.[1] In another tradition, some philosophers of the English-speaking world, such as Wittgenstein, Austin and Ryle have also pointed to language as being of prime importance in the understanding of human activities.[2] But regardless of these intellectual forerunners, *if* they may be so regarded, the major step in establishing the new empirical discipline of conversation analysis was taken by the late Harvey Sacks who, while considering tape recordings that had been made of phone calls to a suicide prevention agency, proposed that instead of treating such talk as being about something other than itself, it should be taken as an object for description and analysis.

For Sacks and his co-workers, then, talk and the sets of behaviour otherwise known as 'non-verbal behaviour' became the topic and focus of investigation. The task was aided by the availability of a whole technology of recording, such as tape and video machines, and which had one consequence important to note, distinguishing conversation analysis from other areas of social science. By being able to record and thereby preserve the raw data of actually occurring talk, innumerable competing and extended analyses could be performed upon it, unmarred by any prior conceptualization of the interaction into pre-conceived packages. Thus, one major hindrance to the development of a cumulative body of analysis was removed, namely, the inability to decide whether competing sociological accounts were the result of a different aspect of the social world being examined, or due to differing data collection techniques. Conversation analysis, by using 'bottled' raw data, and by restricting itself to what is describable in that data, in accordance with the precepts of ethnomethodology, is potentially able to circumvent this particular problem.

How does one go about analysing a segment of talk? Are there any rules of procedure involved? What are we to look at first of all? What is to be included as talk and what as random 'noise'? These are the kind of questions which might initially strike someone asked to analyse conversation. However, there were really only two considerations which guided the first investigators. First, the assumption that talk is organized, and organized by the parties to that talk. Second, that this organization, this orderliness, must be shown and displayed in whatever fragment of naturally occurring talk constitutes the 'raw data'.

But even these minimal considerations do not adequately convey the necessary work which goes into showing what the talk contains, what features it displays, what phenomena are attended to, and so on. While answers to these and other questions of a similar nature are a matter for analysis itself, an important, indeed essential, aid is the transcription system used for displaying and preserving the acoustic and international qualities in the 'raw data' as produced by the speakers. The following is an example of what is involved:

A:	Wha:t did you come *in* for.
B:	*He*'s never told us really,
(A):	N ⌈ o:,
(K):	⌊ ( ).
(A):	Cause he doesn't ⌈ kno:w *does* ⌉ he,
D:	⌊ N*o* : , ⌋
(D):	No hohoho
G:	( ) cause I coll*a*psed once or twice before I could find out what it *was* (you see).

In the transcript, emphasis on a sound is marked by underscoring as in 'wh*a*:t'. The colon : marks a stretching of the sound 'wha:::t' where the length of the prolongation of the sound relates to the number of colons. Unclear or possible hearings of an utterance are placed in brackets such as (you see). When two or more persons are talking at once the 'overlap' is marked with $\begin{bmatrix} & \text{as in} \begin{bmatrix} \text{kno:w } does. \\ No & : & , \end{bmatrix} \end{bmatrix}^{3}$

These transcripts have not always been so detailed. Indeed many of the early ones looked little different from what might be found in the text of a play, with a pause marked as (pause) and laughter entered simply as (laughs). The transcription system has developed in detail and complexity as workers in the field have become aware of the incredible fineness with which people organize their interactions with each other. After all, as analysts have pointed out, people do not merely 'laugh' or 'pause' or 'utter', but do things with them: things which may depend upon their volume, or lack of it, pace, length, and so on, of the laughs, pauses, and utterances and, accordingly, are features which have to be reflected in the data.

Also, it is because of the detail involved in the organized ways in which people produce their talk in relation to each other that conversation analysts generally restrict themselves to transcripts of talk which they themselves have recorded for research purposes. All too often the transcripts produced by other agencies, such as courts, contain amendments and deletions or are otherwise unfaithful records of the talk that actually occurred. Hesitations, false starts, overlaps between speakers, etc., all of which may be of little concern to the particular organization making the transcribed record, are of major interest to those who wish to describe the working of conversation.[4]

In addition, researchers also show a marked preference for using material which has been gathered in 'natural' settings. There are, again, a number of reasons for this. One which is of especial importance is that the type of conversational activities which take place within, say, an interview or in an experiment might very well be restricted. In courtroom interactions, for example, the pacing of the talk could be slower and the incidence of overlapping talk few and far between because of the kind of occasion it is. However, the tendency to avoid such settings is, for most researchers, a matter of preference; much of the data analysed by Sacks in his lectures was taken from group therapy sessions involving teenagers although this rarely surfaces as relevant to the analyses undertaken. The simple conclusion is that the data is to be obtained from wherever possible. After all, there is a whole world and a wide variety of mundane and exotic settings in which talk takes place and so anything brought back for investigation is to be regarded as data. At this stage of the game one might compare conversation analysts with the early botanist who, interested in the structures and varieties of plant life, could as perfectly well go and look in his own garden as conduct an expedition to more remote and rare regions. For, given that one has little idea about the domain for which the structural descriptions hold, then there is little point in collecting data from a 'sample' of settings simply because one has no knowledge of the parameters of the population of settings. Group therapy sessions and Tupperware parties might well be recognizably different to members, but in what regard and with what relevance to the ways in which people produce their talk is, as yet, hard to determine. Since the problems on which conversation analysts work are derived from the data which they examine and nowhere else, this would seem to leave us with an unbounded set of social settings and occasions as places from which materials could be extracted.

But, having suggested that virtually any occasion of social interaction involving talk is a possible place from which to draw data for conversation analysis, nevertheless, it is true to say that, by and large, the majority of the data that has been analysed has been recordings of telephone conversations. This has certain advantages. First, it enables the researcher to obtain a complete conversation: an important matter if one is interested in the overall organization of *a* conversational episode. For example, the way that a participant takes and understands a particular utterance can turn on what has been talked about earlier in the conversation. This can be seen in one way in which parties to a conversation see that the conversation is heading towards closure through the fact they are again talking about 'arrangements' mentioned earlier in the conversation. 'Arrangements to meet' are typically reinvoked in the closing sections of conversations. Obviously, this point can only be analytically displayed as a feature if the whole of the conversation is available. Similarly, one of the ways in which we can talk about the several levels at which conversations are organized involves not only the utterance by utterance level, such as commonly displayed in questions and answers where an answer can be seen as an 'answer' by virtue of its location after a question, but also in the way a 'section' of a conversation can be located and related to other 'sections' of the conversation. Clearly, working purely with fragments of otherwise complete interactions and conversations, such observations, and the eventual analysis to which such observations might lead, would be difficult. For these and other reasons, telephone conversations afford the coverage required.

Further, while many researchers might wish to build an analysis that depended upon gestures and other non-verbal displays to decide 'what was going on in the talk', these are unavailable in audio recordings and, as yet, in transcriptions. The fact that such 'information' was available to the parties to the talk, and not to the analyst, puts the latter in an inferior position. Accordingly, consistent with the methodological precepts mentioned earlier, restricting the material for analysis, at least in the beginning, to 'phone calls means that the researcher has open to inspection the very same features available to the interactants. All the parties, including the researcher, have the talk available and any analysis built upon such talk is constructed on the basis of what was available to the participants in *their* construction of the conversation.

What has been said so far might indicate that the data for conversational analysis could, in principle (practical considerations apart), be gathered from almost anywhere where talk is exchanged. One type of data, however, which researchers in this field assiduously avoid is the constructed or invented piece of talk. While invented talk might have some point or place in other fields, conversation analysts are, above all, interested in describing the methods and procedures persons use to construct interaction, and, accordingly, it would seem sensible to use actual empirical instances of such interaction. There is another aspect to the use of constructed data which is worth mentioning since it highlights some of the difficulties we have in 'seeing' that conversation is organized. The sense and the point of a constructed illustration, in this case of talk, depends upon some notion of 'plausible usage'. The reader or the hearer is able to 'fill in' the contexts in which the illustration might be used, infer what circumstances it might apply, and so on. Similarly, it is not uncommon to find this kind of phenomenon among researchers learning to transcribe conversation. Novices often 'mishear' the talk because, not knowing or attending to the *actual* ways in which people talk, it is the 'imagined' or the 'plausible usage' which is transcribed. Surprisingly, we are not very skilled at describing talk in a way that handles all the fine details of its real instances. The act of transcribing conversations, having to face the task of dealing with all the complexities of the ways in which people actually talk to one another, with all the repeats, hesitations, throat clearings, pauses, and so on, weakens the hold of our everyday conceptions of the way in which talk proceeds and, in so doing, increases sensitivity to the type of 'objects' which can occur in conversation and so bring to the fore the organized relationships between them.

THE DESCRIPTION OF CONVERSATION EVENTS

In the programme outlining the phenomena that ethnomethodology seeks to display and describe, Garfinkel and Sacks propose that this be envisaged as the analysis of the formal structures of practical action.[5] Ethnomethodology is only beginning this task and one of the difficulties it has to face is deciding what the analytical properties of such a description might be.[6] In the last chapter we discussed Sacks' remarks on the 'problem of description' within social science.[7] He argued that one solution to the 'problem of description', which points out that a description of any object can be indefinitely extended given the uniqueness of the object it purports to describe, is to produce purportedly scientific 'general descriptions'. These could be produced by the Weberian technique of assembling the rational features of a social institution into an 'ideal type' or, for the more thoroughly empirically minded, by some process of aggregation and then averaging the individual objects to obtain a summary characterization to 'stand for' the whole. Sacks' main objection to these procedures, as we have pointed out, centred on the fact that they failed to solve *the* central problem which initiated the search for a solution in the first place: namely, how can the relationship between any given actual person, event, institution, or other social object and the purported general description of such objects be articulated? Sacks' own resolution of this difficulty was that since there appears to be no gain in attempting to provide a 'general description' of the kind mentioned earlier, then one might as well proceed with the attempt to produce descriptions of interactional occurrences which will enable us to understand not only the interaction as a general type, but understand also any given individual instance. It is to seek a position analogous to that of the mathematician. The mathematician is not only able to handle equations such as $x^2 - 3x + 2 = 0$, but also the more general form $ax^2 + bx + c = 0$ where, most importantly, the features or properties of the latter general equation are to be found in detail in the properties of any particular quadratic. This not only enables the mathematician to pose and solve matters relating to quadratic equations in general, but to know that the properties so outlined will be preserved in any given quadratic. In this sense we could say that the properties, as *formal* properties, are *context-free* in that they are independent of any of the actual values assigned to the parameters a, b, and c. In addition to this context-freedom, however, the general form can be also considered as *context-sensitive*. Further, given specific values of constants a, b, and c in the general equation above, certain types of quadratics may emerge with differing qualities. In the particular equation $x^2 - 3x + 2 = 0$, for example, x has two 'solutions' or roots which are $x = -1$ and $x = -2$, whereas the quadratic $x^2 - 3x - 2 = 0$ has only 'imaginary' roots. These can be considered as two different types of equations within the more general form.

Now the terms 'context-free' and 'context-sensitive' are not terms taken from the field of mathematics, but are, in fact, a way in which conversation analysts have formulated the manner in which the structures they describe in conversation can be seen to operate. It is, if you like, a way of describing structures which can be seen as operating transituationally, independent of such things as the interactant's age, sex, social class, time, date and place, and so on, and are yet able to handle, organize and arrange the 'oriented to' features of any actual given instance. The mathematical analogue was used in order to illuminate, we hope, what conversation analysts are attempting to produce when they spend significant time and attention in analysing what would otherwise appear to be isolated, single or 'one-off' fragments of talk. The 'excavation' of a single fragment of conversation is conducted not only to reveal how that particular fragment was put together but also to arrive at descriptions of formal structures and the formulation of analytic problems which could be found elsewhere, rather in the manner of a linguist analysing a single sentence in a language.[8] The linguist suggests that to understand the sense or meaning of a certain sentence presupposes a knowledge of the language of which that sentence forms a part. Hence, an analysis of the structure of that sentence could reveal wider properties of the language itself. In a similar sense, a conversation analyst would say that a whole set of cultural competences and social knowledge go into the production of particular fragments of interaction and, accordingly, a proper analysis of fragments of conversation can illuminate wider and deeper aspects of interaction.

We hope that the above will give some indication of certain 'principles' which inform conversation analysis. The nature of the work is such, however, that more particular methodological issues can only be discussed in relation to data and not in some abstract, disembodied way. So we now turn to look at conversational materials and, perhaps naturally enough, we begin with openings as one aspect of the overall structure of conversation.

ASPECTS OF OVERALL STRUCTURE OF CONVERSATION

Openings and closings as strategic concerns

Conversations are interactional episodes recognized by members and, as such, are segmented events which are marked off in some fashion with beginnings, middles, and ends. It is these 'oriented to' features which are seen by analysts as belonging to the overall structure of a conversational episode. We can begin our discussion by noting that conversations 'open': they do not simply start. In other words, it is not the case that if one wants to begin a conversation then one just starts to talk. A conversation is a joint activity engaged in by at least two parties and, hence, entry into the conversation needs co-ordination by the potential conversationalists. Conversations then, 'open', and they do so by the *in situ* interaction of the people who eventually come to develop the conversation. This way of looking at the beginnings of conversations focuses sharply on the analytical problem of how persons come to jointly achieve the opening of a conversation.

It is important to be aware of the stance being taken here. As it is posed, the problem is one for analysis rather than a practical problem of social etiquette which might arise, for example, in trying to begin a conversation with a stranger. Although such analytical problems might indeed coincide with everyday practical problems we can all face in starting up conversations, it is not being claimed that members always experience the openings of conversations as a strategic problem to be thought about deeply. Rather, analytic problems arise out of the perspective the conversation analyst brings to bear on the analysis of conversational organization. Admittedly, given the perspective, analysis should be able to reveal the organizational basis of the practical problems members can face in attempting to open any particular conversation.

One fairly obvious and common way in which members can 'solve' the problem of co-ordinating the opening of a conversation is through an exchange of greetings. Greetings normally occur at the beginnings of conversations, but we have yet to see what features they have which enable them to deal with this problem of co-ordinating entry into conversation.

First, it can be observed in two-party conversation that an exchange of greetings involves two utterances, 'Hello' – 'Hello', and, second, that the utterances are produced by two different speakers. A third observation would be that there is a first greeting and a second greeting. This is not a trivial point. For it is not the case that there happens to be a first greeting and a second greeting simply by virtue of the fact that one was uttered prior to the other. The 'firstness' of the first greeting in part resides in the fact that it makes a return greeting, a second greeting, *relevant*. To use the technical phrase of conversation analysis, the production of a first greeting *sequentially implicates* the production of a return greeting. Having produced a first greeting a second greeting *should* be produced as part of a *proper* sequence. (Some further aspects of sequential implication will be discussed later.) By way of contrast, the second greeting does not implicate a return greeting. The 'firstness' and 'secondness' of greetings are then features that greetings can have and are features produced and attended to by the interactants in the conversation.

So we can now begin to see how an exchange of greetings deals with the issue of co-ordinating entry into a conversation. The production of a first greeting implicates a return by another party and this second greeting displays to the producer of the first that his greeting was heard, understood for what it was, and accepted as an opening move into conversation. A co-ordinated opening is achieved. But greetings, though common conversation openings, are not the only method available.

One of the earliest papers to deal with the issue of the openings of conversation was written by Schegloff. He dealt with the way in which conversation opened in telephone calls made to a police desk.[9] He developed his analysis by noting an observation made by Sacks, that in two-party conversation the distribution of turns at talk approximates the sequence abababab, where a and b represent each persons turn at talk.[10] This distribution of the way in which speakers sequence their talk, obvious though it may at first appear, allows us to ask the question: who gets to be the first speaker? Schegloff in investigating this and related matters proposed, as a first solution to this problem, that, for telephone calls at least, the answerer speaks first. That is, the person who picks up the ringing telephone speaks the first words into the receiver. This 'rule' covered all but one of the telephone calls Schegloff examined. But, given the ethnomethodological injunction that each and every occasion be examined as the product of methods used by members for the production of orderliness, then that single case could not be dismissed as, say, sampling error, a freak, or counted as a deviant case through the *ad hoc* invocation of other rules. What was needed was an excavation of this exception.

Briefly, Schegloff's re-analysis involved the development of the notion of a Summons – Answer sequence whereby, in the ordinary case, the telephone ring acts as a Summons to which the person picking up the telephone, as first speaker, provides the Answer. We have then: Telephone ring = Summons, followed by 'Hello' = Answer. Schegloff is then able to talk about the one case in which the caller spoke first in terms of the fact that an Answer was not produced upon picking up the phone. In which case, the item of talk produced by the caller is, in fact, another Summons, rather in the manner in which, having knocked on a door and finding no answer, then one might call out a person's name in a further attempt to summon them to answer the door.

We have here been talking about telephone calls but of course many more interactions take place in face-to-face settings, passing people in the street, meeting people in shops, football matches and a host of other occasions. While we have little to say about *all* these encounters, nonetheless, it can be suggested that in these settings the matter of 'first speaker' is also organized: it is not mere happenstance, chance, or whatever, that people find themselves as having spoken first.

One way to discuss this is to observe the ways in which 'strangers' interact with each other in public places when they are mutually visible. Goffman has suggested that one of the features of such settings is that people pay 'artful inattention' to others. For example, people in launderettes can become 'self-absorbed' in whatever they are doing, thereby displaying both that they are properly engaged in some 'accountable activity' and also that they are 'safe' persons for others.[11] In this event, there is unlikely to be any unwelcome intrusion into their affairs. In a similar vein, though to different effect, Sacks has noted how people can orient to making themselves invisible, at least in the sense of not coming to the attention of others.[12] Between 'strangers' interaction would seem to be governed by the rule: 'don't intrude, don't say hello.' However, for at least two categories of person this is overridden and people who are otherwise strangers can attempt the initiation of an interaction. First, as Goffman among many others has noted, attractive women are often the subject of male attention and attempts at interaction. One way in which women can deal with this possibility is through studied inattention: eyes at middle distance looking 'through' the persons around, set face and demeanour which would brook no conversation, invitation to a drink, or query about having met somewhere before. Perhaps, unsurprisingly, this method, adopted in an attempt to avoid unsolicited and unwanted interactions, is one way in which such people come to be seen as 'snobbish', 'stuck-up', or 'haughty'. From a slightly different angle we have the not dissimilar circumstances surrounding the famous, such as television actors, film stars and sports heroes. Typically these people complain or otherwise make comment on the fact that complete strangers approach them on the street, in bars, in lifts and other places, and talk to them as though they were 'friends'.[13] Quentin Crisp, in his own words 'one of the stately homos of England', has written that his recent fame or notoriety in New York had produced in him the 'watery smile of the famous'.[14] Walking round the streets of New York he adopted a facial expression which was solicitous of, or at least accepting of, recognition and potential interaction. Here one can begin to see the notion of the 'insincere smile', a smile that is given to anybody and everybody and, hence, not produced for any particular person: it is not a smile that *you* get but a smile that would have been produced for anyone. This is the other side of the coin to the resolve of the 'model' to set her face in such a way as to rebuff any potential first move to open a conversation.[15] Of course, the famous and the beautiful are not the only people who can find themselves in the position of being potential interactants for otherwise strangers. People can be 'well-known' in offices, factories, schools, social clubs, universities and neighbourhoods and thereby come to use a version of the available interactional options. Some analyses of social life suggest that the categories of male/female organize the initiation of inter-sexual talk and conversation. That is, males approach females in the first instance or, as the homily has it, 'It is for men to try and women to deny.' However, given that the problem is more general than this and that the interactional strategies available can be used by either sex it would appear that the sexual categories rather than organizing the way in which interactions begin are, instead, parasitic upon a deeper level of conversational organization which is independent of the sexual categories and whatever organization might exist between them.

To see what might be involved here we can suggest that such things as the 'watery smile of the famous' act as a 'pre' to any first opening move in a conversation. It is a preliminary move to a sequence proper as, for example, the question, 'Are you doing anything this evening?' is normally heard as a preliminary to an invitation which will be forthcoming given an appropriate negative reply to the question. 'Pre's' are part of the step-by-step entry into conversation for, to repeat, it is not through merely beginning to talk that one can legitimate one's right to talk to another: such claims have to be recognized and acknowledged. Conversely, the women's 'studied inattention' is a discouragement to any 'pre' or opening move in an attempt to begin interaction.

To return to the opening of conversations, one of the 'problems' that has to be dealt with is the auspices under which the interaction is being initiated. Here we want to touch upon the questions of 'identity' and 'topic'. In telephone calls, for example, we can distinguish in the opening of calls a number of different types of response that serve as the answer to the summons of the telephone bell. If one telephones a department store the answer is likely to be of the following order, 'Dingles', 'Woolworths', 'Adult Aids', not 'Peter', 'Albert', 'Jacky', or some such. In a set of data culled from calls into a Canadian police station, the initial answer to a phone call was, 'Newton Police'.[16] Responses like this are the kind received in telephone calls to business and other institutions suggesting that the calls themselves are organizationally defined and, in addition, that the persons producing those answers stand simply as 'Answerers' to the call. The Answerer is not the person to whom the call is actually addressed, though, of course, he or she can act as proxy for such persons. Sacks has talked about these as 'conversationally generated identities'. The identity of the person who produces the answer, 'Woolworths' and similar types, is referred to as 'Answerer-not-called', while 'Hello', or similar, that of an 'Answerer-possibly-called', it being left to further talk to indicate that not merely has the connection been made, but that the Answerer is or is not the person the caller wants. For example,

Co: Hello, Lifeliners can I help you?[17]

indicates both that the Answerer is a 'possible-called' and specifies the proper organizationally defined nature of the call. It should be held in mind that the import of this typology of Answerers of a telephone call resides in the fact that they are locally generated identities, or as Garfinkel might put it, they are identities generated from within the interaction itself and have import within that setting; the identities are, in other words, reflexively tied to the interaction and are not abstracted disembodied categories of persons. Bearing this in mind we can note how Sacks has used the notion of 'Answerer-possibly-Called' to illuminate aspects of behaviour when a number of people, for example, are in a room when the phone rings. To put it simply, who gets to answer the phone? This is a matter that, in some independence of the ecological distribution of persons around the phone, is resolved through a selection among these persons present of who are the 'possibly-called'. One of us can recall the anger and hostility that was generated by 'staff' against a 'student' who would quite commonly 'answer' the phone in the departmental office. The student was seen as improperly claiming the status of a 'possible-called'. However, we are not saying that these kinds of responses are in some way determinative of identities and of the way in which a conversation develops. It is not as though having embarked on a certain course with, say, an institutional opening such as 'Newton Police', that the conversationalists are thereby inevitably committed to this line of talk. For, of course, it regularly happens that people are able to turn what might initially appear as 'institutionalized talk' into 'personal talk', as in the following,

A: Police Desk

B: Who's this?

A: Sergeant Brown

B: Do you know Sergeant Smith?

A: Yes

B: Well I'm a friend of his, I think we met once.
       I'm Bill Jones.

A: Yeah, I think so.

B: Well look can you give me some information about. . . .[18]

Of course, the relevant conversational identities of the parties to the conversation can alter through the course of the talk. A person who initially stands as 'Answerer-not-Called' can have that status changed into the one of 'Answerer-not-Called but talked to' in the sense that, although the call might be intended for another person, nevertheless, the caller engages in talk with the 'mere' answerer and this can change the nature of the relationship between the two parties. As Sacks has pointed out, it is not uncommon for persons to generate relationships out of interaction in which there is no contact other than that which exists on the phone.

There are, then, different ways in which the answer to the summons of the telephone ringing can be produced. Within these there can be seen a whole set of delicate tactical moves in the very short space of interactional time that constitutes the opening of the conversation. As we pointed out earlier, conversations do not simply 'start', they are opened, and the various ways in which they are opened enable a variety of interactional tasks to be accomplished. Related to one of these we have just mentioned, that of identification, is that of establishing what the telephone call is about which we can approach through the notion of 'first topic'; that is, the way in which conversationalists approach that part of the talk which they might later refer to as being 'what the conversation was about'. This way of expressing 'first topic' relates it directly, in the context of telephone calls, to the 'reason-for-call'. However we must be careful to distinguish between 'first topic' and the topic which happens to be talked of first.

We can perhaps put the matter this way. The proper place in which to put the 'reason-for-call' is up front in the talk as first topic, whether the topic be one of making arrangements for a later meeting, an enquiry about the progress of somebody's illness, or the returning of a call to someone who had phoned earlier. Having the 'reason-for-call' as first topic is, in part, one of the ways in which people can come to see what is the reason for call. After all, one can perfectly well report what somebody on the phone 'rang about' despite the fact that many things were talked of, none of them prefaced with, 'The reason I rang was . . .'. 'Reasons for call' can also be preserved and reported in other conversations and the preservability and reportability can be invoked and used by people in reference to some topic as being 'first topic'. This being the case, then, people can come to have various concerns with regard to first topic and in the visibility and preservability of something as a 'reason-for-the-call'. For example, a person might wish to call somebody for a particular reason but not wish the other to take it that that is the reason why they called. Or, it might be that they would like it to be seen that the call was made for 'no reason' in the sense that, occasionally, people who are in specially close relationships specifically do not need a reason to call each other. By contrast, there are also persons who only call or 'drop in' when they want something and it is known that such persons are negatively evaluated. Hence, for these and other reasons, even if the caller does have a reason for calling, he or she might not wish that reason to be visible. After all, it is known that people can orient to the preservability of 'first topic – reason-for-call' and this may be something they wish to control.

'First topic' understood in this way is, then, a place or object in a conversation about which people can have strategic concerns. One of the ways in which we look at the opening sections of conversations is through the various methods conversationalists use to get to the first topic. Here are some examples with some comments on the nature of the issues involved.

```
        TC1     (b)     13
        (phone rings)
1.  :  J:   (W' chuhrdihbluepri:nt)
2.  :  L:   Hey Jerry?
3.                    (●)
4.  :  L:   ●hh
5.  :  J:              Ye:s
6.  :  J:              hHi:   ●h h
7.  :  J:              HI:  :
8.  :  L:              He: y: – you don' haftuh
9.  :  :    bring'ny paper plates I think ah'll jus:t use the plates ah've
            go::t, h h¹⁹
```

One of the first things that we can observe in this transcript is that in the first place at which the Caller can speak, line 2, she claims recognition of the Answerer while the greetings are displaced to lines 6 and 7. Ignoring for the moment that this is a phone call to an organization (it transpires in the call that Linda is Jerry's wife and is calling him at his work place), we can ask what strategic benefits there might be in claiming identification of Answerer right at the beginning of the call?

One facet of the strategic interactional use of claims to identification is that the person making the claim is often using it as an intimacy ploy. In this case, it could be argued that Linda is claiming that she is in such a relationship to Jerry that she can identify his voice from the minimal amount of information available to her on his answering the phone. She doesn't give her name which is, incidentally, one of the games people play on the phone when they invite others to guess who is calling merely through voice recognition. This, of course, can turn out to be a very tricky business since people can feel wounded or upset if they are not recognized and, further, can be a basis for bringing the nature of the call, and thereby the relationship, into question.[20]

So '*Hey* Jerry?' in line 2, claims recognition of the Answerer. It also might be seen as a way in which the Caller can attempt to get to first topic as fast as she can. Consider that she is phoning into an organization and that there are a number of potential Answerers of the phone. Thus, although her first opportunity to speak, that is, line 2, might be the place where she says that the paper plates are not needed, it would not work as a general procedure. However, compare,

P: Newton Police

L: Yes, I'd like to repor – report a stolen car
    and

P: Hello, Newton Police,

C: A yes, I had my car towed away from – eh Parkway and – eh Regent; it was in the alley-way. Could you tell me whereabouts it would be?[21]

In these cases the first place at which the caller can speak is the place at which the first topic, reason-for-the-call is introduced. We can now perhaps begin to appreciate the skill with which Linda gets herself to be in the position to deliver the first topic fast. For it is not simply a matter that, by virtue of the fact she is the Caller she is automatically, as it were, able to produce the first topic, or that she can get to the first topic quickly. Again compare:

Clara: Hello: ;,

Agnes: Good *morni*ng

Clara: How'r you::

A: Hello::,

B: Hi:::

A: Oh::i:: 'ow are you Agne::s

In these cases the Answerers have recognized the voice of the caller and are, accordingly, able to delay the move to first topic through 'How are you' and thereby possibly wrest the first topic for themselves. Linda, however, maintains control for herself although she could have produced the first topic earlier than she did if the 'Hellos' as greetings had been omitted as in,

Margy:	Hel*lo*:,
Edna:	Hello Margy?
Margy:	Ye: s
Edna:	•hhhh *We* do pai:::nting, a:ntigui::ng

What we can begin to see now is the strong sense of saying conversations do not merely start, do not merely begin. There are organized patterns to the features that people use to begin a conversation. There is not just a beginning, say an exchange of greetings, but commonly an opening section to a conversation which may vary in length and which may comprise a number of things, such as greetings, 'how are yous' and the responses to such enquiries into 'personal states'.

We hope to have given some sense of the detail with which one can begin to approach an area of conversation as seemingly devoid of interest as openings. There are, of course, other aspects of conversation than openings. There is the obverse issue of how conversations come to a close. Two people having a conversation do not end that conversation by simply ceasing to talk. To do this would be to invite something more than curiosity. The conversation is brought jointly to closure through the construction of a closing sequence. Briefly what this points to is that the closing of a conversation has to be warranted, often announced, by particular preliminary moves so that all parties can, in effect, jointly end the conversation. Among the devices identified by analysts are 'preclosings' such as 'well . . .', 'o:h . . .', 'Sooo . . .' which may serve as a marker for the move to closure or may well offer the floor to another speaker. If no one wishes to continue these can become the first part of a closing section and a way, thereby, of jointly warranting the closing of a conversation. Not perhaps surprisingly, other closing devices depend more heavily on the course of the preceding conversation giving, incidentally, support to the idea that participants orient to the unit we might term a 'single conversation' throughout a conversation's course. In other words, materials can be picked up during the course of a conversation and preserved for use in the conversation's closing. An earlier enquiry by the caller, for example, about what the called was doing, can be used to announce a closing section by, 'Well, I'll let you get back to Crossroads', or some such. Often the closing of a conversation can be coterminous with the closing of some social activity, such as a seminar, a visit to the doctor, and so on, and it is the closing section which can be used for such things as making arrangements for next meetings, parking briefcases, closing notes, and so on.

A fairly commonplace feature of the closing of conversations is the use of conventional, ritualized phrases such as the following:[22]

Marge:	Okay honey
Laura:	Okay
Marge:	Bye bye
Laura:	Bye bye

The conversation ends with Marge saying 'Bye bye' followed by Laura saying 'Bye bye': a pair of utterances strikingly similar to the ways in which conversations often open:

Nancy:	H'*llo*:?
Hyla:	Hi :

They are similar in these three ways: first, the sequence of utterances has two parts; second, one part is produced by one speaker and the other part by the second speaker; and, third, the two utterances are placed in immediate juxtaposition. This brings us to the second area of conversation analysis with which we are to be concerned and that is the close order organization of adjacency pairs. Just as conversations can be analysed according to the overall level of organization it displays as a unit of conversation in terms of such things as opening and closing sections, so it can be looked at in its fine detail; that is, the ways in which it is closely organized utterance by utterance. Adjacency pairs have a large role to play at this level.

CLOSE ORDER ORGANIZATION OF CONVERSATION

Adjacency pairs

Adjacency pairs are adjacent utterances produced by two different speakers where the production of the first part of the pair makes the production of the second part sequentially relevant or, as we expressed it earlier, when the first part of an adjacent pair is produced it sequentially implicates the production of the second part of the pair. More generally 'sequential implicativeness' means 'that an utterance projects for the sequentially following turn(s) the relevance of a determinate range of occurrences (be they utterance types, activities, speaker selections etc.). It thus has sequentially organized implications.'[23] It becomes evident that adjacency pairs are ubiquitous in conversation. Summons and answer sequences, greetings, closings are all instances of adjacency pairs. Questions and their answers can also be seen as adjacent pairs as can proposals, requests, offers, invitations, and their respective acceptance/rejection. As interactions composed of two elements, each of which is performed by separate persons, the completion of a full sequence, say, a greeting, or a proposal, means that a first pair part cannot be followed by any second pair part. After a question one properly obtains an answer not a greeting. We have already noticed that conversations often close with terminal exchange pairs, such as 'Byebye' – 'Bye-bye' and that conversations often begin with an exchange of greetings, such as 'Hello' – 'Watcha'. Now, instead of asking why conversations open with greetings and close with terminal exchanges, with the notion of adjacency pairs we can try to move to a more abstract level in an effort to gain more analytic generality, and ask: Why do conversations both open and close with adjacency pairs? Clearly, this will involve us looking at some of the formal properties of adjacency pair phenomena rather than, say, examining particular greetings, or particular terminal exchanges. To do this let us discuss some examples.

The first draws upon an observation referred to earlier in this chapter that in two-party talk, the turns at talk are distributed A B A B A B . . . where A and B are each one party's turn. Now, although the distribution A B C A B C A B C . . . is logically possible in three-party talk it rarely occurs. Instead, one is likely to get a distribution of the following kind: A B C B C A C B . . . In other words, in more than two-party talk a salient 'problem' for all parties is to select the next speaker, given that there is no precedence rule to dictate who shall speak next. In the following example, we can see how an adjacency pair construction, a question, is used by Ken to select the next speaker:

Jim: Those guys are losing money.

Roger: Gut you go down-low-down to the New Pike there's a buncha people oh:: and they're old and they're pretending they're having fun, but they're really not.

Ken: How cn you tell. Hm?

Roger: They're–they're tryna make a living, but the place is on the decline . . . [24]

Adjacency pairs then are to be found in the turn-taking system of conversation.[25] Similarly, where there is a 'breakdown' in a conversation, such as a failure to hear or understand, interruptions, silences, and the like, adjacency pair devices can be used to effect a remedy, as in the question, 'What did you say?'

So we have the following areas in which adjacency pairs are used: openings-closings, the operation of the turn-taking system, and the repair of the turn-taking system. How can we account for this? What properties do adjacency pairs possess which enables them to be used in these variety of ways? Is it possible that there is an answer that relates all of those and other uses? Before we attempt such an answer, let us briefly examine two more areas in which adjacency pairs are to be found.

For reasons which we cannot dwell on here, the construction of long, multi-causal or multi-sentence utterances requires collaboration between the speaker and the listener(s) such that the listener does not take a turn at talk at points where he otherwise might do so, say, at natural pauses or at the end of sentence units. A common example would be someone telling a story or a joke.[26] Contrary to the impression given in novels and in plays, long turns at talk by one person are not normally bounded by the talk of others. In natural conversation, long utterances are interlarded with 'hearers' producing such utterances as 'Uh huh' or 'Mm'. The interest in these lies in the further observation that hearers do not normally offer these anywhere in the speaker's talk, but that the speaker specifically constructs places in his talk for these 'Uh huh's to be placed. That is, they are routinely offered at the end of clauses or sentences signalled by the use of 'question intonation'. Following the clause or sentence with question intonation one can regularly find the listener offering an 'Uh huh' or its equivalent. Here again we find, then, an adjacency pair format involved in the construction of long utterances.

Finally, and to refer again to the turn-taking system, persons engaged in talk organize the turns at talk to minimize any gap or overlap between speakers. When one person is talking, then at the place where that person stops and the other starts up there is a coordinated effort to produce this turn transition in a way that avoids either a silence or both parties talking at once. One means of systematically producing this effect is through the use of adjacency pairs. The reason for this hinges on a special rule which operates for the use of adjacency pairs. This rule is that if a first pair part is produced, then at the first possible completion of that part the speaker should stop and the hearer should immediately produce the relevant second pair part. From the hearer's point of view, then, it is known that it is safe to take a turn at talking at the first possible completion point. In addition, many first pair parts, most especially questions, can be signalled right from the start of the utterance as projecting an adjacency pair: e.g. 'Why, Where, When, etc.'

We have considered five major places in conversation where adjacency pairs occur: at openings and closings, in the operation of the turn-taking system, in the repair of local trouble, in the building of long utterances, and in the achievement of no gap/no overlap at turn transition points. This would suggest that the adjacency pair format is in some way fundamental to the organization of conversation and that this is due to the properties we have illustrated: they are two utterances long, adjacently placed and produced by different speakers. They have, that is, the general properties of a discrimination and an ordering of parts.

We can illumine the question of why they come to be used so powerfully especially in the close order, utterance by utterance, organization of conversation by looking to see whether there is any organization or rule involved in determining where they are to be found in conversation. Recalling the fact that adjacency pair second parts are conditionally relevant upon the production of a first pair part then the question of whether there is any organization to the distribution of adjacency pairs, amounts to asking whether there is any organization to the distribution of first pair parts? The answer which Sacks offers is as follows: adjacency pair first parts can go *anywhere* in conversation *except* directly after another first pair part, *unless* the second first pair part is the first part of an 'insertion sequence'. Since we have not dealt with an 'insertion sequence' let us describe this first. The rule proposed by Sacks for the distribution of adjacency pairs would allow the following as legitimate:

AP₁ ⎡──────── A: What are you doing this evening?
      ⎢ AP₂ ⎡ B: Why?
      ⎢   ⎣ A: I thought of going over to Dave's.
      ⎣──────── B: Well actually I'm meeting Sally this evening.

Here we have two adjacency pairs, AP₁ and AP₂, where the latter is embedded in the former, AP₂ being the inserted sequence. Apart from this type of instance the rule states that adjacency pair first parts can go anywhere except after another first pair part. The only object that constraints the first pair parts are, therefore, first pair parts themselves. While this is a large degree of freedom for the distribution of a conversational object, some organized restriction upon its occurrence is retained. Specifically adjacency pairs first parts, in terms of placement, are only bound by themselves. In addition, the notion of 'anywhere' involved here is much wider than might be suspected at first glance. It does not simply mean that one can place a first part anywhere in a conversation, within the constraint mentioned by the rule, after an utterance has been completed. One can place a first pair part prior to the completion of an utterance. For example, speakers can have problems in the course of an utterance, such as being lost for a word or, more severely with stammering, and in these cases a hearer can offer a continuation of the utterance with the sort of inflection carried by a 'question' or with a tone which says, 'I'm guessing'. This, thus, then makes the speaker's own completion a second pair part of a question or the acceptance or rejection of an offer. In addition, we have already seen the operation of adjacency pairs in the construction of long utterances. If Sacks' rule is in anyway correct then something rather important follows relating to hearership especially in regard to the issue of next speaker. Sacks asks why it is that people who are not talking bother to listen. Of course, there are many reasons why people listen to other's talk, out of politeness, because they are interested, because they like the other person, because family obligations demand it, and more. What Sacks is after, however, is a motivated basis for listening which is independent of the whims or the passions of the persons engaged in the conversation, and it might well be that the system of talk itself, the way in which conversation is organized can provide this motivation. After all, the interest, the politeness, the liking, the family obligations, and so on, will have to be displayed using the machinery which organizes the structure of conversation.

Sacks begins by proposing, as a starting position, that a person is willing to talk only if he is selected to talk. This, at least on the face of it, seems a reasonable supposition given the fact that persons unwilling to talk on such occasions can be subject to all kinds of interactional sanctions extending to imprisonment, or incarceration in a mental asylum. Even within this minimal supposition, a person willing to talk only if selected, would have to listen to find out if and when he is selected. It is not the case, moreover, that a person can always tell at the beginning of an utterance whether it is going to select him to speak next. For example, 'isn't it so, John' and other tag questions can always be tacked on at the end of the utterance to select next speaker, as every school teacher knows. So, given the pervasiveness of adjacency pairs, and the close ordering they demand, in the use of speaker selection, including their use in the tag questions just illustrated, a person can find that although he has not been selected to speak, nevertheless, he has *had* to listen since he might have been selected. In other words, within conversation there is simply no rest, even for some person who intends to talk only if selected. One cannot tell definitely at the beginning of another's utterance that it is not for you, and so go to sleep as it were, because it can always turn out to have been for you. Not only is this true for non-speakers but it is also true for speakers as well. The speaker has to listen to his own talk for the simple reason that upon completion of his talk someone could do things like ask 'why' or 'what'. The motivation to listen is, then, built into the system of conversation and this motivation operates for both speaker as well as non-speaker.

We have been led to a consideration of the motivation for listening through our examination of the distribution of adjacency pairs but it is not just in regard to 'listening' that adjacency pairs play a part. Of possibly greater import is the role they have to play in the step by step manner in which understanding is displayed and achieved in conversation.

One of the ways in which persons demonstrate that they understand each other is by one party paraphrasing, rewording, or otherwise formulating what another has said. This enables any speaker to check on the hearer's understanding or sense of the talk thus far. While, as we noted in Chapter 4, people do produce formulations as ways of attempting to demonstrate that they have understood the other speaker it is, nevertheless, a cumbersome technique in that if it were consistently applied speakers might never get past an initial utterance since they would continually be asking for clarifications of clarifications of each other's talk.

This possibility, of course, is generated by the indexical quality of language and powerfully illustrated by Garfinkel when he asked students to make clear the meaning of a fragment of talk. Students were asked to report an ordinary conversation by writing what was said by the parties down one side of a page. On the other side they were then asked to write down what they understood the utterances that constituted the conversation to be about. The data is as follows:[27]

Husband:	Dana succeeded in putting a penny in a parking meter today without being picked up.	This afternoon as I was bringing Dana, our four-year-old son, home from the nursery school, he succeeded in reaching high enough to put a penny in a parking meter when we parked in a meter zone, whereas before he had always had to be picked up to reach that high.
Wife:	Did you take him to the record store?	Since he put a penny in a meter that means that you stopped while he was with you. I know that you stopped at the record store either on the way to get him or on the way back. Was it on the way back, so that he was with you or did you stop there on the way to get him and somewhere else on the way back?
Husband:	No, to the shoe repair shop.	No, I stopped at the record store on the way to get him and stopped at the shoe repair shop on the way home when he was with me.
Wife:	What for?	I know of one reason why you might have stopped at the shoe repair shop. Why did you in fact?
Husband:	I got some new shoe laces for my shoes.	As you will remember I broke a shoe lace on one of my brown oxfords the other day so I stopped to get some new laces.

| *Wife:* | Your loafers need new heels badly. | Something else you could have gotten that I was thinking of. You could have taken in your black loafers which need heels badly. You'd better get them taken care of pretty soon. |

The students found the task of writing out the conversation easy enough but writing down what they understood was being talked about more difficult. As Garfinkel began to impose higher standards of clarity and accuracy the task became more laborious and eventually was seen to be impossible. This was because the writing of the 'meaning' of the talk developed the conversation as an ever increasing set of relevant issues. The attempt to accomplish the task merely multiplied its matters.

By contrast, the uses of adjacency pairs permit people to monitor each others' talk in such a way that 'understanding' can be seen as 'displayed' through the positioning of items of talk and actions. When someone asks the question 'What time is it?' then the answer, 'Five o'clock' is seen as an answer by virtue of its placement next to a question and thereby 'displays' that the question was understood by virtue of the fact that a 'correct' response had been produced. As Sacks and Schegloff put it:

Past and current work has indicated that placement considerations are general for utterances. That is: a pervasively relevant issue (for participants) about utterances in conversation is 'why that now' a question whose analysis may also be relevant to find what 'that' is. That is to say, some utterances may derive their character as actions entirely from placement considerations. For example, there do not seem to be criteria other than placement (i.e. sequential) ones that will sufficiently discriminate the status of an utterance as a 'statement', 'assertion', declarative', 'proposition', etc., from its status as an 'answer'. Finding an utterance to be an 'answer', to be accomplishing 'answering', cannot be achieved by reference to phonological syntactic, semantic, or logical features of the utterance itself, but only by consulting its sequential placement, e.g. its placement 'after a question'.[28]

We are now in position to see much more clearly the basis for the observation that presaged this section on adjacency pairs. It was noted that the closings of conversation contained items such as 'Bye-Bye', whilst openings contained greetings, 'Hello-Hello'. These are two utterances, adjacently placed and produced by different speakers. What the second speaker can do by virtue of placing his item of talk in second position is to *show* (not claim) that he understood what the first speaker was aiming at (opening or terminating a conversation) and also show that he is willing to go along with that action. Conversely, the first speaker can see from the talk of the second that what he, the first speaker, had said had been heard and understood. And of course mishearings, misunderstandings of disagreements can all be made available in the same way. The co-ordinated entry into and the co-ordinated exit from a conversation, both requiring close local organization, can be accomplished through the use of the adjacency pair format which provides for the 'sense' of 'why this utterance at this point'.

Of course, the adjacency pair relationship between one utterance and another is not the only method of relating utterances together. Utterances can be 'tied' by other means and 'understanding' achieved in other ways. One of those ways is through the use of pronouns by which persons can display in their talk that they have understood the prior speaker.

A: John and Mary went to the pictures.

B: They did?

Here the proper names 'John' and 'Mary' are replaced by B with the pronoun 'they' which 'ties' the two utterances together, in the sense that the referents of 'they' are to be found in the prior turn.

Sacks has talked about the operation of pronouns in conversation as the 'tying' of one utterance to another. The display of understanding thus shown is one of the central tasks of the use of pronouns. In this sense it would be mistaken to believe, as some writers do, that pronouns are substitutes for nouns in the way that a local band can appear as a substitute for the main act which failed to appear.[29] Indeed, not only does this way of proceeding fail to notice the work that pronouns perform, it also fails to see the real difficulties that would be encountered if one tried, as an exercise, to talk without using pronouns.

In this section we have concentrated on the close order level of conversational organization as displayed in the use of adjacency pairs. We have seen how, because of their properties of discrimination and the close ordering of parts, adjacency pairs can powerfully yet finely be involved in such matters as the turn-talking system, the selection of next speaker, the opening and closing sections of conversations, the tying of utterances, the building of long utterances, and so on, as well as in the accomplishment of understanding through their use of fitting utterances together to build a conversational episode. There is clearly much more than could be said, not only to do with adjacency pairs but also in reference to the close order organization of conversation; however, we wish now to turn to the matter of 'topic', what the talk is about, regarded by some as the central organizing feature of talk.

TOPIC ORGANIZATION

Central as this might appear in the study of conversation, it has proved to be one of the more difficult areas for analysts. One of the main reasons for this is that 'topic', as an area for direct analysis, has a tendency to dissolve into more abstract structural concerns. Sacks himself notes, for example, that in the history of linguistics, considerations of content dissolved into consideration of form.[30] He illustrates this general tendency by means of the following:

1. *A:* But uh how've you been? – How's Vi?
2. *B:* Oh fine / / fine
3. *A:* Howdjuh survive the quake? en the fires en the floods and everything?
4. *B:* Oh we had em all.

One way of proceeding in terms of topic would be to engage in some kind of content or semantic analysis. Using such a method one might gloss the set of items 'quakes', 'fires' and 'floods' with the term 'disasters'; this, here, being the obvious term which expresses the similarity of the items in the list. Proceeding further along this line of analysis we might end up considering how talk about 'disasters' is related to other topics such as talk about 'minor' troubles, aches, pains and the like, or contrastively, perhaps with 'good news' topics.

Sacks suggests, however, that this way of looking at the data, an approach based upon content considerations alone, might well be incomplete if not inadequate. He points out that the way in which 'topic' is organized might have much to do with the way in which other aspects of the conversation are organized. Failure to see this possibility might well mean that we also fail to see, for example, what the questions in the above transcript are as conversational activities. We have already looked at aspects of two levels of conversation organization: first, the overall structural organization of the talk in terms of the various parts that compose a conversation; second, the way in which utterances are locally organized through such devices as adjacency pairs. In terms of the latter focus we can see in the above extract that utterance 3 is an adjacency pair first pair part, and, as we discussed above, can be placed anywhere in the talk. But is that all that can be said about the local organization of this utterance? Is it possible that another level of organization is implicated in some way? Let us look at what this question might point to.

One link we can perhaps suggest for the utterance 'Howdjuh survive the quake? en the fires en the floods and everything?' is to 'how've you been?', rather than, say, to other things characterizable as disasters. In this light, the 'Howdjuh survive . . .?' looks like a request for up-dating on events that have occurred since the conversationalists last met. People regularly up-date each other in the sense of passing on news of various people, events or other items, in order to bring the persons concerned into a 'state to talk'. Besides avoiding problems and embarrassments that might arise if one party directly asks another about, say, their spouse only to discover that they have recently been divorced, people can also make 'noticings' about another's appearance, say, a new hair style or item of clothing, and in so doing display that they have kept the other person in mind since the last meeting. Given, then, that people can and do perform these interactional activities we can see that such 'up-dating' talk, and the various 'noticings' people can make about each other, indicates that the type of talk and content of the talk is orientated to relevant features of co-participants and the relationship between them.

In so far, as we *can* collect together the set of terms 'quake', 'fires' and 'floods' under the tag of 'disasters', this fails to recognize that 'disaster talk' is only an instance of a more general organization geared to more general ends. To focus directly on topic through its manifest content, such as 'disasters', is not then necessarily the most fruitful way of proceeding.

How then does Sacks suggest that topic might be handled? One way is through an examination of 'topic openers', the structural ways in which people can elicit topic talk from another person. In the fragment 'Howdjuh survive the quake en the fires en the floods en everything?', it was initially suggested, following Sacks, that this could be taken as a version of 'How have you been?', a member of that class of conversational components that elicit 'up-dates' from the other person. It also, however, has features of its own which enable it to do other tasks in the sense that it selects for a more specific talk than simply 'how've you bin'. Considered in relation to topic, 'How've you bin' permits something like 'Fine' as a proper response which, in itself, does not develop any topical talk. 'Fine' holds off from the introduction of a topic at this point in the conversation. We can note in this conversation that it is not unusual for one person to ring another and for them both to claim that they have nothing to say and yet manage to produce a lengthy conversation.

Nancy:	H'll*o*?
Hyla:	Hi
Nancy:	Hi::
Hyla:	Howaryuh?
Nancy:	Fine How'r you?
Hyla:	Okay
Nancy:	Good
Hyla:	mhhh
Nancy:	What's doin?
Hyla:	aAh, nothing[31]

The conversation then proceeds for many pages of transcript. 'What's doin' in the above transcript could be called a 'topic elicitor' who's job is to attempt to get the other speaker to produce a topic for talk. These elicitors commonly occur in environments in which normal topical flow is not operating. Normal topical flow being the way in which 'topical talk' is maintained despite the fact that the topic of talk has changed. By contrast 'Howdjuh survive . . .' is aimed at producing more focused talk.

We can see then that from initially examining a specific topic, 'disasters' we have already moved off onto more structural concerns regarding topic elicitors and topic flow. Briefly developing the latter notion for the moment, Sacks suggests a distinction between 'topical talk' and talk which is 'on topic', where in the latter case all the talk would be focused on a particular topic.[32] Topical talk by contrast involves a way of talking with a coherence which is recognizable but, nevertheless, if one listed 'the topics' involved in the talk then one might well find that each person talked about a different thing. In this way topical talk does not mean that one will find whole segments of talk devoted to 'the same topic', but instead that one topic will flow unmarked into another. The way in which this flow is achieved while maintaining topical coherence and understanding, depends in large part upon the way in which items of talk from a prior utterance are picked up and transformed by a next speaker, often by the use of pronouns and other pro-terms. Casey illustrates these aspects of topical flow in the following data:

Agnes: I wanna see the game, Glady's ast us
over et one thirty tuh see the game,
I had her over las' night for a
minnet.

Portia: How's *she* doin

Agnes: Oh FINE, SHE HEARD FROM BILL, HE ARRIVED
SAFELY, end, AND IS doin fine[33]

Here Portia is able to shift and yet topically tie her utterance to the prior talk by the use of the pronoun 'she' which picks up the reference to Gladys and, by this means, is able to shift the topic from 'the game' to Gladys. In the turn in which Agnes replies to Portia's enquiry about Gladys, Agnes is able again to shift the topic from Gladys to Bill by a series of steps which, while linked to the prior talk, effect a gradual shift of the topic, via 'oh FINE, SHE HEARD FROM BILL'.

This type of topic flow attests to the ways in which conversationalists attend to the problem of understanding in the sequential production of talk. We have already seen how 'understanding' can be handled in part through the use of adjacency pairs, among other devices. Here we have another way in which topics come to be understood. Given a general orientation by hearers to the question, 'Why that now?' then analysing out of an utterance its connection to the prior utterance and producing an utterance which displays that just such a connection has been found, is one method members can use to answer the question. Speakers can regularly display through the course of their talk that they have understood a previous statement, by producing topically coherent utterances. Sacks has suggested that this is a way in which we can come to an understanding of signalled 'touched-off' utterances; that is, utterances signalled by such items as, 'Hey...', 'Mh...', 'Oh by the way...', etc.:

A: God any more hair on muh chest an'
I'd be a fuzz boy

B: 'd be a what

C: A fuzz boy

A: Fuzz boy

B: What's that

A: Fuzz mop

C: They you'd have t'start shaving

(1–0)

B: Hey I shaved this morni – I mean last night for you.[34]

Here, the signalled 'touched off' utterance, 'Hey I shaved this morni – . . .' contains the content word 'shaved' which also occurs in the previous speaker's utterance. In this respect it would seem to preserve topical coherence. In which case, then, why the signal in B's last utterance suggesting that it is produced as non-topically coherent? According to Sacks, what is happening in cases like this is that the analysis by the next speaker of the previous speaker's utterance produces 'a thought', that is, something they can say, but which is not something that stands in the appropriate topical relationship. So, while the term which would have been used if the utterance were fully topically coherent, in this case 'shave' or relevant variant, is produced by B, it now simply recurs with some thoughts attached to it. That is, B is signalling that he has produced an utterance which is not 'fully right'.

This example of signalled 'touched off' utterances suggests that the issue of topical coherence is not a simple semantic matter of, say, moving from 'Gladys' to 'she', from noun to pronoun, as in the previous example, or in producing the same key terms, such as 'shave'. It is fundamentally a matter for speakers to select appropriate items for the topic *at hand*. We can illustrate this in the following transcript taken from a telephone call to a police station where the caller is making complaint concerning some young boys:

C: Ah gee I hate; I do: one of them; but I don't like to say anything you know. I mean I don't know he sounded like an awfully nice boy to talk to an yet

P: Oh some of them are some of the worst crooks are very nice

C: Ya

P: I married a woman that talks beautifully but oh she's rough on me

C: Oh (laughs) you're terrible not even letting her defend herself.[35]

In this extract 'talking beautifully' is co-classed by P with being 'nice' and enables the topic at this point to shift to the policeman's wife while remaining topically coherent. However, while seeming 'nice' and 'talking beautifully' might be seen as an appropriate fitting together in some ways, it is perhaps better to see this co-classification not as the result of some semantic consideration external to the conversation but as produced by the speakers as items of a 'to be analysed' co-class in relation to some particular 'here-and-now' conversation topic. In other words, topical organization, like other levels of conversation organization, is very much a matter attended to and done by parties to that conversation at the time it takes place, and which requires them to analyse, *in situ* as it were, moment by moment, utterances for their topical implicativeness. Thus although one might be puzzled at an IQ test which required children to co-class dogs and children, for the purpose of renting a flat, such a connection might be very appropriate.

A: I have a fourteen year old son

B: Well that's alright

A: I also have a dog

B: Oh, I'm sorry[36]

Consideration of topic as a conversational phenomenon, then, entails more than a consideration of 'what the topic is' simply as a matter concerning the semantic components of the items used. We have seen that other considerations such as the overall structure of conversation can have a bearing on the *sense* of the talk at any given point. Again issues related to the display of the sequential understanding of talk as a pervasive problem, that is, 'Why that talk now?', also need to be brought to bear to obtain some leverage on the sense of the terms used. Furthermore, what the topic is, or might be, in a particular conversation can often turn on the manner in which terms are co-classed by speakers, rather than these being organized in respect of something called 'the topic' which, as it were, externally constrains which items can legitimately be fitted together. In other words, conversationalists create and organize topics by what they say at that time.

SUMMARY

In this chapter we have treated the analysis of talk as if it is concerned solely with conversations. This is, indeed, an impression that can easily be gained through reading the relevant published work. But, the potential range of application and concern is much wider. Some work has been done, for example, on data provided by newspaper reports, using methods very similar to those developed by Sacks in his earlier work, especially those concerned with naming and categorizing objects and events. In recent years there has also been an increasing interest in and awareness of the potentialities of video recordings of naturally occurring interactions. Considerable potentiality exists in the use of video materials but, currently, progress appears to be somewhat limited given the lack of a medium into which to transcribe the visual actions and activities for more continuous inspection.

Finally, we must reiterate that the work of conversation analysis embraces far more than we have been able to touch upon in this chapter. There is little point in us apologizing for this, since space, as well as competence, prevents fuller treatment. What we hope we have achieved is a presentation of the concerns of the discipline and an indication of how the analyst works with the materials at hand. Above all, what we have tried to do is demonstrate that whatever the style or the level of analysis involved in the study of naturally occurring conversation, there is always a link with the central concerns of ethnomethodology: namely, the description of the procedures which members use in the construction of the sense of social order. Its notion of social order is that produced by a local cohort of speakers and it examines this order production through a description of talk as a naturally occurring phenomenon.

NOTES AND REFERENCES

1. See, for example, selections in P. Luckmann (ed.), *Phenomenology and Sociology*, Penguin: Harmondsworth, 1978, and also J. Coulter, 'Transparency of mind', *Philosophy of the Social Sciences*, 7, 1977, pp. 321–50.

2. For example, L. Wittgenstein, *Philosophical Investigations*, Blackwell: Oxford, 1958; J. L. Austin, *How to do Things with Words*, Oxford University Press: Oxford, 1965, ed. J. O. Urmson; and R. Turner, 'Words, Utterances and Activities', in his *Ethnomethodology*, Penguin: Harmondsworth, 1974, pp. 197–215, details some of the implications of this thought for sociology. More recently, J. Heritage, 'Aspects of the flexibilities of language use', *Sociology*, 12, 1978, pp. 79–103.

3. Data collected by C. Scott as part of SSRC financed project, 'Community Reactions to Deviance', directed by Dr M. Atkinson. Transcription done by G. Jefferson. A fuller version of the transcription system is to be found in G. Psathas (ed.), *Everyday Language*, Irvington Publishers: New York, 1979, pp. 287–92.

4. There is no *bar* on the use of transcripts made by other persons. It is mainly a matter of the nature of the problem under consideration. Clearly if one was interested in 'overlap' then a newspaper reporter's verbatim account might be of little value. For other matters, such as how people name things, it might be perfectly adequate. As is usual in CA, one's methodological techniques are not formulable in advance of the particular problem being discussed. This is one reason why there is such difficulty in writing *about* CA; its practice cannot be divorced from the substantive problem at hand. Hence, also the difficulty found in 'explaining' CA to outsiders who typically want disembodied accounts of methods, scope, proof procedures, and so on.

5. H. Garfinkel and H. Sacks, 'The Formal Structure of Practical Actions', in J. C. McKinney and E. Tiryakian (eds), *Theoretical Sociology*, Appleton-Century-Crofts: New York, 1970, pp. 337–66.

6. R. J. Anderson, 'A Sociological Analysis of Some Procedures for Discerning Membership', unpublished Ph.D., Department of Sociology, University of Manchester, 1981 discusses this matter in more detail.

7. H. Sacks, 'Sociological descriptions', *Berkley Journal of Sociology*, **8**, 1963, pp. 1–19.

8. The notion of 'excavation' is taken from H. Jacobs and J. Schwartz, *Qualitative Sociology*, The Free Press: New York, 1979, pp. 345–6.

9. E. A. Schegloff, 'Sequencing in Conversational Openings', in J. Laver and S. Hutcheson (eds), *Communication in Face-to-Face Interaction*, Penguin: Harmondsworth, 1972.

10. The reason why the talk only 'approximates' this sequence, turns on the distinction between 'slots' for talk and the actual talk which fills a slot. Thus, after the question 'What time is it?', a slot is indicated into which the answer ought to be placed. If, for some local reason, this slot is not filled, the question not being heard for example, then the original question can be repeated at that point giving the sequence a, ab. This highlights one of the ways in which analysts come to say that talk is absent given that some talk is 'expectedly' to be produced as a relevant next action. Although we largely confine ourselves to two-party conversations, it will be no surprise to anyone that there are multi-party conversations. The addition of other entitled speakers obviates the regular distribution of

talk characteristic of two-party conversations. In these cases the selection of 'next speaker' is otherwise handled. See H. Sacks, E. Schegloff and G. Jefferson, 'A simplest systematics for turn-taking in conversation', *Language*, **10**, 1974, pp. 731–4.

11. For these kinds of behaviour, see E. Goffman, *Behaviour in Public Places*, The Free Press: New York, 1962; *Relations in Public*, Basic Books: New York, 1971.

12. H. Sacks, 'Notes on the Police Assessment of Moral Character', in D. Sudnow (ed.), *Studies in Social Interaction*, The Free Press: New York, 1972, pp. 280–93, and Ch. 5 of this volume.

13. The killing of John Lennon also shows, most pointedly, that hostility can also be produced.

14. Q. Crisp, 'A Day in the Life of', *Sunday Times Colour Supplement*, Dec. 1980.

15. Schegloff recounts a cautionary tale of the dangers of 'first moves':

    That conversational oaks may out of conversational acorns grow is a frequent theme in folklore. One version of such a story, starting from a somewhat different acorn, is the following:

    On the express train to Lublin, a young man stopped at the seat of an obviously prosperous merchant.

    'Can you tell me the time?' he said.

    The merchant looked at him and replied: 'Go to hell!'

    'What? Why, what's the matter with you! I ask you a civil question in a properly civil way, and you give me such an outrageous rude answer! What's the idea?'

    The merchant looked at him, sighed wearily, and said, 'Very well. Sit down and I'll tell you. You ask me a question. I have to give you an answer, no? You start a conversation with me – about the weather, politics, business. One thing leads to another. It turns out you're a Jew – I'm a Jew. I live in Lublin – you're a stranger. Out of hospitality, I ask you to my home for dinner. You meet my daughter. She's a beautiful girl – you're a handsome young man. So you go out together a few times – and you fall in love. Finally you come to ask for my daughter's hand in marriage. So why go to all that trouble. Let me tell you right now, young man, I won't let my daughter marry anyone who doesn't even own a watch!!' in Laver and Hutcheson, *op. cit.*, p. 402n.

16. These phone calls were collected by Rudiger Krause.

17. This example belongs to data collected and transcribed by

D. R. Watson from calls made to a suicide prevention agency. 'Lifeliners' is a pseudonym.

18. This piece of data was collected by E. Schegloff and is referred to by Sacks in his 1970 Lectures, mimeo.

19. Data from a corpus of materials at UCLA, transcribed by G. Jefferson.

20. Indeed, in the conversation we are looking at, while at 7 and 8 Jerry and Linda have both produced recognitional 'Hi's' and thereby establishing the claim to mutual recognition, the call actually continues as follows,

10. : *J:* Who's *thi:*s

11. : *L:* Linda. ehh hhhkhhh

12. : *J:*   OH(h):.

13. : *L:* ·henh·

    : *J:* hi::: (laugh particle)

    : *L:* *W*uhdiyar *m*ean uwho (h)'s this

In other words, claims to recognition can be accepted for a period only to be undercut later in the conversation.

21. From material collected by Rudiger Krause.

22. These extracts, too, are from the UCLA corpus noted in footnote 19. On 'closings' see H. Sacks and E. Schegloff, 'Opening Up Closings', in R. Turner, (ed.), *op. cit.*, pp. 233–64.

23. *ibid.*, p. 239n.

24. Data in Sacks' Lecture, 5 Apr. 1971.

25. The turn taking system for conversation has been extensively analysed by Sacks and his co-workers. A lengthy summary of this analysis is to be found in the paper by Sacks, Schegloff and Jefferson, *op. cit.*

26. These places where a listener might possibly become a speaker are places of 'transition relevance'. See Sacks, Schegloff and Jefferson, *ibid.*

27. H. Garfinkel, *Studies in Ethnomethodology*, Prentice Hall: Englewood-Cliffs, 1967, pp. 25–6.

28. H. Sacks and E. Schegloff 'Opening Up Closings', in R. Turner (ed.), *op. cit.*, p. 241.

29. We are thinking here of some of the work of B. Bernstein and his co-workers, who count pronoun frequency as a way of distinguishing between 'restricted' and 'elaborated' code usage. the restricted code, it is proposed, employs more.

30. Sacks, Lecture, 17 Apr. 1968.
31. Data provided and transcribed by G. Jefferson. Transcript simplified.
32. Sacks, Lecture, 17 Apr. 1968.
33. N. Casey, Ph.D. thesis 'The Social Organisation of Topic in Natural Conversation: Beginning a Topic', Plymouth Polytechnic, 1981. The data was transcribed by Gail Jefferson and is presented here in a simplified form.
34. Sacks, Lecture, 17 Apr. 1968.
35. Data from Rudiger Krause. Transcript simplified.
36. Sacks, Lecture, 17 Apr. 1968.

Chapter seven
CONCLUSION

As we indicated in Chapter 2, from the nineteenth century social thought, especially in Germany, was particularly concerned with the distinctions that could be drawn between the natural and the human sciences. To some degree this was, perhaps, a reflection of a romantic rejection of science as manifest in the industrial and other social changes being wrought in its name; the growth of a factory system of production, a free market in labour, urban growth on a massive scale, and their darker corollaries of poverty, industrial unrest, squalor and exploitation. In addition, science as a mode of human knowledge seemed to denude the world of its specifically human qualities. The worlds of symbol, of religious mystery, of ethical concern was, it was felt, rapidly disappearing under the cold gaze of scientific scrutiny. The rainbow, to use a rather romanticized symbol, was no longer a reminder of the covenant between God and his people, but was merely a natural phenomenon explicable even by a schoolchild. The physical world was rapidly being divested of its mystery, its beauty and its awesomeness, and human life, it was feared, would soon follow this arid path. Nature became the physical world, God a manifestation of irrationality, morality reduced to self-interest or the spasm of conditioning, community to economic organization, politics to ideology and human life nothing more than a field of vectored forces.

Of course, the proponents of science had much to point to as beneficent consequences of the use of science in human affairs. For one, it had broken the shackles that had tied men to the fearful domination of the Church and promised to replace dogma by a more adequate and rational means of ordering human social life. Science also promised an end to scarcity and the eradication of the age old problems of disease, poverty and want. In penal and psychiatric reform, in education, in welfare, to mention but a few areas, the scientific approach to human problems promised an end to superstition and the cruelties this inflicted.

In the face of such 'advances' the romantic reaction and humanist critique seemed to have little to offer as the last desperate throw of a die-hard reactionary social philosophy. As far as the social sciences were concerned, many of its arguments and ideas about the unique nature of social life and the special methods required to study it, were easily rebutted and even ridiculed. Man was, after all, an animal and a member of the physical world and his actions and behaviour accountable in much the same way as thunder and lightning, the movement of the tides, and the motions of the planets. Against this prevailing view, efforts to establish credible and intellectually respectable alternative foundations of knowledge, especially about human life and society, wandered off into the excesses of 'empathetic understanding', 'introspection' or 'reflective contemplation', or some such vague and empty methodological rhetoric. The absence of agreed clear and public criteria against which the results of such processes could be judged, did these alternative epistemologies little good against the 'obvious' success of science.[1] In the social sciences, the 'subjective', and its various conceptual affines, became disreputable, transformed into a repository of various human failings such as a lack of objectivity, irrationality, partial viewpoints, ideological contamination, and more. In psychology, for example, many rejected the whole idea that it was a discipline which studied 'the mind'. The so-called 'behaviourist movement', as one of the more extreme proponents of this view, deliberately chose to forego any attempt to deal with 'inner' mental processes and, instead, concentrated its attention on what was observable. In sociology and economics, human agents became 'variables', 'actors', 'consumers', 'producers', 'inputs' or 'outputs', and in political science persons intruded only during the vote or in biographies.

Although the battles between these opposing traditions of social thought have been largely fought at the philosophical level, a major drawback for those wishing to give due weight to the 'subjective' element in human life, to bring back, to put it another way, the human agent as a creator of social life, has been relative lack of success at the methodological level. It is at this point where we see Garfinkel as making the decisive step. As we saw in Chapter 2 he transformed the philosophical issue of whether mutual understanding is possible given the 'subjective isolation' of individuals, into a methodological one, by conceptualizing acting persons as interpretative agents who *use procedures to arrive at mutual understanding*. The philosophical 'whether' becomes the researchable 'how'. It is this which is given in the sense of the concept of 'member' which we have used throughout this book. A 'member' is not a breathing, living, sweating person but a set of procedures, methods, recipes, activities, and doings that are used to achieve sense in the world. In short, 'it refers to mastery of natural language...'[2] Strictly speaking, the terms 'procedures', 'methods', 'recipes', etc., should be understood as indicating the *in situ* construction of sense and understanding. Indeed, the idea involved here might be better captured, if somewhat inelegantly, by the term, 'membershipping' as a 'present continuous' activity. As Garfinkel and Sacks express it, 'the mastery of natural language is throughout and without relief an occasioned accomplishment'[3]. As a small contributor, then, to the great debates we alluded to at the beginning of this chapter, ethnomethodology is that sociological discipline which takes for its programme the investigation of the intersubjectivity of practical reasoning and action.

Of course, what this involves for ethnomethodology (and sociology for that matter) is another question, though in the previous chapters we have tried to give some idea of the work done to date. In the remaining pages what we intend to do is make some concluding remarks and, at the same time, deal with, if only in a cursory manner, some other matters which concern the relationship between ethnomethodology and conventional sociology.

As we have argued throughout, ethnomethodology is interested in that most traditional of sociological questions: how do patterns of stable actions occur and reproduce themselves? This was the problem that prompted sociological theories from Adam Smith to Comte, Marx, Spencer, Durkheim and Weber, Mead, Parsons, and the rest. Ethnomethodology differs in at least one important respect in seeing this orderliness as originating in the activities themselves, and subordinates all other matters to this.[4] Nor is this a philosophical claim. It is better seen as an investigative policy or programme.[5] As such it involves a shift in perception to 'see' the phenomena it points to in order to make them observable and amenable to empirical investigation. In this respect, ethnomethodology connects with its phenomenological precursors who proposed the process of 'epoché', in which the 'natural attitude' was suspended, as a way of viewing the everyday world anew. Garfinkel's 'breaching experiments', in which he set out to produce bizarre or unusual happenings as a way of bringing to view the interpretative work persons do when things as 'as usual', are perhaps a methodological equivalent of 'epoché'. As social scientists we are normally, as is any member, so overwhelmed by the utterly commonplace and mundane nature of much of our social activity, that we are blind to the work which goes in to accomplishing and ordering that activity. The stranger, as Alfred Schutz noted, is in a different position to those 'at home' in a situation and is, perhaps, rather better placed to notice occurrences which would otherwise pass unnoticed.[6] Similarly conversation analysts achieve much the same sort of effect by the sheer effort of transcribing tapes. This not only brings to notice features to talk that might not otherwise be 'heard', but also distances the analyst from the data.

Another and crucial consequence of this investigative stance is to see orderliness as an outcome of the methods employed by actors to accomplish the sense and the accountability of their daily life and the activities they perform within it. In this sense, what is conventionally talked about in sociology as 'the actor's point of view', is better thought of as a process of analysis rather than a picture of the society as seen from a particular vantage point. The world as seen by members is a world of 'here and now' objects, events and persons; an occasioned world identified, recognized, made visible, created in and through the methods members have for making sense with each other. The work involved in making sense is, essentially, practical work directed toward realizing aims and aspirations; the purpose is not knowledge for knowledge's sake. Moreover, it is work done as interaction; as part of the activities it organizes, and of which it is constitutive. The member is, above all, an investigator of his or her social world, as much concerned with how a social scene is organized, what kind of persons are parties to it, what relationship they have with each other, what they are doing and why, as is the professional sociologist. Both the professional and the lay sociologist are pervasively engaged in finding out about social structures. In other words, it is not the case, as might be implied by the notion of the 'actor's point of view', that the member of society knows in advance how the society works. Members can also be ignorant or mistaken.[7] What is supposed is that the members of society have ways of finding out about the society 'from within'; indeed, much of their lives are devoted to precisely this. They are concerned in a way that the conventional sociologist would find familiar, in that they make enquiries about the powerful, the causes of crime, ways of improving their lot, how to predict the course of social change, and more, and these are practical enquiries and questions, made asked and answered, as part and parcel of their lives.

Another aspect of the notion of 'actor's point of view' as commonly held, is that in most sociological theories it is the last residue of the 'subjective' element in the conceptualization of human social life. Although social scientists may, or so is the aspiration, chart and measure all the systemic forces which propel human behaviour along its courses, there remains the unexplained variance, no matter how small, which will not disappear. In accordance with a very old principle, a virtue is made out of this irritating defect, this residue, this unexplained variance, by treating it as evidence that the social actor retains, if only by default, some measure of autonomy, however mean.[8] Indeed, it becomes researchable as enquiries into the imperfections of the socialization process, disjunctions between contrary forces, or even a separate domain of enquiry which belongs to psychology. One reflection of this might be the hybrid discipline of social psychology which is at least some recognition of the fact that neither a purely individual nor a purely collective perspective is likely to get at the full truth about all the complexities and perplexities of human life. Be this as it may, the distinctions we are pointing to here, however loosely we may characterize them, between the 'subjective' and the 'objective', between the 'mental' and the 'physical', between the 'individual' and the 'collective', are still very much with us, more often than not as unreflected upon presuppositions of our investigations.

Ethnomethodology, however, rejects, as does Schutz, this dualism so pervasive in Western social and philosophical thought, or, perhaps more precisely, rejects it as an organizing analytical and investigative principle. Instead, it emphasizes that human social life is an intersubjective phenomenon. As we saw in Chapter 3 when comparing Parsons and Schutz, the world on this view is a world as experienced by an experiencer and nothing else. Accordingly, making sense of experience along with others becomes an intersubjective process carried on in and through language. But, what becomes of such entities as mind? Is the process of intersubjectivity merely another version of those inaccessible and uncriticizable ways of knowledge that so confuted the early opponents of the idea that human life could be studied using the methods of science? Coulter, who in addition to using the ideas of ethnomethodology has also employed those of linguistic philosophy, is in no doubt about this. He shows that the traditional mental categories, 'thought', 'understanding', 'intention', and so on, can be treated as 'mechanisms of social reality production and sense-assembly in everyday, practical commonsense affairs'.[9] His studies focus on the common-sense procedures for ascribing mental predicates and the work they do in everyday interaction. Far from being relegated to an 'inner' and inaccessible subjectivity, these notions, because they belong to our language, are very much public and social phenomena; in other words, part of our cultural knowledge and common-sense competence for making sense. As Coulter puts it:

Member's practical employment of mental categories in their routine affairs testifies to the transparency of mind in the only terms that preserve the integrity and intelligibility of our reasoning . . . We lose our bearings when we detach our questioning about psychological phenomena from their anchorings in the mundane world of everyday interaction and its organisation.[10]

Although there is a great deal more which could be said on this matter, one point we do want to draw attention to is the greater emphasis the concept of intersubjectivity places on the individual, conceptualized as member, as an agent, a creator with others of the social order. One methodological counterpart to this is ethnomethodology's commitment to the particularities of phenomena. As we have pointed out in a number of places, the often unwitting strategy of conventional sociology is to produce generalized descriptions of phenomena, but from which it is impossible to recover the individual instance so described without the use of 'ad hoc' practices. Such generalized descriptions, in the end, usually add up to normative idealizations of the activities they purport to describe. Ethnomethodology's insistence on the greater particularity of descriptions is not only a desire to achieve more recognizable descriptions of everyday social activities than those usually found in sociology, but also a recognition that the construction of social organization is very much a localized matter produced in particular places at particular times. Attention to this fact, it is intended, will avoid imputing to the member the sociologist's theoretical problems and, instead, focus on the extremely fine detail involved in the work in which members engage, moment by moment, to construct the activities of daily life.

Finally, let us deal with a criticism, albeit briefly, often levelled against ethnomethodology: that is fails to give an analysis, or even address the matters of, power, class, and inequality: in short, that it is blind to the significant issues 'of our time'.[11] Clearly, it would be absurd to deny that power, stratification, and more, matter to the members of society. Ethnomethodology does not deny this. What it does say is that just because these are issues, and commonsensically regarded as such, to the members of society, there is no necessary reason why they should be central problems for sociology. Moreover, as should be expected from all that has been said so far, ethnomethodology does not talk about these kinds of phenomena in the approved causal ways, as determinants within a system of action. Its methodological injunction to view the social order, as a member does, from 'within' inhibits the use of this kind of theoretical schema. Its approach is more oblique. For example, as we saw in Chapter 5, ethnomethodology has much to say about identification, of which 'class', 'status' and 'power' are merely a few of the ways in which persons may be described. And, it might be suggested, this is to focus on the more fundamental issue of what part identification plays in the organization of collective life; an issue presumed in discussions of class, status and power, among others. In any event, ethnomethodology is not in the business of going into competition with the ordinary members of society, using their methods to subvert the versions they produce, as it were.[12] Its questions and its data are circumscribed by the task of showing how members organize their activities using their knowledge, their categories, their methods, as topics and resources for the analysis. Nor can it tidily be incorporated into conventional sociology as a micro companion to the prevailing macro emphasis. Its picture of social organization is altogether too different, not to mention its methodological principles.

To some extent this charge against ethnomethodology, that it is largely an irrelevant discipline, is, more often than not, predicated on a view of the social sciences which sees one of their more important tasks as that of providing 'useful' knowledge about society. Quite what this involves is certainly variable, ranging from gaining knowledge directly usable in effecting social reforms of various kinds, such as the reduction in crime, to fighting insurgent movements more effectively, to awakening the revolutionary impulse in exploited peoples. What all of these have in common is an image of the social scientist as social engineer. An image which, to a greater or lesser degree, permeates all of the social sciences from economics, as perhaps the best example, to political science to sociology. But what the image ignores, and which ethnomethodology takes as one of its main presuppositions, is that the social world is already in full working order. Persons can and do understand each other through talk despite philosophical doubts about whether knowledge of other minds is possible, or problems about the analysis of meaning. Letters get posted, and sometimes delivered, goods are produced, people starve and die because of decisions made many thousands of miles away. The phenomena of investigation are already there, as are the methods for investigating them, making decisions about them, arguing about the decisions, collecting data on which to base the decisions, etc., which are themselves part and parcel of the phenomena. Social engineers, to put it this way, are already there in the society as its members, continually producing it. So, to push the image a little further, the ethnomethodologist, as a social scientist, is not an engineer among mechanical idiots, but another engineer who happens to be interested in the practices of engineering.

Where might this interest lead? To better engineering practices? More humane ones? Or simply to the creation of a useless lot of narcissistic engineers collected together in a mutual admiration society? Although it is perhaps far too early to even make guesses about where ethonomethodology might lead, it is worthwhile, nonetheless, to consider briefly how Garfinkel expressed the relationship between ethnomethodology and sociology and what, respectively, they might promise.[13] He made the comparison between chemistry and alchemy. Alchemy promised the world; a promise to be redeemed by the transmutation of base metals into gold and the discovery of the elixir of youth. Chemistry's aims were more modest. Although they used much the same painstakingly developed technology of alchemy, these were put to different ends. Different sets of questions were asked about the world, and different theoretical schema developed. For many years the chemists did not have it all their own way. Alchemists kept pointing out that they were getting nearer all the time to the final goal of transmuting lead into gold. Certainly, they had been able to take lead and with the addition of a few essential ingredients, egg yolks, a full moon, and the sweat from a hangman's noose, managed to obtain a dark yellow compound that had some of the properties of gold. Indeed, so close were they to the final goal that government departments began to fund a number of more promising monks, seers, and soothsayers, some even brought in from overseas, set them up in research establishments in the hope that the final hurdles would soon be overcome. In this kind of climate, the early chemists had very little chance, especially when they occasionally remarked that they were not much interested in making gold but much more fascinated by what happened when a glass was placed over a lighted candle. No doubt as time went on some of the more generous-hearted alchemists began to admit that perhaps chemistry did have a part to play in alchemy, though only of some limited 'micro' relevance.

We, with all the benefit of hindsight, know what happened in the rest of this rather fanciful story. But, of course, we are in no position to say what will happen to sociology and ethnomethodology. Moreover, given the promisory notes handed out in the past by all the social sciences, it is perhaps best to keep silent on this matter. What is more certain is that ethnomethodology and conversation analysis have established themselves as much more than distinctive approaches to the study of social life. They constitute a radical rethinking of the whole way of conceptualizing issues of description and analysis. Conversation analysis in particular has gone beyond programmatics to produce a new discipline which is capable to generating observations and findings of a cumulative nature.

These developments of ethnomethodology are not supplementary to those of conventional sociology, they do not 'fill out' the gaps left by other approaches to the study of social life. It is perhaps not too strong to suggest that ethnomethodology constitutes a fundamental break with a whole tradition of social scientific thought, and while the polemics surrounding ethnomethodology may have abated, the challenge for conventional sociology remains: to stay committed to common-sense problems and rest content with analyses that can never be more than yet another folk version of the world; or to subject the everyday, mundane, routine world to analysis in an effort to describe how common-sense understandings themselves are generated. The two are not compatible. While there is always room for discussion there is no possibility of integration or talk of macro and micro levels of interpretation. The phenomena which Garfinkel pointed to and suggested ways of studying, present a challenge for investigation. We hope that this book will draw some people towards this. After all, the social world is there to investigate.

NOTES AND REFERENCES

1. A good and less bowdlerized account of these debates is to be found in Z. Bauman, *Hermeneutics and Social Science*, Hutchinson: London, 1978.
2. H. Garfinkel and H. Sacks, 'On Formal Structures of Practical Actions', in J. C. McKinney and E. A. Tiryakian (eds, *Theore-*

tical Sociology, Appleton-Century-Crofts: New York, 1970, p. 342.

3. *ibid.*, p. 345.

4. This way of putting the point is owed to W. W. Sharrock and R. J. Anderson, 'Ethnomethodology and British Sociology: Some Problems of Incorporation', paper given at BSA Conference, Lancaster, 1980. A number of points are owed to this provocative but sensible paper.

5. This implies that it is an open question as to just what orderliness is to be found and recognized.

6. A. Schutz, 'The stranger', *American Journal of Sociology*, **49**, 1944, pp. 499–507. The same impulse of throwing the 'familiar' into relief, this time by the researcher becoming involved in strange and exotic groups, appears in symbolic interactionism. See P. Rock, *The Making of Symbolic Interactionism*, Macmillan: London, 1979, p. 212. Ethnomethodology, however, seeks to render the familiar strange, rather than vice versa.

7. This is explicit in the model of documentary interpretation in which subsequent appearances or events can retrospectively result in a reinterpretation of what earlier experiences 'really were'.

8. An excellent paper on some of the issues here is C. Taylor, 'Interpretation and the Sciences of Man', in R. Beehler and A. Drengson (eds), *Philosophy of Society*, Methuen: London, 1978, pp. 156–200.

9. J. Coulter, *The Social Construction of Mind*, Macmillan: London, 1979, p. 34. Also his *Approaches to Insanity*, Martin Robertson: London, 1973. In addition, A. F. Blum and P. McHugh, 'The social ascription of motive', *American Sociological Review*, **36**, 1971, pp. 98–109 is also pertinent.

10. Coulter, *The Social Construction of Mind*, *op. cit.*, p. 62. Another good example is D. Smith, 'K is mentally ill', *Sociology*, **12**, 1978, pp. 23–53.

11. The accusation, of course, presupposes that conventional sociologists analyse these phenomena. They do talk about them a great deal, it is true, especially about how they should be conceptualized and measured. Whether this amounts to more than conceptual confusion is another, and debatable, matter. Once again, this observation is owed to Wes Sharrock and Bob Anderson.

12. In this vein, see M. Pollner, '"The very coinage of your

brain": the anatomy of reality disjunctures', *Philosophy of Social Science*, 5, 1975, pp. 411–30; J. Coulter, 'Beliefs and Practical Understanding', in G. Psathas (ed.), *Everyday Language*, Irvington: New York, 1979, pp. 163–86.

13. Presented in talk and discussions at Manchester University.

INDEX